THE AUSTRALIAN LOVE LETTERS OF RAYMOND CHANDLER

Alan Close was born in Sydney in 1955. His first book, *The Romance of the Season*, was published by McPhee Gribble in 1989, and his stories and poems have appeared in many Australian newspapers and magazines. He has most recently earned a living as an extremely casual steward on cruise boats on Sydney Harbour. He lives in Bondi.

The
Australian
Love
Letters
of
Raymond
Chandler

Alan Close

McPHEE GRIBBLE PUBLISHERS

McPhee Gribble
Penguin Books Australia Ltd
487 Maroondah Highway, PO Box 257
Ringwood, Victoria 3134, Australia
Penguin Books Ltd
Harmondsworth, Middlesex, England
Viking Penguin, A Division of Penguin Books USA Inc
375 Hudson Street, New York, New York 10014, USA
Penguin Books Canada Limited
10 Alcorn Avenue, Toronto, Ontario, Canada M4V 3B2
Penguin Books (NZ) Ltd
182-190 Wairau Road, Auckland 10, New Zealand

First published by McPhee Gribble 1995

10 9 8 7 6 5 4 3 2 1

Copyright © Alan Close, 1995

All rights reserved. Without limiting the rights under copyright reserved above, no part of this publication may be reproduced, stored in or introduced into a retrieval system, or transmitted, in any form or by any means (electronic, mechanical, photocopying, recording or otherwise) without the prior written permission of both the copyright owner and the above publisher of this book.

Produced by McPhee Gribble
487 Maroondah Highway
PO Box 257 Ringwood 3134 Victoria Australia

Designed by George Dale
Typeset in 11/12½ Garamond Stemple by Midland Typesetters, Maryborough, Vic. 3465
Printed in Australia by Australian Print Group

National Library of Australia
Cataloguing-in-Publication data:

Close, Alan, 1955-
The Australian love letters of Raymond Chandler.

ISBN 0 86914 318 2.

1. Chandler, Raymond, 1888-1959—Correspondence.
2. Gantrell, Deirdre—Correspondence. I. Chandler, Raymond, 1888-1959. II. Gantrell, Deirdre. III. Title.

A823.3

Cover still-life photography by Jo Grant.

Publication of this title was assisted by the Commonwealth Government through the Australia Council, its arts funding and advisory body.

to
Ray and Dee

Acknowledgements

This is a true story. The letters Raymond Chandler wrote Deirdre Gartrell are authentic, although some names within them, and of people in Deirdre's life, have been changed at her request. The characters in Chandler's life, as portrayed in this book, are based on actual people, but to those with speaking roles I have given names, personalities and body types of my own invention.

My information about Chandler's life is drawn almost exclusively from Frank MacShane's *The Life of Raymond Chandler*, published by Johnathon Cape, London, in 1976, and from Chandler's *The Selected Letters of Raymond Chandler*, edited by Frank MacShane, and published by Columbia University Press, New York, in 1981. Without these two books this offspring would never have drawn breath. For readers interested in Raymond Chandler and his letters these two sources are the benchmarks of Chandler scholarship, something which this book is not intended to be. I would also like to thank Professor MacShane for his personal help with this project.

For permission to quote from Chandler's published letters and to print his previously unpublished letters to Deirdre, I thank the Ed Victor Literary Agency, London. Grateful acknowledgement is due to the *Sun Herald* and the *Sydney Morning Herald* for the use of quoted material.

For permission to reproduce their letters to me, I thank Frank MacShane, Judith Priestman (Dr), Miss Kathrine Sorley Walker, Mr Graham C. Greene, the Ed Victor Literary Agency, and Lilace Hatayama.

In Australia I am indebted to Sophie Cunningham for faith from the start, Rose Creswell, Tim Curnow, Fiona Inglis, all the fine women on the phone from Armidale, The Eleanor Dark Foundation for a 1990 Fellowship at Varuna, the NSW Government for their 1990 NSW Writer's Fellowship, and I offer special thanks and deserved acknowledgement to my editors, Sandy Webster and Peter Nicholls.

Many friends have borne the brunt of my involvement with this book, not least for suffering the half-remembered *bon mots* of Raymond Chandler which have been my excuse for conversation for its duration. This book, of course, is for you. I would particularly like to thank my parents and brothers, the Mears family *ad extentum* of Grafton, the Cadell family of Merrigula, Jolyon for the biography in the first place, Steve Wright for the tape, Stuart Coupe of *Mean Streets*, Gerard Lee, Clare Taylor and Leonie Lane for their many years of friendship and encouragement, and, despite usually disastrous consequences, Sean Kidney and the staff of Social Change Media for repeatedly allowing me in the vicinity of their photocopier.

Most importantly, without the cooperation and kindness of Deirdre Gartrell and her family, and without Deirdre's permission to publish the letters written to her by Raymond Chandler, this book most certainly would not be in your hands today.

No number of letters, however loving, can add up to one long clinging kiss.

Raymond Chandler, 1957

Contents

Prologue
1

Part one
the business backfires
3

Part two
I don't quite know why you are so close to my heart,
but you are
31

Part three
I miss everyone very much, even the
people I didn't like
65

Part four
trouble, brother, is something we is just fresh out of
95

Part five
the tug of a magnet
127

Part six
why do they do it? why do they always go off with lunkheads?
163

Part seven
if you marry this fellow your life'll be rooned
181

Part eight
a hindu at his own funeral
219

Part nine
trout fishing in america
263

Part ten
green pastures parched brown
293

Part eleven
letters
319

notes on quoted materials
385

Prologue

Katoomba, New South Wales, January 1994 They sat opposite each other, a pile of paper two inches high between them. It was her suggestion to meet there, halfway, on neutral ground. It was an indication of the state of affairs between them.

He watched her eyes move down to the manuscript on the table. A clock ticked. Books lined the walls. What a strange, unique relationship he had with this woman. There was no one else in his life like her. He hadn't seen her for four years, she was not in his life in any physical way. And yet he had spent more time with her over those years than the people he saw every week.

She looked up. 'I won't let this be published as it is.'

His impulse was to not betray any emotion. He felt his eyes flutter, his face redden. In the garden birds sang, a small woman in a terry-towelling hat bent over a flower bed.

'I don't like what you've done. I don't like the words you've put in my mouth. I don't like the person you've made me. I've decided I want the true story. I want the facts to be right. I won't sign your paper. I'm sorry, but that's it.'

'You want the true story? You didn't want that before.'

'No. I've changed my mind.'

She kept her eyes on him. She was older, heavier, greyer than the last time he'd seen her. She was fifty-six this year. Things had changed, she was changed, her life had changed. There was a new assertiveness here. Determination. Nervousness. He closed his eyes and counted to ten, very slowly.

He opened his eyes. She was still there, watching him.

'All right, the true story. Tell me what changes you want. We'll go for the truth. The facts. The real thing.'

He turned to the first page.

Part one
the business backfires

the light of my life

La Jolla, California, 12 December 1954 The phone rings in the hallway of a house. Outside the sun shines but the hallway is silent and dark. Diffused light slants through the frosted glass of the front door. In it dust motes are disturbed by the fast approach of a man to answer the phone. He is in his sixties. He stoops slightly, is dressed in a grey cardigan, a dark tie, brown gabardine trousers and leather slippers. His hair is thinning and grey. The hand which picks up the phone wears a yellow cotton glove.

He listens in silence then says, 'Thank you, nurse. My wife's nephew will drive me. We'll be about ten minutes.'

The man's voice is soft, slightly wheezy. It is tired, slurred perhaps with alcohol. It is not the voice of an American. It is the voice of an Englishman who has lived in America for many years.

Minutes later a large convertible bumps backwards out of a driveway on to a steep street lined with middle-class California bungalows. At the bottom of the hill the car screeches into the main road and follows the coastline north on the right-hand side of the road. The young man driving leans into the corners, his mouth set seriously, his hair flying. Palm trees rise against the blue sky; at the base of the cliffs is a skirt of white water. Beyond that is the ocean, black and cold in the late afternoon light.

In the passenger seat the older man clutches the handle above the glovebox, still wearing the yellow cotton gloves.

His jowls bounce, his bottom lip protrudes. He is wearing horn-rimmed bifocal glasses and has a tweed coat over his cardigan.

At the hospital the older man walks quickly down a long corridor, tugging the gloves from his hands and pushing them into his coat pocket. He reaches the door to a private room and enters without knocking. An elderly woman lies in the bed, struggling for breath. She could be his mother. Perhaps his wife. A doctor has his stethoscope at her chest. A nurse stands at his side, another opposite her on the other side of the bed. They turn when the man enters. He goes to stand beside the nurse opposite the doctor. Nothing is said. The woman's hand is lying limply on the counterpane. The man pulls the bedside chair under him and takes the woman's hand in both of his. His face shows no emotion. The nurses and the doctor lift their eyes to him momentarily then return their attention to the woman.

She labours for breath. It rushes into her and falls back out. Her eyelids flutter and her arms flap weakly like wings. The man watches impassively, his bottom lip protruding. After each breath the wait is so long it seems there will be no more – then her chest rises suddenly again, only to collapse immediately as before.

The rhythm continues for several minutes. Nobody looks up. Then, without warning, the woman lets out a long sigh and lies completely still.

The doctor keeps his stethoscope at her heart. After a moment he steps back, tugs the metal arms from his ears, looks at the man and nods. The man's expression does not change. The nurses glance at each other then look down at the floor and the three of them leave the room in silence. The man remains holding the woman's hand for several minutes then reaches forward to close her eyes and leans down to kiss her. When he stands his cheeks are wet.

Of course in a sense I had said goodbye to her long ago. In fact, many times during the past two years in the middle of the night I had realised that it was only a question of time until I lost her. But that is not the same thing as having it happen. Saying goodbye to your loved one in your mind is not the same thing as closing her eyes and knowing they will never open again. But I was glad that she died. To think of this proud, fearless bird caged in a room in some rotten sanitarium for the rest of her days was such an unbearable thought that I could hardly face it at all ... For thirty years, ten months and four days, she was the light of my life, my whole ambition. Anything else I did was just the fire for her to warm her hands at. That is all there is to say.

there is a moment after death

Requiem

There is a moment after death when the face is beautiful
When the soft tired eyes are closed and the pain is over,
And the long, long innocence of love comes gently in
For a moment more in quiet to hover.

There is a moment after death, yet hardly a moment
When the bright clothes hang in the scented closet
And the lost dream fades and slowly fades,
When the silver bottles and the glass, and the empty mirror,
And the three long hairs in a brush and a folded kerchief,
And the fresh made bed and the fresh, plump pillows
On which no head will lie
Are all that is left of the long wild dream.

But there are always the letters.

I hold them in my hand, tied with green ribbon
Neatly and firmly by the soft, strong fingers of love.
The letters will not die.
They will wait and wait for the stranger to come and read them.
He will come slowly out of the mists of time and change,
He will come slowly, diffidently, down the years,
He will cut the ribbon and spread the letters apart,

And carefully, carefully read them page by page.

And the long, long innocence of love will come softly in
Like a butterfly through an open window in summer,
For a moment more in quiet to hover.
But the stranger will never know. The dream will be over.
The stranger will be I.

>Raymond Chandler, unpublished poem,
January 1955

too young to rock and roll

I'd just done the Leaving so it must have been December 1955. I was down in Bathurst babysitting for my sister. I often caught the train down from Orange and stayed the night so she and her husband could go out and do something. Bathurst was the big smoke then. Anything was more exciting than Orange. This night they were going to an APEX dinner. It was a Henpecksian night, which meant that members were allowed to bring their wives. That was the sort of thing they did then. Although knowing APEX it probably hasn't changed very much.

The dinner was at the RSL, I think, or perhaps the local church hall. Lerida and Trevor didn't have a car and they had arranged for the German boys to collect them. The German boys were older than me but everyone in the town still called them boys. They were builders. Their names were Walter, Wolfgang and Karl. They came out after the war with a German company which had a contract to build project homes in Lithgow. Afterwards, when the contract was finished, the three of them went out and started a company of their own. Everyone knew them in Bathurst. You just had to say 'the German boys' and everyone knew who you meant.

I was nervous because although I'd heard a lot about them, I'd never met them. They were extremely eligible and I'd guess that every girl in town dreamed about them at least a little. They had a good reputation for being hard-working and honest. And they were very polite. It was one of the things which made them stand out, their manners. Compared to Australian men they were very proper.

This night they didn't come inside. They pulled up in their utes and waited until Lerida and Trevor came out, and the kids and I went out too, to wave them goodbye. It was dusk, six or seven o'clock. The kids were in their pajamas all ready for bed.

When they saw us coming they got out of their cars to say hello. They were scrubbed up after work, clean-shaven and smelling nice. Trevor introduced me and they each stepped forward, one by one, and shook my hand. And they were so different! Karl was Prussian, and very debonair. He stepped forward, bowed slightly, took my hand, clicked his heels and smiled – and then turned immediately and started talking to Trevor. He was like that. Very polite, but cool somehow at the same time.

Wolfgang was next. His handshake was soft and he sort of melted away immediately afterwards. He was very shy. He missed his family and his home and he seemed nervous, a bit awkward.

Walter was the last. Even from a distance he attracted me most. When they got out of their cars he was the one I looked at twice. When it was his turn Walter smiled and shook my hand firmly then stepped back as if to be clear that that was all he was doing, saying hello. I was probably blushing wildly, terribly embarrassed and excited. Walter has since told me that he was just as interested in me as I was in him. But I was only, what, seventeen? That meant he would have been twenty-six. That was all it was. I was too young.

If I'd been a few years older then none of this might have happened.

a gunshot rings out

La Jolla, 22 February 1955 A gunshot rings out in a confined space, the sound lingering in the after-silence. A woman makes a startled noise and runs down the hall and pushes the front door open. Light floods the hallway. Holding the screen door she goes out to the porch and calls to a police patrol car pulling away from the kerb outside.

'Officer, don't go! Quickly, don't go!'

The car jumps to a halt and a young policeman throws open the door. He runs up the front path, taking the steps to the porch two at a time. The woman holds the screen door open and he passes her, and stops inside the front door.

'Mr Chandler? ... Mr Chandler? ... Ray?'

No answer. The young policeman creaks up the hall, pushing each door, stepping back as it swings open. The woman is several steps behind, clasping her hands in front of her. There is cordite in the air.

The living room door is open. The policeman enters and looks around, then says loudly, 'Ray? You all right, Ray?'

No answer again. He goes back into the hall, following the bitter smell towards the back of the house.

'Ray?'

The bathroom door is ajar. The policeman pushes it open. At the back of the bathroom is the toilet, beside it the shower cubicle.

'Ray?'

He takes two further steps into the bathroom, then stops. The woman follows, clutching her hands, suppressing whimpers.

Sitting inside the shower cubicle with the curtain ripped from its rail and wrapped around him is Raymond Chandler. He is dressed in a shirt and tie and mutters to himself as he attempts to locate his mouth with the barrel of a small pistol. The shower drips on the top of his head, his glasses are misted and beaded with water. The weight of the gun is tugging open his bottom lip, revealing the pink flesh inside. He still wears the yellow cotton gloves.

The policeman takes one more step.

'Okay, Ray. Just give me the gun. Take the gun away from your mouth and hold it out to me real slow. You're safe now. Everything's going to be all right. We'll take the gun away and Nita will see about getting you dried up and sober.'

He reaches out. His hand is shaking.

'Hold it out to me. That's right. Real slow.'

Chandler's eyes curve into a smile. He gives a soft snort, removes the gun from his mouth and holds it out, loose in his hand. The policeman makes a lunge for it, then lets out a sigh.

The woman, Chandler's former secretary, Juanita Messick, bustles around him.

'Oh Ray, you didn't oughta do that. It ain't that bad. Nothing's that bad, Ray.'

She unwinds Chandler from the plastic curtain. His clothes are wet from the shower above. The policeman puts one foot inside the shower recess and together they lift the old man to his feet. He gives no opposition. When they get him standing and out of the shower Nita embraces him and he leans against her with his arms by his sides, his cheeks wet, eyes staring straight ahead at nothing at all.

the hell with it, I'm going home

Gary Davis: I had a column in the *San Diego Bugle* and I met Ray when they sent me up to do an interview after he and Cissy moved to La Jolla in '46. We'd stayed in touch – although from the news on the radio that Monday morning, not close enough, obviously. Penny came in when I was in the shower. 'It's Ray,' she said. 'He's tried to shoot himself.'

This time he'd really done it. He was still alive. But that's all they said. The gun didn't go off, or he missed. Something like that. We didn't know.

We knew Ray was bad, but that's different to actually trying. He'd been ringing the cops every other day since Cissy died, threatening. It got so they almost stationed a car outside his house, just in case. The La Jolla cops had a soft spot for Ray. He called them 'the boys with the beautiful shirts' because they wore these tan uniforms which were always perfectly pressed. They were gentleman cops up there. You talk crime in La Jolla you talk jay walking. If they ever had a real incident, a shooting or something, you can bet the first thing that'd get done'd be the dry cleaning.

I called and they told me he was in the psychiatric ward of the county hospital, which is the law here in California. You're allowed to try and kill yourself, but if you don't do it right the law says a doctor has to try to find out why you wanted to in the first place. He went easy, the sergeant said, but cussing, of course. He'd been soused pretty well full-time since the day Cissy died so he was in a bad way.

I dropped in to the hospital on the way to work. He was propped up in bed in clean pajamas and they'd given him a shave and a wash and he looked perkier than he had in months. He was their celebrity patient and enjoying the attention, charming the butts off everyone. The nurses were giggling among themselves and even the doctors were walking away smiling and shaking their heads.

'Gary.' He saw me and held out his hand. I pulled up a chair and we talked for a while. He was still shaking and breathing real heavy. He might of looked good from a distance but you got close up and you could see exactly where he'd been those last months.

I asked what I could do for him and he said, 'If you really want to help me, get me a decent cup of coffee. But to do it you'll probably have to get me out of here first. Which is fine by me.'

We talked to the doctor. I posted myself as guarantor and they let him out on the condition he go straight down to Chula Vista, which is a private drying-out joint on the border south of San Diego.

On the drive down he was trying to be light-hearted. We joked about Errol, the young cop who found Ray in the bathroom. I knew all about Errol. His mom and my mom used to sew together. He was a nice kid. But about as tough as a poached egg.

'It's a helluva gorgeous day, Gary,' he said after a long silence.

'Ray,' I said, 'thank God you're alive to enjoy it, is all I say.'

He grunted and kept looking away out the window at the sea. 'I guess you're right, Gary. But you know, and I know too, it doesn't matter how many gorgeous days you get, they don't add up to a life.'

I looked across. His lip was set but it was all show. He looked old and he looked scared. I reached over, and he took a grip of my hand so hard it could have been all that was keeping him from drowning in a stormy sea.

When we got there, I took him up to the desk and helped him sign in. We went through all the papers and when it came to saying goodbye he had tears in his eyes. I held on to him and said, 'Ray, you're going to be all right and eventually you're going to be glad things ended up this way and not the other.'

'Gary,' he said, 'you're young and what the young haven't got in experience they make up for with hope. When you get to my age it's the other way round. But I love you, and thank you for all your help.'

I turned to go. When I looked back he had his wrists out like he was waiting for handcuffs and the nurse, a young black guy, was having trouble keeping from laughing. 'Take me,' I heard Ray say. 'I'm yours.'

I came back two weeks later and he was tan and happy and looked like he'd put on ten pounds at least. He knew all the nurses by their first names and kissed them all goodbye – all except Nelson, the nurse with the handcuffs. He even had some of them wiping their eyes to see him go. That's Ray for you.

But his mood didn't last. He got lower as we drove up the coast. He didn't want to go back to that house and I couldn't blame him. I offered for him to come stay with me and Penny and the boys, but he wouldn't. When we got back to La Jolla, he went straight inside and rang one of the local realty offices. He already had a tumbler of Scotch in his hand and he stood there glowering at me over his glasses while he waited for the phone to answer.

When it got answered he said, 'This is Ray Chandler. You boys know where I live. My house is on the market as of now. I'll sell to the first buyer who comes along.' And he hung up and stood there teetering, hitting his drink and breathing heavy. He already had a glow on. His top lip was lined with sweat and he looked at me and laughed that wheezy little snicker of his.

'The hell with it, Gary. I'm going back to England. I'm going home.'

I've since learnt the word for it

On Christmas Eve, or maybe it was New Year's Eve, only a few weeks after that first meeting, Lerida and I were out taking the baby for a walk in the stroller and we passed the house where the German boys lived. They lived together, as well as working together. They were inseparable. You'd always see them together. I liked that about them. I liked the way they relied on each other. For reassurance, I suppose, in a strange country.

This night they were having a party. There were a lot of cars outside and singing and laughing from inside. And piano-accordion music. I remember the accordion particularly, because it was so exotic and wonderful. It was dusk, and the day was cooling off and the air was full of rich thick smells, you know what it's like, that delicious, soft time of day, and the sound of the accordion and laughing and singing was so happy and friendly I was overwhelmed. Entranced. I remember this very well – just from that waft of the sort of life they led being totally intoxicated. That's when I really got hooked. That party seemed to epitomise all the richness of their culture, and everything ours wasn't.

I've since learnt the word for it, *Gemütlichkeit*. It means cosiness, warmth. Snugness. That's what I felt missing from my life. That was what I wanted.

a gaping hole in the roof

Gary Davis: Ray went to England to forget but all he did was remember. He stayed at the Connaught, where he was with Cissy in '52, and he wrote me that he couldn't sleep because the place was full of ghosts. He kept seeing her places. In the corridor, standing in the doorway of the bedroom struggling for breath. He'd get the heebie-jeebies and reach for the bottle. Then he'd wake up at lunchtime with a hangover and start over again. It was the only way he knew to keep the remembering at bay.

At least he had things to distract him. He was a bigger shot in England than he ever was in the US and he was getting a lot of attention. Interviews. Photo sessions. Luncheons. This filled the time. He wrote me about one interview he did:

The *Express* – at least I think it was the *Express* – sent a seven-foot walking cadaver to interview me. He had to get on all fours to make it though the doorway and when he stood up to shake my hand and had untangled himself from the cut-glass chandelier he loomed over me like the photos you see in the *Guinness Book of Records* of the tallest man in the world with his mother. He'll be dead before me, no doubt, and I should be thankful I met him. They always die young, these giants. Their pituitaries pack it in. He had me scared though. Everything he wanted to know I answered yes to before he could take offence. I asked him where he ever found a bed long enough to stretch out on and he said he hadn't. He sleeps on the floor, and has, I imagine, since he was twelve and his parents woke up one day to find themselves face to face with a pair of knees and above them a gaping hole in the roof.

what heaven would have looked like

December in London. Outside rain hit the pavements, but in his suite at the Ritz Raymond Chandler sat in shirt sleeves, drinking a gimlet, that concoction of gin and lime juice created by the British who lived in the Far East for when the tonic water ran out. A gimlet was Chandler's drink when he knew he shouldn't be drinking. He discovered it – or decided it wasn't as bad for him as straight Scotch – on board the *Mauretania*, crossing the Atlantic with Cissy in 1952.

Over the next two years, while he watched Cissy 'die by half-inches', he sat with her in the evenings and took one gimlet, one only, while she sipped her sherry and tried to breathe. Later, when she got worse, he moved back on to the harder stuff. When writing *The Long Goodbye* in 1953, he set gimlets on the bar at Victor's for Marlowe and Terry Lennox.

Watching Chandler drink was a reporter named Merrick Flynn. He and Chandler were getting on well, at least Chandler was thinking so. Merrick was one of those extremely tall, thin men who disappear side-on. His belt stretched tight across his hip bones and he seemed to bow in a permanent stoop. Chandler had decided to like him for his ungainliness alone.

Merrick sat on the sofa opposite Chandler. He had a notebook open on the coffee table between them and jotted in shorthand as Chandler spoke. Every now and then he attempted a sip at the pale green drink in front of him. It was only eleven in the morning. He was young and not used to this sort of thing.

Chandler spoke generally about his career, leaning forward on his elbows and staring at the carpet beneath the coffee table as he answered Merrick Flynn's questions. He spent quite a bit of time looking at the reporter's shoes. Size 14s, he would guess later as he sat at lunch with some of the boys at the Garrick Club.

'You work for ten years, Merrick, and arrive in ten minutes. Here I'm regarded as a major American novelist. In the US I rank slightly above a mulatto.' He set his lip and shrugged. 'But what the hell. I've taken a cheap, shoddy genre and given it literary respectability. With *The Long Goodbye* I took the detective novel probably as far as it can go. I'd be a damned fool not to dine out on that if someone else is paying.'

Merrick scribbled in his notebook, smiling. 'And Mr Chandler, could you tell me a little about your early years?'

Chandler raised an eyebrow over the top of his glass. 'How early?'

Merrick shrugged. 'You were born in America?'

Chandler studied him for a few moments, then took a deep breath.

'I was born in Chicago in 1888. Although I was conceived in Laramie, Wyoming, and if they had asked me I should have preferred to be born there. I always liked high altitudes, and Chicago ... ' He cocked an eyebrow. 'Well, it's not a place where an Anglophile would choose to be born.'

Merrick smiled.

'My mother left my father when I was seven years old and returned to live with her mother and sister in London. My mother was Irish, one hundred per cent Waterford Protestant, in case that distinction means anything to you. My father was descended from Irish Quakers who settled in Pennsylvania in the seventeenth century. I presume this generosity of Irish blood accounts to some degree for the more argumentative aspects of my temperament.'

He raised his drink and caught Merrick's eye, his face grim behind his glasses.

'My father was a railway engineer. In the course of his job he travelled widely – or, should I say, narrowly – and my mother suffered a good deal from his absence. And his intemperance. My father was an utter swine who, even at my age then, I could see was treating my mother abominably. She was absolutely right to leave.

'In the house of her own mother, however, she was to suffer further cruelty. She was made to feel guilty for her dependent place in the household and her unfortunate choice of husband. I recall, for instance, that she was the only adult not offered wine at the table. Petty humiliations such as these drew me very close to my mother. Even at that age I understood how unfair they were.'

He stopped for a breath.

'Our family money came from my Uncle Ernest, who carried on his father's legal practice in Waterford. It was my

Uncle Ernest who paid for me to attend Dulwich College.'

He waited, ensuring Merrick had registered the name.

'It is Dulwich College to which I directly attribute my success as a writer. Had I not been thoroughly grounded in Latin and Greek I would not have been so sensitive to the American vernacular. And it is this sensitivity which has stood me apart from my crime-writing contemporaries, who to my eyes are largely unable to distinguish a trumped up *faux naïf* from the genuine vernacular. This doesn't seem to bother most people, but it certainly does bother me.

'When I left Dulwich I was destined for business. This was my uncle's decision, and the reality of my situation. I spent some months on the Continent studying languages – I was for a time interested in a career as a comparative philologist (I used to sleep with a chart of the 214 key ideographs of Mandarin Chinese over my bed) – then returned to sit the Admiralty Civil Service examinations. To do this I had to swear allegiance to the Queen.'

He looked down.

'Over the years in California, Merrick, I have been proud to be British. It has been a matter of pride to have a family history behind me. Over there . . . ' He looked up. 'Family history means little more than trying to find out where the children were last afternoon. A bloodline is something you find on the pavement after a shooting.'

Merrick laughed.

'Now, due to the draconian British tax laws, that youthful decision is causing me considerable distress. Anyway, of six hundred candidates in these examinations I was placed third – and first, if you don't mind me boasting, in Classics. I was offered a position in the Admiralty, keeping records of supply movements between fleets. I wanted to write, even then, and I thought the routine and easy hours of the Civil Service would allow this. From the first day, however, I loathed my job. The office passion of the time was a bitter battle over the introduction of carbon paper. And the very idea of being expected to tip my hat to the head of the department struck me as verging on the obscene.'

Chandler took a sip of his drink.

'After six months, much to the horror of everybody around me, I left, and holed up in Bloomsbury – where the writers lived then – and followed my passion. I had several jobs, including some weeks at the *Daily Express*. As a reporter, however, I was a complete flop. Every time I was sent out on a story I got lost. I was fired, and I deserved it. That left me, how do they say it, a man with nothing to do who wanted something to do – and I took up poetry.

'My first poem was composed at the age of nineteen, on a Sunday, in the bathroom. It was called 'The Unknown Love'. We are all fortunate that I no longer possess a copy.

'I still write poems. I wrote several after my wife died last year. The *Atlantic Monthly* have one called 'Requiem'. Haven't run it, of course. They'll probably wait till I'm dead, then bring it out.'

A thin smile crossed his face.

'Perhaps I'll have a posthumous second career as a poet. Lord knows, the first was not a great success. I was not cut out to be a poet. I have the sort of mind which could make me a good second-rate anything. But as a poet I knew that was not enough. Between 1908 and 1912 I published twenty, perhaps thirty, poems – thankfully all of them now lost – and was earning a living writing reviews and lifting paragraphs from the foreign press. In 1912 I threw it all in, borrowed five hundred pounds from my rich uncle – all of it repaid, at six per cent interest – and returned to my homeland.'

He looked down into his glass, and Merrick waited.

'I arrived in New York City with an accent you could cut with a baseball bat and no practical gifts for earning a living. And naturally, for no reason, except that most people eventually do, I ended up in Los Angeles – which then, I might say, was not the smog-congested crime pit it is now. It was then quite a fair city, with a gentle year-round climate. This is what attracted the movie studios. Beauty, as they say, dies an ugly death.

'Los Angeles was rough, but not without its intellectual and artistic circles. We would meet and have musical evenings, and discuss terribly highbrow topics, such as Art versus Truth, and even, God forbid, compose poems together. There were, to atone for this, quite a deal of gorgeous young women, and I was not lonely.' He sighed. 'A memory which today is altogether of another man's life, if not another world.

'To gain employment I took a bookkeeping course at night school, but within six weeks the instructor took me aside and said that I had done the three years' course, and that was all there was. I then took a job in the Los Angeles Creamery, as a bookkeeper – a position no different, essentially, from my damnation in the Admiralty, except that I recorded the movement of milk, not missiles. It was, you may imagine, not the future I had had in mind when I approached my uncle for a loan to return "home".

'Then, finally, the States entered the War. We were all waiting for it over there. It was just a matter of time. But when the US did declare war it felt more proper to me, perhaps not surprisingly, that if I was going to go into battle, I should fight under the Union Jack. I went up to Vancouver and joined the Canadian Expeditionary Force. The War ...'

He leant back in the sofa.

'I was almost killed in France. A shell landed on my unit and I was the only survivor. I tried to write about it, but not surprisingly did not write about it well. I believe I did a good line in a Henry James pastiche at that time, and almost sold an example of this to the *Atlantic*. But they saw sense and withdrew. I had, at that stage, nothing to distinguish me. No style. Even if what I did write was already quite nasty in tone.

'After the War I took a job working for an oil company as a bookkeeper and soon became office manager. I was good at the job – even, I was told, extremely good – and I soon became director of a number of subsidiary companies and manager of several more. It was a hard business, but I was fair, and I had the most loyal office staff in Los Angeles. But I was not content. I did not see my future in offices. I was under enormous strain and some in the company did not like my style. The office martinet gained the ear of the Big Man and poisoned him against me and in 1932 I lost my job. I was forty-four years old.

'I was not young, and a decade of increasing despair had

taken its toll on me. But I suppose at such junctures in one's life certain choices become apparent. Mine was very clear. I wouldn't get another chance. I listed myself in the Los Angeles telephone directory as a writer, and set about looking for something to write.

'These were the good years of Hemingway, and I was very taken with his directness and honesty. I knew I couldn't take myself seriously enough to play his game, but quite accidently I happened across a game I thought I could play. My wife and I used to take weekends motoring up and down the California coast, and on these journeys, looking for something to read which I could throw away when I was finished, I discovered the pulp detective magazines. *Black Mask* was the most famous. It struck me that the writing was forceful and honest, even if it did have its crude aspect, and I decided this might be a good way to learn to write and earn a little at the same time. I spent five months writing an 18 000 word novelette and sold it for one hundred and eighty dollars. One cent per word.

'After that I never looked back, although I have had a good many uneasy periods looking forward.'

He looked Merrick in the eyes, then lifted his hands.

'And probably you know the rest. My first novel, *The Big Sleep*, was published in 1939. It didn't change the world, but it didn't go for a bath either, and encouraged by this I finished *Farewell, My Lovely* a year later. The others followed. *The High Window*, *The Lady in the Lake*, *The Little Sister* and *The Long Goodbye*. And I am now working, or I should say not working, on another.'

He sighed heavily.

'Early in my publishing career I realised that I could not make a living from book royalties alone and in 1943 I was invited to work in Hollywood. Even at my commencement I earned as much in a week there as book royalties brought me in a year. And as my name and experience grew that amount increased out of all relevance to reality.

'When I couldn't take any more, I wrote an article exposing the lowly status of the Hollywood writer and debunking the whole goddamn myth-making machine. I expected to be blacklisted, but as a consequence of this public outburst, or perhaps in spite of it – the *Atlantic Monthly* is not what Hollywood reads – I received even higher paying contracts than before.'

He shook his head.

'Hollywood. It'll steal your soul if you let it. But some of the people you meet there – some of them – are real gold. Film writers, Merrick, by and large are better company than book writers.'

He tipped back the last of his gimlet, and stood. Merrick watched him walk to the bar. His shirt was clean and freshly pressed, his trousers were a fine grey worsted, the bottom half of a suit. He had sleeve elastics high on his arms and leather slippers over his socks. He was sixty-seven years old and walked with a slight stoop. He had large ears, fleshy jowls and a tendoned neck. He was average height, perhaps 5'10". His glasses were thick bifocals with heavy black frames. Merrick felt his heart open.

The bagginess of Chandler's trousers, the tail of his shirt puffing out, the creases across its back, his yellow cotton gloves ('For my eczema. I feel like a fading beauty of the stage') – all made Raymond Chandler, the toughest hardboiled detective writer in the world, seem very vulnerable, very human, very alone. Merrick looked across to the window. The grey London day outside seemed to be almost seeping through the glass.

Chandler returned with two more drinks. He set them on the coffee table, tugged up the knees of his trousers and dropped back into the sofa.

'Hollywood. I doubt it could have existed at any other time in history. Only America could invent it because only Americans could believe in it. Don't die before you see Hollywood, Merrick. And Las Vegas. That's what Heaven would have looked like if Sam Goldwyn had been in charge.'

He laughed wheezily and lifted his glass. His eyes, magnified in the round reading lenses of his bifocals, loomed over its rim. Merrick reached down and tried another sip of his drink. Chandler set his glass down and leant back into the sofa with his hands dangling in his lap.

I don't recommend it

'And Mr Chandler, could you tell me a little about Mrs Chandler?'

Merrick leant forward with his elbows propped on his knees.

Chandler's face dropped. 'What about Mrs Chandler? She's dead. Died last year.'

His voice cracked.

'I've not got over it yet. And call me Ray, goddamn it.'

He looked the reporter straight in the eyes and a tear rolled down his cheek. It fell onto a trouser leg and disappeared. Merrick looked down at his fountain pen hovering above the notebook, capped it and laid it down on the page.

'I'm sorry.' He paused and then looked up.

'And ... Ray, would you mind talking about your attempt at suicide?'

'What do you want to know?'

Chandler glanced momentarily into Merrick's eyes then reached down for his glass. 'It was the most inefficient attempt at suicide on record.'

He leant forward.

'Merrick, have you ever lost someone you loved? Or are you too young? Do you know what it's like to wake up every morning and find no reason in your life to keep living? That's assuming you've had some sleep to wake up from. Do you know that feeling, Merrick?'

Merrick shook his head and said softly, 'No.'

Chandler reached for his glass and leant back into the sofa. 'Well, I don't recommend it.'

He took a drink and set the glass back on the coffee table. There was a footfall outside the door to the suite and steps continued down the corridor. A car horn sounded on the street below. Other than that, silence. Crackling silence. The lime juice on Merrick's tongue tasted hard and metallic. In the front of his mind the sweet chemical aroma in the room identified itself as carpet cleaner.

Suddenly Chandler said, 'The charge was rotten. The humidity must have decomposed it. The second shot, the business didn't even go off. The first shot ricocheted all around the room and went up though the ceiling. It could just as easily have gone into my stomach.'

Merrick waited. 'Are you glad now that it didn't?'

Chandler, staring under the coffee table at the Ritz carpet, with Merrick Flynn's size-14 brown brogues planted squarely on it, considered his answer. In his article Merrick wrote: 'It would have been easy for him, not wishing to shock, to answer "Yes". He did not.'

Chandler said, 'I think so, yes. And I think this year will be better than the last. But believe me ... ' He looked up. 'I'd take poison rather than live again through the year I have just had.'

Chandler held the reporter's gaze for what seemed like minutes. Then the ice fell in his drink and he looked down, saying nothing.

the sort of person who has to stay at the ritz

'I'll tell you how I've been living here in London, Merrick.'

Merrick nodded.

'I've got a string of women, all about thirty years younger than me, all of them beautiful, all intelligent, all of them sorry for me. They let me take them out to lunch. I buy champagne and make jokes and they laugh. They all love me, after a fashion, and I love all of them. And although they give me enormous pleasure, every one of them also causes me pain. Why? Because I can see what they're doing. They're propping an old man up in his final days. And I laugh and go along with it and drink and drab, but really ... But really, all I want is to die.'

He looked straight at Merrick and took a slow sip of his drink.

'I can see what people are doing, Merrick. Everybody has been friendly beyond reason, I can see that. But I'm testing them. Acting like an utter swine, more often than not. Do you know why I'm here, at the Ritz?'

Merrick shook his head once, a tiny movement.

'I was thrown out of the Connaught for having a woman in my room. The manager came up and bawled me out like a schoolboy. My wife used to say ... '

He glanced around at the gold and chintz furnishings.

'My wife used to say that the people who went to the Ritz were the sort of people who couldn't get into the Connaught.'

Sweat was breaking out on his forehead. Behind his glasses his eyes were shining.

'This would not have happened while my wife was alive. I would not have been the sort of person who had to stay at the Ritz.'

He reached for his glass, then set it back down.

'You know Natasha Spender? Wife of Stephen Spender, the poet. Heard of him?'

Merrick nodded.

'She's a concert pianist. Very beautiful, very successful. An absolutely wonderful woman – except she's married. And she wants to stay married. She's got two children and a loving husband and a house to run and social commitments which would kill most women. And on top of that she's got her career. And if she was to say tomorrow she'd drop it all – the family, anyway – for me, I'd ...

'I love her Merrick. I love her in a way she doesn't love me, and probably never will. But that doesn't stop me sending her flowers and gifts and taking her out and staring into her eyes in a completely inappropriate way. Why? Because I'm desperate. All I want in the world is to replace what I had with my wife. I can't, of course. You can't build thirty years of marriage overnight. I have more women offering themselves to me than I have deserved in a lifetime. But where does it get me? Sex is delicious, but without love it is nothing.'

He stared Merrick in the eyes, then threw his hand in the air. 'But what the hell, you know that. Everybody knows that.' He looked down into his glass. 'I only want one thing. But it's the biggest thing and you've got to be lucky to find it once in your life, let alone twice. I won't find it again. I know that. And that's why I'm like this. That's why I did what I did in the bathroom last year, and why, still, without having to do it myself, what I really want is for it all to end.

23

Anything else I say, all the attention I am getting, is just a window-dressing of soiled merchandise.'

He reached out and made a wide grab for his glass, poured its contents down his throat, and tried to push himself up from the low sofa. Merrick reached out to help but Chandler waved him aside. As he crossed the room he continued to speak over his shoulder. He dropped ice into his glass, poured on lime juice and added a long splash of Tanqueray.

'You know Merrick, when I arrived it was the most wonderful spring. The squares were flaming with tulips three and even four feet high. Kew Gardens was a paradise of green and colour, rhododendrons, azaleas, amaryllis, flowering trees of every kind. It caught me by the throat after the hard dusty green of California. I loved it. It was like coming home after spending years in exile. But now I've become so damned refined here that at times I loathe myself. I suppose you'd say I hang around with the St John's Wood-Chelsea literary-artistic crowd. They're lovely people, some of them, and I love them back. But most of them no decent man would want to associate with. They're people dripping with intellectual and witty small talk who don't wash their hands when they go to the bathroom.'

He swizelled his drink with a teaspoon, and looked at Merrick over the top of his glasses. Merrick smiled uncomfortably. Chandler let the spoon fall onto the silver tray with a clatter and started back towards the sofa.

'And the queers. So many queers.'

Merrick felt himself bristle. What was Chandler about to say?

'My wife hated homosexuals. She could pick one out just by walking into a room. I feel the same way. They have no emotional depth, these people. They're all surfaces, glitter and gold paint. And in London, as you know, in the artistic circles at least, one man in every three is a goddamn queer. Which is hard on the women.'

A smile curled his lip.

'But I guess not at all hard on me. Except at dinner parties where I've got to put up with their goddamn squeals and chatter. Do you know, Merrick, how many dinner and luncheon invitations I receive? More than seven days in a week can see me through. And at every one I'm expected to perform, to be charming and witty and impeccably behaved. Well, I'm not. Half the time now I get so stinking before I go that I don't even go. I'm behaving atrociously and I know it. I simply see no reason not to. It would never have been like this while my wife was alive. Oh, I subject my hosts to the rigmarole of apologies and flowers and reconvened functions, but the logical thing is happening. I'm not getting invited any more. The word is getting around. "Chandler will be soused, don't even bother." I know what's happening. I can see. I didn't get to be one of the most successful mystery writers in the world by walking around with my eyes closed. I'm not blind and I'm not stupid.' He lowered his voice. 'Only desperate.'

He took some more of his drink.

'You know Ian Fleming? You must know Ian. James Bond? Yes? Well, we met somewhere. One of those fancy dinners. Got on immediately. We're both outside the normal swim of things, you see. Neither of us are really approved of. The intelligentsia, the goddamn literary mafia, look down their noses at us. They keep telling me to write a 'serious' novel. The sort of book people read because they're told to by the goddamn primping second-guessers who call themselves critics. People read our books because they want to, because they want a story with blood in its veins. Not the lifeless posing, the smokescreen of waffle, which comes from the Steins and Pounds and Eliots in this racket.'

He voice was raised, and he realised it.

'Anyway, Ian visits me here. I've always been a horizontal man, always preferred to lie rather than sit. I make us drinks and we flop down on the bed in there and blab away – for an hour or two sometimes – and then he goes home.'

He stopped to think.

'I've never had a friend who's dropped in like that before. I've never had a friend I've ever really wanted to. Where I live – where my wife and I used to live – a town called La Jolla, on the coast near San Diego ...'

He waited. The reporter gave a slight nod. Chandler pronounced it 'La Hoy-ya'.

'Well, there isn't anybody there you'd want to talk to. It's an expensive retirement town. A friend of mind once described La Jolla as a good place for old people, and their parents.'

Merrick smiled.

'Wish I'd said it. In Spanish La Jolla means "The Jewel".' Chandler smiled. 'What gleams brightest in the La Jolla I know is the kitchens. In my part of America, Merrick, the modernisation of one's kitchen is virtually the meaning of life.

'When I first went to La Jolla my impulse was to get out on the streets and shout four-letter words. Everyone is dead from the neck up. It's a consequence of the Californian way of life. The department-store state. The most of everything, the best of nothing. So, I've been denied the pleasure of a thinking companion over there.

One day Ian dropped in and we were propped up side by side on the bed, cuddling our glasses of Scotch and trying not to sick up over that goddamned fake Turner in there, and he commented that he had never met my wife. It was true, I realised. He hadn't. So I pulled this photo out – a photo I have of her that I used to keep on my desk in La Jolla – and poor Ian, he really had no idea ... I was awash with tears before he knew what to say. And it wasn't because I was suddenly overcome with grief. It was because I could see exactly what my life had become without her.'

He leant forward, trying to stand, but fell back into the sofa. He tried again and this time had the momentum. He stood wavering on his feet. Merrick reached up to steady him.

'Sorry, bit dizzy.' He took a step around the coffee table and started crossing the room. 'I'll show you. I want you to see what my wife looked like. She was a beautiful woman. On her death bed she was still beautiful.'

He disappeared through the doorway into the bedroom. Merrick reached for his glass. He sat with his elbows on his knees, looking down at the blank page of his notebook, his fountain pen lying across it. How in hell was he going to write this?

He could hear Chandler in the bedroom, searching in drawers. He turned back through his few scribbled notes, and after a while he became aware of silence from the bedroom. He looked across at the doorway then pulled himself to his feet and crossed the room.

'Ray? Mr Chandler? Are you all right?'

He went in. Chandler was sitting on the edge of the bed. On his knees he held the framed photo of his wife. His forehead was shiny with sweat, his bow tie was crooked. He looked at Merrick as if he wasn't there at all.

Due to a printers' strike Merrick Flynn's interview never appeared in London. But it was syndicated internationally, and on 22 January 1956, eleven months to the day after the 'business backfired' in Chandler's bathroom in La Jolla, the article was run by the *Sun Herald*, Sydney, Australia.

I was half asleep myself

I was home for the summer holidays. And it must have been January because the cherries were finished. We picked the cherries at Christmas and didn't take a day off until they were all in. Some years they were over before Christmas, other years, depending on how dry it was, we went into January.

It was definitely a Sunday because we'd had a big Sunday lunch and I was the only one who hadn't stumbled away to bed to sleep it off. I was out on the verandah reading the *Sun Herald*. I know it was Sunday also because I'm sure it was the *Sun Herald*. It was smaller than the *Herald*, and the only other paper we got in the house apart from the *Herald* was the *Sun Herald*.

I had the paper out on my knees and I was turning the pages without really reading them. I was half asleep and almost drifting off, then I came to an article which attracted my attention. It was on the left-hand page. No, wait. Left side, right-hand page.

are they all like this?

Gabrielle Mercy: I met Ray at a dinner at Natasha's. I suppose he would have said I was one of his London 'girlfriends', as he liked to call us. There was Natasha and Helga and Jocelyn and Alison and me. We formed a sort of shuttle service to keep an eye on him. Made sure he ate when he was drinking, watered down his whisky when he wasn't looking, kept him company at critical times, that sort of thing. He couldn't be left alone or he'd drink until he passed out.

To get him into a more stable environment, Natasha found a flat around the corner from her at Carlton Hill. We packed him up from the Ritz and took him over there in a taxi. It was a nice little flat – bedroom, small lounge, kitchenette. Everything he needed. But, as it happened, Ray loathed it, I think because it reminded him exactly of the home he no longer had – a home and someone in it to love.

We used to take turns to call around and make sure he wasn't drinking himself to death. You never knew what you'd find. Every day he was up and down. You could find him dead drunk on the sofa in the middle of the day or clean-shaven and sparkling, ready for a walk in the park.

One day I knocked on the door and said loudly, 'Ray, it's me, Gabrielle.' I was fearful, as usual, about what condition I might find him in. Ray pulled the door open almost immediately. He took my hands in both of his and said, 'My dear, I have the most charming letter to show you. Come with me.' I followed him into the flat and he said over his shoulder, 'Do you know many Australians?'

'Well, I know some, yes.'

'Good. You can tell me. Are they all like this?'

We reached the dining-room table, which was always covered with letters and papers, and he put a letter in my hands.

It was from a girl in Australia, handwritten on a ruled pad. She had read an article about Ray in one of the newspapers out there. She said she was writing to offer her condolences 'for his sadness'.

It was a very sweet letter. Ray watched me as I read it, his eyes twinkling.

When I reached the last paragraph I realised why he was watching. I burst into laughter and handed the letter back.

'Well,' I said, 'you'll certainly be answering that one, won't you?'

Part two
I don't quite know why you are so close to my heart, but you are

philip, mate

A flat in Bondi, first floor at the front, overlooking the street. The building is a small block of four, 1930s black brick. The street runs off Bondi Road, high on the hill. In the distance over the red rooftops is the blue sea.

At midday a man leaves his desk and eats a sandwich at the kitchen table in the sun. He reads while he eats, leaning over the pages of a hardcover library book.

It is winter. The warmth leaves the kitchen and the man takes the book into the lounge-room. He lies in front of the electric heater and keeps reading. He is into the last quarter of the book. He is familiar with the plot now, he turns the pages with patience, drawn on as with any good novel.

A large ginger cat joins him. It lies between the man and the heater, his head out on his paws, his tail swishing slowly. The man greets the cat and plays with the fur at its neck. He reads on; the afternoon passes beneath him. Sometimes he reads a whole page chuckling; several times he laughs out loud, and turns the page shaking his head and smiling.

Suddenly he sits up, his face intent. Keeping his place with his finger, he turns to the index at the back of the book, looks something up, then flicks forward again to find other specific pages. After glancing through these he goes to the front of the book and looks down a list.

'Hah.' He exclaims out loud.

He looks into the glowing element of the heater, a smile at the corners of his mouth.

After a minute he stands, hits a button on the heater, and takes the book to his desk a few yards away on the closed-in balcony. As the element cools the cat lifts its head and blinks sleepily, raises itself to its feet, stretches back on its haunches and follows the man on to the balcony.

A wide sliding window overlooks the street. The cat leaps onto the windowsill and positions itself. Its tail slaps slowly against the bricks as it watches a big Newfoundland pace sloppily back and forth on the path below.

On the wall above the man's desk is a notice board with index cards pinned haphazardly over it. On one is typed:

The secretary, I should perhaps add, is a black Persian cat, fourteen years old, and I call her that because she has been around me ever since I began to write, usually sitting on the paper I wanted to use or the copy I wanted to revise, sometimes leaning up against the typewriter and sometimes just quietly gazing out of the window from a corner of the desk, as much as to say, 'The stuff you're doing's a waste of time, bud.'

The man inserts markers between the pages of the book and makes some notes on a piece of paper. When he is finished he swings his chair away from the desk, props his feet on the windowsill and looks out the window. The cat watches, then swipes at the air to attract the man's attention.

The man laughs and reaches out. 'Philip, mate.'

The book the man has been reading is *The Selected Letters of Raymond Chandler*.

this was the moment

The letters didn't stand out at first. I was coasting along in that level below applied concentration, not really thinking about what I was taking in, not even registering who the letters were addressed to.

Then I came to this:

May I comment on the fact that in none of your letters to me have you ever told me about anything external to your own thoughts? You have never described your room, your university, the buildings, the place, the atmosphere, the climate, what sort of place Armidale is.

Armidale? Armidale, NSW?
Australia?
When did Armidale come into it? Why is he talking about Armidale? Had I missed something? Had I dozed off? Gone dreamy for the last hundred pages? I couldn't understand it. I was stumped. Total blankness.

I went to the top of the letter. 'To Deirdre Gartell' read the editor's note above. Deirdre Gartrell. Who was she? Chandler had addressed her as 'Deirdre Darling'.

The letter was almost at the end of the book. 1957. Late in Chandler's life. At this stage he had several women friends whom he addressed as 'Darling' and 'Dearest'. Mostly these were London 'girlfriends', all twenty or thirty years younger than he, women he met when he went to England after Cissy's death. Was Deirdre one of these? If I'd noticed her name at all, it had left me now.

I turned to the index in the back of the book. Listed beside Deirdre's name were five letters, all grouped within twenty pages. I went back to the text. They were all dated 1957. I re-read them, feeling my heart start to race. I thought for a second then went to the front, to the list of recipients, and found this: 'Deirdre Gartrell: Young Australian correspondent whom Chandler never met.'

Whom Chandler never met!'
This was the moment. This was when I got up and went to my desk.

deirdre darling

La Jolla
2 March 1957

Dearest Deirdre

Courage is a strange thing: one can never be sure of it. As a platoon commander very many years ago I never seemed to be afraid, and yet I have been afraid of the most insignificant risks. If you had to go over the top somehow all you seemed to think of was trying to keep the men spaced, in order to reduce casualties. It was always very difficult, especially if you had replacements or men who had been wounded. It's only human to want to bunch for companionship in the face of heavy fire. Nowadays war is very different. In some ways it's much worse, but the casualties don't compare with those in trench warfare. My battalion (Canadian) had a normal strength of twelve hundred men and it had over 14 000 casualties.

Ray

La Jolla
20 March 1957

Darling Deirdre

Love is a strange thing. I smoked a pipe from morning to night when my wife was alive and I loved it. I can't smoke cigarettes at the typewriter. I'm not much of a smoker anyhow. I used to drink a great deal of tea, and my wife loved that, just as she loved to see me smoking a pipe. I have a large collection of them, all

English. Since she died I don't smoke a pipe or drink tea; I suppose it may be wrong, but everything intimately connnected with her likes has died in me when she died. I don't mean I am unhappy – not at all. I was for a long time, but not now. The irrevocable can finally be endured. It would in a way be far worse if she had divorced me (this is just an example, we adored each other) and had married some other man and I had to think of her living with and loving that man, and saying to him the same tender things she said to me ... You pay me a great compliment in feeling sure and happy when you put your thoughts and feelings in my hands, but you are quite right. I do have a strange sort of instinct for understanding people, especially women. And I can always be trusted, although by bourgeois standards I am no moralist. I am more than twice your age and it may be out of place for me to be saying these things to you, but it is nevertheless a simple fact that I could never hurt, cheapen or demean a woman, and often, when I was young and unmarried, I had to think for the girl too, to prevent her sometimes from doing something which I knew would shame her later. I always seemed to know. I don't have any idea why. I don't go too far with this, because after all I am writing to a well-bred young lady, and I don't want to offend her. I could go much further, but would it be right?

Surely you realise that when you write so frankly to me it is because I am far away and because we may never meet. I rather hope we shall, unless it destroys an illusion. You need the illusion. And it might be that if we did meet, and even if I didn't too much disappoint you, you would never again be able to open your heart to me. As for your being born too late or I too early, I shouldn't have had the marriage I had, if it had been otherwise. Do you understand what it is to love a woman so deeply and be so deeply loved that no day in thirty years was not in its way a

...hip? I always held her chair for her at the table – until she couldn't come to it anymore. I ...ys opened the car door for her and helped her in. I never let her bring me anything. I always brought things to her. I never went out of a door or into a door before her. I never went into her bedroom without knocking. I suppose these are small things – like constantly sending her flowers, and always having seven presents for her birthday, and always having champagne on our anniversaries. They are small in a way, but women have to be treated with great tenderness and consideration – because they are women.

Ray

La Jolla
23 April 1957

Deirdre Darling

Most people make do with what is available and seemingly appropriate to their condition. Ferocious romantics of my sort never make do with anything. They demand the impossible and on very rare occasions they achieve it, much to their surprise. I was one of those, one of the perhaps two per cent who are blessed with a marriage which is forever a courtship. I can't, as I think back, find any reason why I should have been so favoured. Above all, since as a young man I was anything but virginal ... You will never lose dignity with me, since it is obviously a part of you. To answer one question, I never proposed marriage formally to anyone. My wife and I just seemed to melt into each other's hearts without the need of words.

With much love
Ray

La Jolla
8 May 1957

Deirdre Darling

May I comment on the fact that in none of your letters to me have you ever told me about anything external to your own thoughts? You have never described your room, your university, the buildings, the place, the atmosphere, the climate, what sort of place Armidale is. You may think this unimportant, but to me it indicates a state of mind; a state of mind which must be unhappy. I am interested in Australia, in everything about it, what it looks like, what its houses are like, how many rooms they have and what sort, what flowers grow there, what animals and birds are there, what the seasons are, what the ordinary life of people of your sort consists of. You tell me a great deal about your thoughts, but nothing about the life around you. Do you suppose I became one of the most successful mystery story writers of any age by thinking about me – about my personal torments and triumphs, about an unending analysis of my personal emotions? I did not. And you should know that very well. But from you all I hear is about you. This is not said to blame you or accuse you of being egocentric at all.

With love and some hope
Ray

La Jolla
25 July 1957

Darling Deirdre

It seems that I have a serious anaemic condition. Not fatal, but quite serious. These diagnoses never make much

...sion on me, since I have lived my whole life on
the edge of nothing. Once you have had to lead a
platoon into direct machine-gun fire, nothing is ever
the same again ... I don't quite know why you are so
close to my heart, but you are. In some mysterious
way you have put me inside you, so that I have to lie
awake at night and worry about you – you a girl I
have not even seen. It must sound ridiculous to you.
All I can say is that in some strange way you have
become a part of me, so that I wake in the night and
wonder what is Deirdre thinking or doing, is she
making a fool of herself with some nice but stupid
man, and if she is what can I do about it? All very
silly, but there is a certain devotion in it also, entirely
because of your letters. I have had thousands of
letters, and I suppose I have written thousands. A
collection of my letters is to be published when I can
weed them out. But that is not the point. Why should
I take Deirdre into my heart when hundreds of
charming people made no impression on me at all
deeply?
   The older you get, the less you know.

With all my love
Ray

something took hold of my heart

The extracts are an eccentric selection when read in isolation, but as I read and re-read them something took hold of my heart about the way Chandler wrote to Deirdre. He was caring and tender. His words revealed a genuine feeling for her. There seemed to have been a real intimacy. Some sort of love.
   And yet they had never met.
   Chandler was sixty-nine in 1957, and if Deirdre was at college in Armidale, she was probably around twenty. She was young enough to be his granddaughter. And yet it

appeared that Deirdre had formed some sort of attachment to him. At first he tried to talk this down. His voice is responsible, he is compassionate but careful, somewhat distancing – but not without an air of sexual flirtatiousness.

However within months something new had developed, and Chandler had to admit: 'I don't quite know why you are so close to my heart, but you are. In some mysterious way you have put me inside you ...'

At first I simply wanted to satisfy my curiosity. How did Chandler and Deirdre Gartrell get so close if they never met? Was their relationship an important one in Chandler's life? How long did they correspond for? How did they start writing? Did the correspondence start with a fan letter from Deirdre? Was she still alive? Did the letters still exist? If so, where were they? Was their relationship public? If so, why hadn't I heard about it before now? Surely someone had written about it. Some Australian literary gumshoe. I was perplexed. I was piqued. I felt left out. What was going on here? I simply couldn't understand why I had never heard of this Australian connection in Chandler's life.

So many questions. Why did it matter to me so much? There is always a 'why'. But when your blood's up and your mind's racing, you don't think of why.

axe murdering, a primer

What the hell, I thought, why not?

I picked up the phone. I rang Directory Assistance. I got a number. I rang Armidale. I got a woman.

'Good morning. University of New England.'

'Yes, good morning. I'm hoping you can help me. I'm trying to locate a woman who I believe was a student at the University in 1957.'

'Yes?'

'Her name was Deirdre Gartrell.'

'Yes?'

'That's all I know about her. Her name, and that she was a student in Armidale in 1957.'

'Yes?'

'Would it be possible to verify that with you? Do you have records going back that far?'

'Oh yes, sir. Our records are fastidiously maintained. We have the finest university archives in the country.'

'Good. So could you tell me if she was in fact a student there? And could you give me any idea what has become of her since she left university? Do you keep track of your old students?'

'We do sir. But I'm afraid I won't be able to give you any of that information without the permission of the person involved first.'

'Sorry?'

'Well, I'm afraid, sir, that the university observes stringent privacy restrictions. There's no way I could give that sort of information over the phone. Not to a complete stranger. You could be anybody. You could be an axe murderer.'

She laughed shrilly.

'You're right. I could be. But I'm not. I'm just a bloke trying to find out something about a woman who I believe was a student at your university in 1957.'

She was silent.

'So you can't tell me anything?'

'Not about an ex-student, sir. The only way I can give you information about an ex-student is for you to obtain his or her permission first.'

'But I don't know her! That's why I'm ringing you, to try to locate her.'

'I'm sorry sir, that's our rule. I suggest you find her another way, then get her to write to us giving us permission to give you the information you require. Then we can help you.'

'But the information I require is her location.'

'I'm sorry, sir. I can't help you with that.'

'Well, do you have any suggestions of another way I might locate her?'

'Yes, sir. You might try the phone book.'

'Which phone book? She could be anywhere. She might not even be in Australia. And she's probably married. She probably hasn't even got the same name.'

'That's true, sir. But still, I'm afraid I can't help you. Now, unless you have another question, I won't waste any more of your time.'

'No, no more questions.'

'Good. Well, thank you for your inquiry, sir.'

The line clicked. I held the receiver away from my ear. I looked at it. I put it down.

Philip picked his way over the papers on my desk, purred in my ear and headbutted my chin, a line of saliva dropping to my shirt. A tough tom in the back alley at night, Philip was a dribbler indoors. I ran my hand along his back. He arched up against me. I swivelled in the chair and looked out the window across the rooftops to the blue Pacific Ocean. I tried to laugh. I shook myself. And I thought it'd be straightforward.

The phone book! What a great idea. Only sixteen million people in Australia. Easy! Easy-peasy.

I never did like Armidale. It's typical of the place that it's got the most expensive petrol on the New England Highway. Some sort of collusion between the servos. It's the sort of town that makes you want to go out on the main street and shout four-letter words at midday. The sort of town which turns harmless, innocent people into axe murderers. It's got an attitude problem, that's the trouble with Armidale. Attitude.

Armidale. It had my heart thumping now. I wasn't going to be brushed off that lightly. I stared out the window and ran my hand down Philip's back. I asked him where I should look next. He closed his eyes and a line of dribble fell to the cover of the Chandler biography on my desk.

I think your project is most interesting

Columbia University
Dodge Hall
9 September 1987

Dear Mr Close

Thank you for your letter about Raymond Chandler and Deirdre Gartrell. I think that your project is most interesting and certainly hope that you can obtain the necessary material to complete your project.

Unfortunately, I do not seem to have Deirdre Gartrell's current address, but I suggest that you write to Kathrine Sorley Walker, 60 Eaton Mews West, London, SW1, with a letter similar to the one you sent me. Kathrine was for many years Helga Greene's associate in the Literary agency and she should have the address. You might also send a copy of your letter to Graham C. Greene, c/o Jonathan Cape, 32 Bedford Square, London, WC1, just in case Kathrine has moved since Helga's death – although I don't think she has.

I hope this has been of use to you. I'd love to write more but I'm just back from a trip and have dozens of other letters to write. In any event, all good wishes and good luck.

Yours sincerely
Frank MacShane

Custard-yellow paper, US letter-sized, electric typewriter, no errors (typed by a secretary?), signed in ink. Impressions? Friendly, but hurried. A bit vague. Baggy corduroy trousers, leather elbow patches. One of those absent-minded professors who knows everything but has forgotten it. Dodge Hall. A good address.

And Kathrine Sorley Walker? A familiar name. She edited, with Dorothy Gardiner, *Raymond Chandler Speaking*, published in 1962 and copyrighted, interestingly, to The Helga Greene Literary Agency. Helga had been Chandler's English agent and close friend. Only months before he died they became engaged and Chandler altered his will in her favour. They never married.

And Graham C. Greene? Some relation to Helga, surely. And to Graham as well?

London
7 October 1987

Dear Mr Close

Thank you for your letter of 28 September.

I think Kathrine Sorley Walker may be able to help you though there will be some delay as she is at present in North America. Unfortunately I personally am unable to answer your specific enquiries.

You might perhaps like to note that a lot of Raymond Chandler's papers are now deposited at the Bodleian Library in Oxford.

If in due course you require copyright permission for the use of anything from Raymond Chandler's works you might care to note that the literary agent of the Estate is Ed Victor Esq, Wardour Street, London WIV 4AT.

Yours sincerely
Graham C. Greene

Fine bond paper, embossed letterhead. Electronically typed (by a secretary?). No errors. Illegible signature in ink. Later I discover, in David Marr's biography of Patrick White, that G.C.G. was one of White's editors at Jonathan Cape. Any relation to Helga and the other Graham? Still don't know.

I try to picture him and I can't get David Niven out of my mind. Long cigarette holders, trimmed moustache, gin cheeks. And this, Chandler's opinion of Graham Greene's *The Heart of the Matter*: 'It has everything in it that makes literature except verve, wit, gusto, music and magic; a cool and elegant set-piece, embalmed by Whispering Glades. There is more life in the worst chapter Dickens or Thackeray ever wrote, and they wrote some pretty awful chapters.' But, a week later: 'The end of Greene's book was great. It atoned for a lack I had felt before.'

London
10 October 1987

Dear Mr Close

I am just writing to acknowledge your letter of 28 September which has arrived during Miss Sorley Walker's short absence abroad. She will, of course, see your letter on her return and will doubtless be in touch as soon as she can thereafter.

Yours sincerely
Elizabeth Robinson

A secretary? Typed with an electric typewriter on a blue aerogramme. How economical. How English! No errors. Sender described as: 'Robinson, 60 Eaton Mews West', etc. Signed in fine black biro, in large round letters. Where do girls learn to write like this? Does adolescent pressure dictate that this is more feminine than the cramped, often illegible handwriting boys seem to end up with? Is some masculine credibility gained by being unreadable? Even more mysteries to solve.

London
27 October 1987

Dear Mr Close

Your letter of 28 September, and a copy of your letter of the same date to Graham C. Greene, were awaiting my return from America.

Mrs Helga Greene was (slightly) in touch with Deirdre Gartrell about the time Chandler died but did not keep up the contact so I'm afraid we have no idea where she is now. As far as I know there were no other letters to or from her in the papers that are now lodged at the Bodleian Library. Sorry I can't be of more help.

You are certainly on the spot to find her if she has stayed in Australia! But I suppose she probably has a married name now.

Yours sincerely
Kathrine Sorley Walker
Literary Consultant to Helga Greene

Small white notepaper, letterheaded. Typed on a manual, probably by Miss Sorley Walker herself. Several errors. Signed in flourishing blue biro. I imagine Miss Sorley Walker with a cameo brooch at the neck of her blouse and a passion for P.D. James. (Claps the hands together, leans forward, eyes sparkling. 'Wicked. Wicked. But wonderful!') For breakfast she would have Twinings tea from a china cup (dash of milk, no sugar) and thin-cut rye toast with a smear of runny Seville orange marmalade. She would take the *Guardian* over the *Telegraph* and lament the demise of the *Times* under Murdoch.

Bodleian Library
23 October 1987

Dear Mr Close

Thank you for your letter of 15 October inquiring about Chandler's correspondence with Deirdre Gartrell. The Chandler papers that have been deposited in the Bodley were formerly the property of Mrs Helga Greene, and are for the most part a business correspondence, though of a fairly lively and personal nature, as you would expect from Raymond Chandler. There is a certain amount of purely personal material as well, together with some literary papers: mainly later, post-mortem typescripts of short stories, though with some original Chandler working papers included.

   I am in the process of cataloguing the collection, and no material – by the terms of the deposit agreement – may be made available to readers until I have finished the catalogue. So far as I am aware we do not have any original letters between Chandler and Gartrell. They are certainly not in Chandler's own personal files of correspondents, arranged alphabetically by surname. What we do have, however, are typed extracts from seven letters written by RC to Gartrell in 1957. These were made by, or for, Dorothy Gardiner for her book, *Raymond Chandler Speaking* (1962), though not reprinted there. I do not know where the originals of these letters are, but the other large institutional holding of Chandler's papers will be found at the Department of Special Collections, Research Library, University of California, Los Angeles.

   If I do find any more Gartrell letters, I will let you know. I am afraid that it will not be possible to offer you photocopies of relevant material until I have finished working on the collection, and even then you will need the owner's permission. I hope to have finished the catalogue early next year, in time for the centenary [of Chandler's birth].

Yours sincerely
Judith Priestman (Dr)
Assistant Librarian

Bodleian letterhead, white bond paper, ref JAP/RMcC. The 'JAP' I presume is Judith Priestman (Dr.). But who is 'RMcC'? Raymond Chandler's middle name was Thornton. The letter is signed illegibly in black biro. Judith Priestman (Dr) would seem to be the real thing. Businesslike, efficient yet friendly and 'lively and personal' herself. The 'Bodley' in the first paragraph is relaxed and possessive. Quaint. At home. Is she young, is she old? I can picture the tea cup and saucer on her desk and her hands moving over the typewriter keyboard [electric, clean copy, not one error]. Why do I assume she typed the letter, not a secretary? I see the wedding band on her finger, but when I pull back the person I see is the sultry long-lashed attendant in the bookshop across the road from Geiger's pornography shoppe in Howard Hawks's 1946 film of *The Big Sleep* – before she pulled the blinds shut and took her glasses off and shook her hair out after Bogart hadn't fooled her with a request for an 1860 *Ben Hur*, third edition with the duplicated line on page 116.

get dressed, sweetheart

No luck. Time went by. Life went on. I didn't lose any sleep. What did I care? I was only curious. Just wondering. Why did I want to find Deirdre Gartrell, anyway? What would I say to her if I found her? 'Oh, hello, I believe you used to have something going with Raymond Chandler, the famous mystery writer. Is this correct?' Why was I doing this? What was driving me on?
    What's the real story here?

Get dressed, sweetheart – and don't fuss with your necktie. Places want us to go to them.
['Bay City Blues']

This is not a story about the more famous Raymond Chandler, the novelist. It is about Raymond Chandler the letter writer, Raymond Chandler, the man.

I first read Chandler's novels as a teenager. My mother was a reader. I slipped her green-spined, sticky-taped Chandler Penguins from the shelf when I was supposed to be studying for the Higher School Certificate and read them, I remember even now, with pure enjoyment. With a smile all across my face. I was swept along by the language – the humour, the characters, the dialogue. I didn't stop, of course, to wonder about the nature of writing and how it worked on me as a reader. It was only later, re-reading Chandler as an adult, I understood that the words were the surface and beneath them was something else.

Plots for Chandler were merely a vehicle for the writing, little more than a tiresome necessity. He said of the Philip Marlowe radio series, 'The plots of these shows don't matter; they're just an excuse for people to go places and say things.' What he was trying to get on paper was the business beneath the story. He wanted to make us *feel*, to touch our emotions, to convey to us his understanding of the world.

Why do we read books? To learn things, to be entertained, to reassure ourselves that we are not alone. To salve our isolation. On one level this is something ancient, spiritual perhaps, satisfying our need to hear truths, to access myths, to feel a part of our culture.

But we also read to fulfill our need for an emotional connection with another human being. I would say that what makes a reader like a book is nothing greater, or less, than the rapport he or she feels with the personality of the author – the connection that the reader makes with the writer within. 'Only connect' advised E.M. Forster. In the words of Chandler:

In the long run, however little you talk or even think about it, the most durable thing in writing is style, and style is the most valuable investment a writer can make with his time ... He can't do it by trying, because the kind of style I am thinking about is a projection of personality and you have to have a personality before you can project it. But granted that you have one, you can only project it on paper by thinking of something else ... Preoccupation with style will not produce it. No amount of editing or polishing will have any appreciable effect on the flavour of how a man writes. It is the product of the quality of his emotion and perception; it is the ability to transfer these to paper which makes him a writer.

A writer's style, the way he or she uses words, acts as a conductor, the connecting tissue, between the writer and reader. This is what I understood when I re-read Chandler's books as an adult and thought about what had lingered with me from reading them as a teenager. What was really affecting me was not merely Chandler's words – what was in fact shining up through the words was the man himself. Chandler had connected. I needed to find out more.

places want us to go to them

It's time to introduce one of the heroes of this book. The maestro. The conductor. The prompter beneath the footlights. The quiet achiever. Professor Frank MacShane.

With that name he could be a character in a novel himself. Inspector Frank MacShane Investigates. Someone on TV. 'And we cross live to Inspector Frank MacShane at the scene of the crime.'

Except he's a professor. 'Professor Frank MacShane Pursues His Interest.' Who is he? According to the fly-sheet of the biography, he is 'Professor Frank MacShane of Columbia University'. According to his letterhead: 'In the City of New York. School of the Arts. Writing Division. Dodge Hall.'

Great address. Very Little Dorrit. But what is his role in all this?

If Professor Frank MacShane didn't exist someone would have had to invent him. Published in 1976, his is the only biography of Raymond Chandler to date. In 1981 he edited *The Selected Letters of Raymond Chandler*. These are the bookends of the Chandler fan's shelf.

There are other Chandler texts. *Raymond Chandler Speaking*, edited by Dorothy Gardiner and Kathrine Sorley Walker, was published in 1962, three years after Chandler's death. This is a book of extracts from his letters, often abbreviated with cavalier disregard for high-fidelity reproduction. It is ordered into chapters: 'Chandler on Chandler', 'On Writing', 'On Cats', 'On Famous Crimes' etc. It also contains some previously unpublished material from his personal files: the short story, 'A Couple of Writers', written in 1950, which his agent couldn't sell, and the start of a new Marlowe novel, *The Poodle Springs Story*, since 'completed' and published by Robert B. Parker in 1989.

An interesting collection, but without MacShane's guidance, this collection of extracts becomes rudderless in the sea of serious Chandler study. Without MacShane I wouldn't have known who Dorothy Gardiner was. (Secretary, at the time of Chandler's death, of the MWA, the Mystery Writers of America association.) And without MacShane I would not have known that Kathrine Sorley Walker was 'for many years Helga Greene's associate in the literary agency'. And without MacShane's biography of Chandler I would not be able to explain why *Raymond Chandler Speaking* is held in copyright to the 'Helga Greene Literary Agency' when all the words are Chandler's.

There is another Chandler text. An American academic named Matthew Buccoli had tracked down all of Chandler's early prose and poetry and collected it in *Chandler Before Marlowe: Raymond Chandler's Early Prose and Poetry 1908-1912*. I found a very dusty copy of this pretty skimpy little book in Powells Bookshop, Portland, Oregon when I finally went to America in 1989. But I couldn't buy it.

I think Chandler would have approved of MacShane's biography. It is compassionate but dry-eyed, not in the least sentimental. But Chandler was not proud of his early poetry. 'I should be grateful I went through the arty and intellectual phase so young and grew out of it so completely,' he wrote to Hamish Hamilton. Of his first ever poem he commented, 'I am fortunate in not possessing a copy.'

I didn't buy the *Early Prose and Poetry*. A man has to draw the line.

When you write the biography of a friend, said Flaubert, you must write as if you are taking revenge for him.

MacShane's biography does this. It creates of Chandler a character more complicated and sad and lonely than any he invented for his own novels; a solitary, unhappy man who, in Chandler's own words, '[possibly] was born a half a century too late and... could so easily have become everything our world has no use for. So I wrote for the *Black Mask*. What a wry joke.'

For the decades of dismissal in the hands of the literary highbrows, for the generalised disregard of the mystery novel as a sub-literary genre, for the sad, proud frailty of Chandler himself, Professor MacShane, in his *The Life of Raymond Chandler*, had his revenge.

the undertaker's parlour

Perhaps I could have put the biography down; having satisfied my curiosity, I could have slipped the book back on the shelf as I did my mother's green Penguins more than twenty years ago. But I did not. One sentence made that impossible. One sentence, on the second last page, gripped my heart and squeezed it.

Chandler had died alone. His life in those last years was dominated by a confusion of emotional instability, which left him, at his end, alone in his rented apartment in La Jolla.

MacShane wrote: 'He lay alone in the undertaker's parlour reaping the neglect his indecisiveness had earned him.'

When I closed the cover of MacShane's 'Revenge' these were the words that left Chandler's life and entered mine.

These were the words which started this story.

I wrote them on the inside front cover of my daily notebook. When that ran out, I copied them into the next. I continued doing this. The words cautioned me every time I opened the book. I copied them on to a card and pinned it to the wall above my desk.

Every day when I sat down to work, the words were in front of me. I didn't read them anymore, they were just there, a part of my landscape, a warning.

This is what was happening.

I was living with Fiona and Philip in a flat in Bondi. Fiona was my girlfriend. Philip was my cat. Out on the balcony where I had my desk I was writing to a woman I hadn't met. In due course... What? Julia was already a presence in my life. A decision would have to be made. I knew that even then – without knowing it, in the place below my mind. It might be an easy decision, or it might turn out to be difficult. But it would, eventually, have to be made.

This was it. This was where it started.

I wrote

Bondi
1988

Dear Julia

I've stumbled across this amazing story...

eighteen pairs of shoes

Yes, I am exactly like the characters in my books. I am very tough and have been known to break a Vienna roll with my bare hands. I am very handsome, having a powerful physique, and I change my shirt regularly every Monday morning ... I do a great deal of research, especially in the apartments of tall blondes. I get my material in various ways, but my favourite procedure consists of going through the desks of other writers after hours. I am thirty-eight years old and have been for the last twenty years. I do not regard myself as a dead shot, but I am a pretty dangerous man with a wet towel. But all in all I think my favourite weapon is a twenty dollar bill. In my spare time I collect elephants.

So, who was Chandler? Did he really collect elephants?

In the public mind – what, he might have said, there is of it – Chandler is the doyen of the tough, hardboiled school of American detective writing. It's either Chandler or Hammett, depending on your taste: cynical/sensitive, or pure tough. But Chandler was not the man most readers might expect. Chandler's hardboiled had a soft centre:

I am engaged, and have always from the very beginning been engaged in the effort to do something with the mystery story which has never quite been done. In one way Hammett came close; in another way Sayers came close. Neither was capable of imparting emotion to the right nerves.

He wanted us to enjoy the writing for its own sake. His aim was 'to squeeze the last drop from the medium [I] have learnt to use'. And he succeeded. In 1948 he was able to write:

Since Hammett has not written for publication since 1932 I have been picked out by some people as the leading representative of the school ... The result is that everybody who used to be accused of writing like Hammett may now be accused of trying to write like Chandler.

Chandler knew that good writing would last – and the result now is that many readers, not only of crime novels, know Chandler's name. But I have found that this is often all they know.

Once the seemingly inevitable confusion with Raymond

Carver is out of the way, most people who do recognise the name Chandler can tell you with shaky assertion that he was a crime writer. But from there the going is bumpy. In particular, Americans I met tended to receive the name Chandler with a blank face.

But even in his lifetime, when his popularity was already spreading worldwide, Chandler knew that in the US, because crime writing itself was not taken seriously, he was only 'a beat-up pulp writer ... ranked slightly above a mulatto'.

It is a reflection of his status – and the genre he chose to write in – that even people who know Chandler's name cannot say for certain whether they have read his books and, if they do remember reading one of his books, are often unable to remember the titles. *The Big Sleep* and *The Long Goodbye* often generate a nod of recognition, but *Farewell, My Lovely* has the certainty trailing off. *The Little Sister*, *The Lady in the Lake* or *The High Window* bring down the blinds of blankness once again; and try *Playback* and even Chandler lovers will shrug kindly and acknowledge that this last novel at least shows he was human and, given his decline, wasn't it a grand effort for him to finish it at all?

Chandler's fame rests on reputation rather than actual page-turning contact. But let's try this. You've got so far with the titles. You've made it over the first couple of potholes. The headlights are shining off into the darkness. Let's go around the next corner. 'Philip Marlowe. Heard of him?' you ask.

Hmm. Hesitation. Sounds familiar.

'What movie did he star in?'

Okay. Accept the inevitable. We're at the crest of the hill. Slip out of gear, rest the engine, just keep your hands on the wheel.

'How about Humphrey Bogart?'

Ahh! Lights flash on all over the place. You're looking down on a city of associations. Chandler would have appreciated the irony of this. He asserted repeatedly that he was writing for a 'semi-literate public'. But even in his day Chandler would probably have agreed that the ability to read was used predominantly to work out which movie to go to next.

Bogart. You can see it, the file comes onscreen, faces open

with recognition. 1930s? 1940s? Black saloon cars screeching around corners into the Hollywood hills. Blackmail rings. Crooked cops. Smart lines snarled from the corner of tough-guy mouths. Dim-lit rooms. Street light shining up through the blinds from below. Black and white, film noir. Late night TV. Arthouse classics.

Bogart. Short guy. Double-breasted suit and pulled-down fedora. Marches into the room with a cigarette hanging off his lips, eyes slitted against the smoke, the bulge of a Smith and Wesson under his jacket, a couple of hoods in the corner with machine guns over their arms.

Fine. We're on the right road. The signs are leading the right way. But that's not Chandler, it's Bogart. Time to head on. We've got detective stories and we've got Bogart. Now push a little further, round the next curve, into the darkness.

Chandler, incidently, approved of Bogart playing Philip Marlowe. 'As we say here [in Hollywood], Bogart can be tough without a gun.'

'Okay, back to Chandler. Where were his novels set?'
'California?'
'Uh huh. Where in California?'
Only two choices, really.
'San Francisco?'
'No, that's Hammett. And Sam Spade. Unsmiling Sam Spade. Marlowe's dour cousin.'
'Then it must be Los Angeles.'

Bingo! 'I was the first writer to write about Southern California at all realistically,' Chandler wrote in 1956. 'Now half the writers in the country piddle around in the smog.'

That's Chandler on a bad day. 1956. A year crowded with bad days.

Okay. Hollywood. Los Angeles. The '30s and '40s. The screen fizzles for a second then up comes the dark, rainy night again, the flash of a single gunshot, a car door slamming, tyres squealing through the over-excited B-grade soundtrack and the black saloon slides into the corners on an empty canyon road, rain slanting through the beams of the headlights.

Stay on that. We're getting an idea of what Chandler wrote

about, and most of that through the movies, but does this lead us to Chandler the man? Vaguely. Follow the lights to this – Lauren Bacall, who met Chandler during Howard Hawks's filming of *The Big Sleep* in 1946: 'He looked like a professor; very quiet, rather shy, quite pleasant. He said nothing memorable, pertinent or enlightening.'

Nice. And perhaps correct. During the filming Howard Hawks sent Chandler a telegram asking who had killed Owen Taylor, the Sternwood chauffeur found early in the book at the wheel of the family limousine under ten feet of water off the end of a pier. Chandler checked the text, considered his answer, then sent the reply, 'I don't know.'

Now we're getting somewhere. Here's José Ferrer, a Hollywood actor who met Chandler once: 'He was wearing a nondescript tweed jacket and gray flannels, seemed cheerful and pleased to meet me, which puzzled me, and was so far from the Philip Marlowe tough image that I was bewildered.'

But Ferrer was an actor. 'Of course, nobody can *really like* an actor,' Chandler liked to say after he'd been around Hollywood a while. Chandler always preferred the company of film writers, and appreciated that they were to do a paid job. 'In Hollywood the average writer is not young, not honest, not brave, and a bit overdressed. But he is darn good company, which book writers as a rule are not. He is better than what he writes. Most book writers are not as good.' Here's overdressed Hollywood good guy, H. Allen Smith, on Chandler: 'He was a mild-mannered guy of medium size with black wavy hair, horn-rimmed glasses, and a sensitive face. He looked like a poet is supposed to look.'

We're getting the picture. Chandler wasn't Philip Marlowe. He wasn't Humphrey Bogart. J.B. Priestley wrote: 'He was a shy, rather a ruminative kind of man biting at a pipe. More English in type than American.'

To Ian Fleming he possessed an 'ugly Hapsburg lip grimace'. Hamish Hamilton found, 'He looked fiercer than I had expected, with his thin lipped mouth, and habit of frowning and jutting out his lower lip.'

That's what others think. Let's talk to Chandler himself:

Every interview makes a different man and that is one reason I don't like them. The photo is rather ugly. The hands are obviously those of a strangler ... The physical description of Chandler is unrecognisable by anyone who knows him. He calls me small. What is his standard? ... Attired for the street I am an inch short of six feet. My nose is not sharp but blunt, the result of trying to tackle a man as he was kicking the ball ... Hair like steel wool? Nuts. It is limp. Walks with a forward-leaning lope, huh? Chandler cantered gaily into the cocktail lounge, rapidly consumed three double gimlets and fell flat on his kisser, his steel wool hair curling gracefully against the pattern of the carpet. No wonder this man thinks me observant. By his standards anyone who noticed how many walls the room had would be observant.

But Chandler's standards weren't always easy to meet. In a letter of 1950 he wrote: 'I am having a feud with Warners. I am having a feud with the gardener. I am having a feud with a man who came to assemble a Garrard changer and ruined two LP records. I had several feuds with the TV people. Let's see who else – oh, skip it. You know Chandler. Always griping about something.'

That's our man. 1950, it seems, had its bad days as well. But catch him off guard and he could be modest: 'While I am compelled by weight of opinion, some of it expert, some frankly prejudiced, to admit being one of the handsomest men of my generation, I also have to concede that this generation is now a little seedy, and I with it.'

How do we know all this? Of course. The Professor's 'Revenge'! Here's MacShane's version: 'He was extraordinarily thorough and liked to be businesslike, organised and prepared for any eventuality. He never ran out of anything, whether gasoline or office supplies. He was the kind of man who ordered everything by the case, and he had eighteen pairs of shoes.'

And the last word? That fashion bible, the London *Sunday Times*, which on 21 September 1952 declared of Chandler: 'Only the young at heart could wear such a necktie.'

all of my best friends, I have never met

A real writer, and at times I think I am one, exists on many levels of thought. Perhaps as a result of my business training I always knew that a writer had to follow a line with which the public would become familiar. He had to 'type' himself ... But that would not be enough for him in his own mind. So I suppose in my letters I more or less revealed those facets of my mind which had to be obscured or distorted in what I wrote for publication.

The particular circumstances of his life led Chandler to rely on correspondence as his lifeline to the world. These circumstances had their roots in his drinking and his marriage.
   When they married in 1924, Chandler was thirty-five, Cissy fifty-three – eighteen years his senior. But Cissy was young for her years, pretty and vivacious. On their marriage certificate she gave her age as forty-three and it appears that even Chandler, at that time, did not know her actual age. At first this age difference was something the couple took in their stride, but inevitably, in crucial ways, it determined the life the couple led.
   During the early years of their marriage, Chandler fulfilled the role of a highly-paid business executive. At weekends he played tennis and went to football games with friends. Due to her age Cissy would usually stay at home on these occasions, and although he was devoted to her, Chandler started to notice younger women.
   A pattern emerged whenever Chandler found himself in periods of social activity. It would be repeated when he went to work in Hollywood in 1943. He was not relaxed in company and covered his insecurity with a shell of diffidence which alienated others and left him feeling distressed. Social occasions inevitably involved alcohol and this suited him. It loosened him up and gave him courage. But it also exaggerated his sexual nervousness. Drinking made him maudlin and reflective of the realities of his own life, of his ageing wife at home, the loss of his own youth, of his nervous desire for young women. Once the drink had started to flow, Chandler's

social weekends would often disappear in an alcoholic stupor.

As the years passed Chandler's drinking had become chronic. He was watching his life pass beneath him, and he was still not doing what he had, since childhood, wanted to do – write. By the end of his oil years in 1932 he was in his mid-forties and Cissy was over sixty. She could no longer hide her age with hair colour and youthful clothes, and the reality of his marriage pressed heavily upon him.

He started making passes at young women in the office and attempted a number of affairs. He rented an apartment for one young secretary and would spend weekends with her there, so drunk he had to ring in on Mondays and make excuses for her absence. Often he would not appear himself until Wednesday. Towards the end he would disappear for days or a week at a time. He rang the office with threats of suicide – often from a hotel room in a distant town – until eventually these calls were ignored. The deterioration in his work, however, could not be ignored, and in 1932 he was dismissed. He was forty-four. Cissy was sixty-two. His dismissal was not due to office politics, or 'the Depression', as he would indicate later on. He was fired because of his drinking.

Chandler made a decision to stop drinking and start writing. This meant a radical change in their lifestyle. Because of Cissy's age, and because Chandler needed alcohol to relax with people, the couple did little socialising. Their life was quiet and regular. They had little money. The standard pulp-magazine rate of payment was one cent per word, and although Chandler was soon earning more than this with *Black Mask*, these first years were still frugal. They lived in rented apartments in suburban Los Angeles and during the hot months rented a cabin in the mountains at Big Bear Lake. In winter they spent time in La Jolla. They saw few people. It was in these years that Chandler started communicating with his friends through letters. Many of these were other pulp writers whom he had never met.

In 1943 he was invited to Hollywood. This was reassuring recognition of his achievements as a writer, and the weekly salary he received was huge after the years of struggle on pulp payments and meagre book royalties – but it also revived his old tensions.

After ten years alone at his desk, Chandler was working once again with other people. Soon he started drinking again, and attempting liaisons with young women in the studios. On one occasion he did go off with a young secretary for some weeks. But he always went back to Cissy. He recognised by then, in his mid-fifties, the value of the stable life that she offered him. He knew he did his best work when sober and alone. At his age Hollywood was exhausting and the process of scriptwriting too disheartening to leave him the energy to do the writing he really wanted to do. In an unpublished article of 'qualified farewell' to Hollywood he wrote, 'I am a writer and there comes a time when that which I write has to belong to me, has to be written alone and in silence, with noone looking over my shoulder, no one telling me a better way to write it. It doesn't have to be great writing, it doesn't even have to be terribly good. It just has to be mine.'

In 1946, with money earned in Hollywood, the Chandlers moved to La Jolla permanently. 'I was a bit of a stinker in Hollywood,' he wrote. 'No swimming pool, no stone marten coats for a floozie in an apartment, no charge accounts at Romanoff's. I kept the money.'

In part the move was Chandler's attempt to repay Cissy for the years of misdemeanours against their marriage, and the hardships she had to endure while he was a struggling writer. But Chandler recognised that in La Jolla the 'air of cool decency and good manners that is almost startling in California' was what he needed for his own well-being. And the house was, he wrote, 'a much better home than any out-of-work pulp writer has any right to expect'.

When they bought the house in La Jolla Chandler was fifty-eight, Cissy seventy-six. It was the only house they ever owned.

The Chandlers resumed their reclusive life. Other writers lived there, but Chandler and Cissy were a stiff, private couple and socialising was never easy. Chandler disliked being disrupted from his routine. He would spend the morning working, then have lunch with Cissy and do errands in the

afternoon. In the evenings, when they didn't have
which was often because they were so hard to pl
cooked dinner. Cissy retired early, and Chandler, who
from insomnia, spent the nights reading, and, 'beca
mind is too active for its own good', wrote letters. After
seeing what his friend Erle Stanley Gardner could do with a
dictaphone (Gardner dictated his books in a week or ten
days), Chandler bought his own, and dictated many of his
letters for his secretary, Juanita Messick, to type up in the
morning. He used the machine for scriptwriting, but never
trusted it for his own novels.

In the flesh Chandler was a shy, awkward man, but on
paper he felt safe, and his wit and intelligence flourished. He
had the control over his friendships he couldn't have in the
flesh. He did much of his thinking in letters, and commented
to Hamish Hamilton that 'in letters I sometimes seem to
have been more penetrating than in any other kind of
writing – at times – and that as I re-read some of them, I am
really astonished – astonished at the facility of expression
and the range of thought I seemed to show even when I was
only a struggling beginner.'

To Juanita Messick he joked that he occasionally came
across letters in his files in which he was staggered to find 'I
could have been so brilliant for no money'. And he added,
'What a pity it is that there's nothing in essay writing. I
could have been a very fine essayist, and should thoroughly
have enjoyed that. Much more so than murder stories, which
part of my mind always looks down on with a certain
condescension.'

Chandler's letters do contain the essentials of good essay
writing and in themselves could almost be used as a textbook
of style and eloquence. He could be personal and intimate,
and at the same time erudite and witty. He wrote, 'I have
more love for our superb language than I could ever possibly
express.' He became one of the great literary letter writers
of the century.

In his letters, having dispensed with the business at hand,
he would range on to whatever happened to be on his mind
at the time – the books he was reading, his own life, his

contempt for the highbrow literary establishment or his despair for Hollywood. He wrote about cats and famous crimes and the mores of Southern California, which both amused and repelled him; he launched into intellectual meditations on the art of the murder mystery. He told bawdy jokes and composed rather dated risqué limericks. He was always forthright, and in the introduction to the *Selected Letters* Frank MacShane makes the point that the publication of many of the letters was prevented by the laws of slander. Chandler wrote with clarity and compassion about the practice of writing. 'I'm awfully sorry for writers', he wrote to Hamish Hamilton. 'They try so hard, are so damn vulnerable, and they look so silly when they overextend themselves.' And to Edgar Carter, 'I suppose all writers are crazy, but if they are any good, I believe they have a terrible honesty.'

In letters, Chandler was able to express the different sides of himself – he could be formal, yet relaxed – and many of his correspondents, perhaps seduced by the ease of his prose, became friends. These were mostly business associates – publishers, agents, magazine editors or other writers of detective fiction. His longest ongoing correspondence was with his English publisher, Hamish Hamilton. Early in the friendship, learning that Hamilton was known to his friends as 'Jamie', Chandler wrote: 'Would you mind addressing me as Ray, and will you tell me how I may most familiarly address you? I live in the world where the use of a last name is almost an insult.'

In another letter to Hamish Hamilton, giving his impressions of Somerset Maugham, Chandler could have been describing himself:

I have a feeling that fundamentally he is a pretty sad man, pretty lonely. His description of his seventieth birthday is pretty grim. I should guess that all in all he has had a lonely life, that his declared attitude of not caring much emotionally about people is a defence mechanism, that he lacks the kind of surface warmth that attracts people and at the same time is such a wise man that he knows that however superficial and accidental most friendships are, life is a pretty gloomy affair without them ... In a conventional sense he probably has many friends. But I don't think they build much of a fire against the darkness for him. He's a lonely old eagle.

Chandler did not have many friends, even 'in a conventional sense'. He had many acquaintances, and most of these may have thought of themselves as friends, but every one of the lasting personal connections in Chandler's life was conducted through letters. 'All of my best friends,' he wrote, 'I have never met.' And it is sad to note that most of these 'friendships' were heavily one-sided. Chandler's letters were, in effect, conversations he had with himself.

In his loneliest years, following the death of his wife, Chandler wrote intimately to several women friends (some of whom were his lovers), but much of this correspondence he destroyed before he died. He formed a close relationship with his English agent, Helga Greene, and in his last years he often exchanged several letters a week with her. In his published correspondence, however, there was no other person in his life – no woman he had not met – with whom he appeared to be on such intimate terms as Deirdre Gartrell.

why?

What happened between Chandler and Deirdre? What prompted the intimacy of this correspondence? Why did Chandler become so intensely involved with 'a girl I have not even seen'?

I knew nothing of Deirdre, but I did know something of Chandler's life. Although I had no certain idea of the exact period of Chandler and Deirdre's correspondence, MacShane's extracts are all from 1957. And by this time Chandler's life was anything but happy.

After Cissy's death in December 1954 he never recovered his equilibrium. His life became a confused succession of attempts to replace the stability he lost when she died. He resumed drinking and was thereafter in and out of drying-out institutions in England and the States. Only with the greatest determination did he complete his last book, *Playback*, at the end of 1957. Compared to his earlier novels it is tired and forced, his least successful book. 'There must be some magic in writing after all. But I take no credit for it,' he wrote in 1949, 'it just happens, like red hair.' The magic, by the time of *Playback*, had run out.

As he shuffled between La Jolla and London, avoiding a confrontation with the British tax and immigration authorities, his life disintegrated around him. He was desperate for someone to love and care for. His letters reflect this. He is preoccupied with his unhappiness. The letters have less of his hard edge; they are often sentimental, sometimes desperate and pontificating. They are the letters of an old man near his end. Everything Chandler wrote after Cissy's death is touched with sadness.

Were his letters to Deirdre no more than an attempt to salve this loneliness? The one reference Chandler made to anyone else about Deirdre in the surviving letters only adds to the mystery. Discussing with Hamish Hamilton the possible publication of his letters, Chandler noted that 'some are analytical, some are a bit poetical, some sad, and a good many caustic or even funny ... There are also love letters and letters to an unknown girl in Australia, which were merely a rather kind attempt to resolve her problems after she had given me more of her heart than (as she said) she had ever given to any of her family.'

If Chandler believed he had such a firm grip on his heart, as this letter indicates, why did he chose to involve himself in the problems of this 'unknown girl in Australia'?

Part three
I miss everyone very much, even the people I didn't like

you've got to

Gabrielle Mercy: In London Ray still drank too much and often complained of being miserable, but his life was more or less on an even keel. He enjoyed playing the role of the literary celebrity. Editors knew they could count on him to be unpredictable and witty. In 1956 the Daily Express conducted a poll among its readers to establish the most popular artists, writers and entertainers according to high-, middle- and low-brow tastes. Ray and Marilyn Monroe were the only people to appear on all three lists. He was very pleased. He rang us all up to make sure we'd seen it.

But he did get very low and we couldn't be there all the time. You'd turn up at the Ritz, or the flat at Carlton Hill, and he'd come to the door in tears. He'd cheer up but you knew you were just keeping him from himself. More than once I held him in my arms while he told me how empty his life was without someone to love.

He could be a terrible emotional blackmailer. He would ring one or other of us – whoever was in favour that week – at midnight, or three in the morning, quite drunk, and demand you come around. If you hesitated, or refused, he would say, 'Don't you love me?' Or, 'Is this the way you wanted it?' And he would hang up, saying he was going to kill himself.

The tragedy of it was that Ray knew he was acting dishonourably, and so loathed himself all the more. He would ring in the morning and apologise, if he remembered the incident at all, and send roses or demand you let him take you out to lunch. It wouldn't happen again for a week or so, but you'd invariably hear from one of the others that he had done exactly the same to them a day or two later.

One day I called in to visit him at the Ritz. It was three o'clock in the afternoon and I was going to suggest we trip down to the British Museum for an hour or so. But he was lying on his sofa, dead drunk.

I was furious. 'I don't know why we're all wasting our time on you, you're a hopeless case,' I said, and stormed out.

A few minutes after I got home the phone rang. It was Ray. 'No one has ever spoken to me that way in my life,' he said.

'More's the pity,' I said, 'or perhaps you wouldn't be where you are now.'

There was silence. I could hear his wheezy breathing on the end of the line.

He said, 'I know I'm bad but, you know, it's tiny steps for tiny feet.'

I knew he wanted me to feel sorry for him. But I was determined not to. I wasn't going to give in again.

'Ray,' I said, 'you've got to stop. There's no choice. You've just got to.'

but he didn't

But he didn't stop, and he was taken off to hospital. This happened several times. He'd go for a cure but it would never last. One doctor at the London Clinic decided that what was wrong with him was a rare strain of malaria. This suited Ray well. Suddenly everything was explained, the vomiting fits, chills, fever, forty-eight hour flu – coincidentally all the symptoms of alcohol poisoning. He was able to build quite a degree of melodrama around this but it certainly didn't stop him drinking.

He loved us all, I'm sure, but Natasha the most, probably because it was such an impossible situation. He was convinced that Natasha couldn't keep living the way she was, juggling her career and her family and a really quite ferocious social life. He saw himself as her saviour. He would take her out to lunch and lecture her about taking better care of herself. He managed to convince himself that her life was in disarray and what she needed was someone to put it in order – someone like him. Which was well-intentioned perhaps, but considering the disorder in his own life, really quite laughable. It was us, it was Natasha, who were rescuing him, not the other way around.

In our turn he made each of us feel special, but what he needed was a marriage, a full-time companion, and he knew that each of us, all so much younger than him, had other plans for our lives. And apart from this he had tax problems and couldn't even stay in England.

Because he was a British citizen, he was not allowed to spend more than six months in England in any financial year without paying income tax. He'd already paid tax on his earnings in America and he wouldn't put up with the perceived injustice of this – not to mention the extra cost. Had he been able to stay in London, his last years may have passed in comfort. He may even have found a reason to stop drinking. He may have kept writing. But this was not to be.

he wrote

He returned to America when his visa expired in September 1955, but hated being back. Even from the *Queen Elizabeth*, on the return passage to New York, he wrote to Roger Machell, one of the directors of Hamish Hamilton, 'I sit in a corner with my back protected on all sides. I once said good morning to a passenger, but it was an accident – I was thinking of something else.'

'I miss everybody very much,' he wrote to Roger in another letter, 'even the people I didn't like.'

Back in La Jolla, he sat in his room at the Hotel Del Charro, smoked Craven A cigarettes, and wrote to Helga, 'Am I comfortable? No. Am I happy? No. Am I weak, depressed, no good, and of no social value to the community? Yes. Outside my window is an illuminated swimming pool. Phooey on it!'

He was miserable. What he wanted was a reason to return to England, and on hearing that Natasha was ill and had to go into hospital for an operation, he had found that reason. He flew back almost immediately, supposedly to look after her, but this was probably more stress on her than if he had stayed away. It meant also that he was over-staying his allowed six months. This caught him up in a wrangle with the tax office which went on for years. Finally, in May 1956, 'determined to stay', he returned to the US, to New York.

without love

In New York he ended up in hospital again. This time one of those no-nonsense Manhattan doctors told him straight out that he wasn't suffering from malaria or any other exotic disease, his system was simply breaking down from alcohol abuse. He was given blood transfusions for sixteen hours straight, put on a high protein diet and in five days was well enough to leave the hospital.

He spent a week recuperating at the Grosvenor Hotel and had lunch with his French editor, Marcel Duhamel, and his wife. 'I'd like to sleep with her,' he wrote to Helga. 'Right now I'd like to sleep with any pretty, soft, gentle woman, but of course I shan't do it (even if I had the chance) because there has to be love. Without that there is nothing.'

He wrote to Ian Fleming, 'I have friends here, but not many. Come to think of it, I haven't many any where. Monday night I am flying back to California and this time hope to stick it out and make some kind of modest but convenient life there.'

gorgeous

Gary Davis: He was on a cure when he came back and I wouldn't describe him as exactly gorgeous to be around. When I called in on him at the Del Charro, just after he flew in, he was sitting in the dark smoking and tapping away at a letter. This with the shades drawn at midday. 'They always give me this room,' he said. 'They know how much I adore the pool.'

He was already sick to death of California. 'Skin like burnt orange and smiles like gashes,' he said. For him, that's all it had to offer. And enough memories to make even Hitchcock nervous.

But he knew there was nowhere else for him to go. La Jolla was the closest place to home he had. So he went looking and found an apartment down in the centre of town and made a brave face of pretending it was just what he wanted out of life. It was a pretty little place, set around a courtyard, big palm tree in the middle, spare bedroom to shove all his stuff in, and a big window overlooking the beach. A lot of people would've thought they'd died and gone to heaven with a view like that. But not Ray. He turned his back to it, took some of his books and furniture out of storage, and then wailed that apartment was so crowded 'only a steeplechaser would feel at home in it'.

If a view ever mattered to Ray, he kept it well hidden. When the *Bugle* sent me up to get the dirt on them after they first bought in La Jolla in '46, Ray and Cissy had a view you'd kill for. The living-room had a picture window which looked south across the bay to Point Loma, the most westerly part of San Diego. At night the lights of the coastline must've just about ended in their laps. On that first day, I sat down in front of the window and almost cried, it was so beautiful. But Ray turned his back and fired up his pipe and said, 'We live here. So the hell with it.'

It was a big house and he could have put his study out the front with the view. But instead he worked out the back overlooking the garden. He said he couldn't work looking at the sea. 'Too much water,' he said. 'Too many drowned men.'

Ray was never exactly the sort of citizen the local chamber of commerce could send off as an ambassador for the tourist trade. In his new apartment in '56 he pulled the shades closed and lit up a Craven A and could've been anywhere, except for the climate. He went to parties but was a lonely sight, glowering in the corner in his cotton gloves, sipping his tonic and lime.

He set his new Olivetti up at the end of the dining table with a stack of the little half-sheets of yellow paper he used for writing and tried to get himself into a routine. He kept taking out the Marlowe novel he'd started before Cissy died but said he had to put it away again before he burst into tears. All he wrote in '56, I'd say, were letters. And most of them complaining about California.

lost it

I know what is the matter with my writing or not writing. I've lost my affinity for my background. Los Angeles is no longer my city and La Jolla is nothing but a climate and a lot of meaningless chi-chi. To write about a place you have to love it or hate it or do both by turns, which is usually the way you love a woman. But a sense of vacuity and boredom, that is fatal.

mr america

Gary Davis: He might have been on a cure, but it got the better of him. He complained about having no one to eat dinner with. He said eating alone when you've spent all day alone is like dying a little every night. So it wasn't long before he was drinking again – drowning himself before the dinners got to him.

One day I was up talking to the Boys in the Beautiful Shirts about Civic Pride week, so I called in. It was about eleven in the morning. I knocked on the door and called out,

'Ray, you there?' And he yelled to come in, so I opened the door and just headed in. I could see his feet on the couch. Ray did a lot of work lying down on the couch. But as soon as I got in the room I knew it wasn't no work he was at.

I started talking, telling him a story I'd heard about this young cop we knew called Errol. Errol Flynn, Ray and I used to call him. He was the cop who found Ray in the bathroom with a gun in his mouth. I just opened the door and launched into it. 'Hey, Ray,' I said. 'I've got one you're gonna like. It's Mr Flynn. You're gonna love this.'

But I reached the door of the main room and stopped. Ray was lying there with this glass of vodka resting on his chest. He was stinko, staring at me with his lip out just like a little kid. He knew he was doing the wrong thing.

'Oh Ray,' I said. 'Whatcha doing, Ray? You know you shouldn't be doing this.'

And then tears started rolling down the the sides of his face and soaking into the arm of the lounge under his head. I went and sat with him and took his hand and he gripped it hard and just let go, weeping away like a baby. And finally he said, 'There was blood in my urine, Gary. I'm passing blood. What does that mean? Am I going to die?'

I said, 'Blood in your urine doesn't mean you're going to die, Ray. But it sure don't mean you're Mr America either.' And I pointed to the glass on his chest and told him, 'You know what you gotta do. The first thing is cut this out. Properly.'

I took the glass out of his hands and put it down on the floor. 'Now,' I said, 'you want to hear this story about Errol?'

He nodded and so I launched on, sitting there on the couch holding his hand. It wasn't much of a story, but if you knew the La Jolla cops, and if you knew Errol you'd appreciate the humour.

Seems there was a shooting at a store in town and Errol went down to investigate. This is La Jolla, right. The only shooting gets done in La Jolla is film shooting. So Errol's pretty nervous. In fact I'd say he'd be just about pickling his toes by the time he gets to the door. He had his gun out, ready to do what he had to do. So he gets to the door and says real loud, 'Nobody move!' And of course everyone moves. The whole shop turns and looks, sees Errol with his Colt .45 shaking all over the ranch, and dives to the floor and starts shrieking for God's mercy.

Remember, this is La Jolla. Folks here don't know the rules like they do in Los Angeles. And Errol is so flustered his trigger finger clamps down on the first shape it sees. Well, unfortunately that shape was the Mayor's wife. Didn't kill her, lucky for him, but it must've made things exciting down at Police Central for a day or two. And put somewhat of a plateau on Errol's career. Meanwhile, of course, the original shooter got clean away.

Not national news but it did the trick. Ray's face was clamped up like a little baby's he was laughing so hard. We were both laughing. I was near shedding tears myself. Then the laughing stopped and Ray lay there clinging on to my hand, neither of us saying anything, just looking at the other, our palms sweaty as a runner's jocks.

The next day I rang Juanita, Ray's old secretary, and he let her drive him down to Chula Vista for another visit.

party's over

Chandler stumbles from his apartment house to a waiting car. He is in shirtsleeves but still wearing his bow tie, yellow with black polka dots. It is a hot day, his tie is askew, he has a bottle of vodka in his hand. He opens the passenger door of the car, slumps in, pulls the door closed and sits still, staring straight ahead.

A minute later Juanita Messick bustles from the apartment house carrying a small suitcase. She opens the back door of the car and pushes the suitcase along the seat. She closes the door and goes around the car to the driver's side and gets in. She starts the car and lets it warm up. Chandler does not acknowledge her. He lifts the bottle to his lips. A woman passes on the sidewalk, being led by a haughty ornamental

poodle. She makes an audible cluck! and scoots the dog ahead of her. 'Hurry along, Chester.'
   Chandler scowls at her back.

A family on the street behind us has a black French poodle, small, toy size, I guess. The animal is taking piano lessons, $35 a month. As of now he can play 'Peter, Peter, Pumpkin Eater', not technically very exacting, but one has to begin, *n'est-ce pas*? Little steps for little feet. Later one hopes he will make his debut in Carnegie Hall. The people can afford it and that's all it takes. It's nice to live in an ambitious neighbourhood, and to live in a milieu where money is spent on Art, not just on Cadillacs, Jaguars and coloured butlers. This is true. $35 a month for lessons. Black toy poodle.

   The car drives slowly through the centre of La Jolla. The people on the streets are old and wealthy. They walk with canes and wear wide-brimmed white hats and white suits. These are the locals; the tourists are in swimsuits and sandals with towels around their necks. Chandler watches them from the window of the car, his lip out, snarling.
   'A good place for old people and their parents.'
   Juanita Messick turns. 'Excuse me, Ray?'
   Chandler realises he has spoken aloud. 'Nothing, Nita, nothing.' He takes another swig from the bottle.
   Nita, her hands high on the wheel, says without turning, 'There's only one thing you've got to do Ray, and you know what it is.'
   The car is on the highway, winding between low brown hills. Chandler stares out the window, the bottle lolling in his lap. Nita tries again. 'They won't let you in with that, you know that, don't you, Ray?'
   They take an exit from the freeway, and wind up into the hills. A sign set in an irrigated green lawn reads CHULA VISTA PRIVATE SANITORIUM.

among friends

The entrance foyer is a large cool grey space with a wall of windows and a glass door looking out over a well-kept garden. The sky outside is high and blue. The sea glitters over the brown hills in the distance. Inside, watched by two nurses, Chandler is steadying himself on the admissions counter. His suitcase is on the marble floor beside him. His voice is slurred.

'I'm paying for this goddamn holiday and, by God, I paid for this too. If I can't take it in ... '

He up-ends the bottle and spills vodka down his chin as he swallows. Nita stands behind him with her hands clasped around the handle of her handbag.

'Ray – ' she says.

She starts towards him but the male nurse motions her back. He steps quickly around the counter and reaches up to take the bottle from Chandler's grip. Chandler tries to sidestep with the bottle still up at his mouth. He loses his balance and topples backwards but the nurse saves the bottle in one hand and grabs Chandler by the arm with the other. He reaches behind him to put the bottle on the counter and lets Chandler subside to the floor.

'Come on, Mis' Chandler, party's over. What say you and me go get a shave and a good hot tub bath?'

Chandler wrenches his arm free and turns on his hands and knees to stand. The nurse helps him to his feet. Chandler tries to brush him off.

'I can stand, Nelson, I can stand.' He steadies himself on the counter, trying to refocus his eyes. The others watch. He locates Nita and opens his arms to her.

'Nita, I would have died many years ago without you.'

'Come on, Mis' Chandler,' says Nelson.

'Good God, am I not allowed to say goodbye to my lady friend? What do you run here? A prison?'

Nelson lifts his hands in the air and backs away. Chandler glares and, turning, offers Nita his arm.

'I'll walk you to the car, my dear.'

Glancing back at the two nurses, Nita supports him to the

door. Chandler walks unsteadily with his chin held high. He stops at the glass doors and turns to take her hands.

'Don't worry, Nita, I'll get them in line.'

He bends down to kiss her cheek.

'Ray, everyone knows you here. You're among friends. But if there's anything you need, call.'

She takes him in her arms. When she releases him, his cheeks are wet. He reaches past her to open the door, waits until she has passed through, then turns and weaves a line back to the counter. The nurses watch in silence. All is silence. Even the rubber plants are holding their breath.

Chandler reaches the nurses and holds out his hands.

'Take me,' he says. 'I'm yours.'

The nurses glance at each other and smile. These are words they have heard before.

looking tight

Nelson picks up the suitcase in one hand and takes Chandler's arm with the other. They move slowly down the corridor into the building. The other nurse takes the half-empty bottle from the counter and pushes open a door in the wall behind. A doctor with his feet up on the desk looks over the top of a football magazine.

'Go peacefully?'

The nurse nods and crosses the room to a sink against the wall, the bottle of vodka in her hand. 'I hate it when they keep coming back.'

The doctor looks back down into his magazine. 'Nah. He likes it here. Mr Take-Me-I'm-Yours. Everyone's special friend. What is he? Actor?'

The nurse stands at the sink looking down at the vodka in the bottle.

'He's a writer.'

The doctor doesn't look up.

'Yeah? Famous?'

'Raymond Chandler.'

The doctor pauses for a moment then looks back to the

magazine. 'The Bulls are looking tight this year,' he says.
The nurse looks over at him. There is no life in her face. She lets herself sink forward against the wall with her arm under her forehead. She up-ends the bottle and watches the vodka gurgle colourlessly down the plughole until it disappears and there's nothing left but the sound of the doctor behind her turning the pages of his magazine.

common sense

I regard psychiatry as fifty per cent bunk, thirty per cent fraud, ten per cent parrot talk, and the remaining ten per cent just a fancy lingo for the common sense we have had for hundreds and perhaps thousands of years, if we ever had the guts to use it.

At Chula Vista a psychiatric appraisal was part of the programme. They let the patients dry out and get back on to solid food, then wheeled them into the consulting rooms for a workout. A week away from whisky, another week from going home, and Chandler was relaxed and ready for a fight.

The room was cool and dim. The psychiatrist, like Chandler, was dressed in an open-necked shirt and loose trousers. They faced each other in leather easy chairs, a coffee table lengthways between them, a vacant couch alongside it. Chandler sat with his legs asprawl and his trousers hitched up, revealing black socks and white ankles.

The psychiatrist was overweight, with pocked skin and a poached face, which made Chandler like him immediately. Anything was better than another tanned Californian.

'Mr Chandler ... may I call you Ray? It's more relaxed.'

'Call me anything you like, doctor. I'm a grown man. I can take it.'

The doctor smiled – slightly.

'My name is Brian.'

He reached forward for Chandler's hand. Chandler pulled himself up to shake it, then slumped back into his chair. His shirt stuck to him. His bow tie – white, with tiny red dots – sat straight at his neck.

The psychiatrist watched as Chandler surveyed the room. French doors led out to a small courtyard with plants in pots. Waist-high bookcases stood against the walls. A goldfish wandered in circles in a fish bowl on the coffee table.

Chandler twisted to read some of the spines in the bookcase.

'Got a few of yours in there,' said the doctor.

'Is that right? You use them to test people?'

'Test them how?'

'See how morally debauched they are. If they smile they're sunk. If they laugh they drown.'

The doctor smiled.

'You're Australian?' said Chandler.

The doctor nodded.

'I knew some Australians in London. Awful accents. One of them was a painter. Very pretty. And very talented. If I'm any judge of things.'

'I'd say you would be. Were they big drinkers?'

'The Australians?' Chandler shrugged. 'No bigger than me.'

The doctor didn't answer. Nor did he fill the silence which followed.

Chandler cleared his throat. 'So. What do you want first? The inkblots? Or the finger painting?'

'Why don't you start by telling me why you're in here?'

'For excessive drinking and cumulative exhaustion. They used to think it was a rare strain of malaria. Then I agreed to hear the truth.'

Chandler paused, his lip pushed out aggressively. The doctor uncrossed then recrossed his legs.

'Go on. Why do you drink too much? Tell me about your life.'

Chandler dropped his gaze to the floor and sighed, rolling the palms of his hands over his knees.

'I was happily married for thirty-odd years. I loved my wife very much. She died in December, year before last. Two months later I tried to kill myself with a pistol. I was drunk. The ammunition was faulty. Otherwise I wouldn't be here.'

The doctor nodded.

'Did you drink through the years of your marriage?'

'No. I stopped in 1932. I used to work for an oil company and my drinking cost me my job. That's when I started writing. I didn't drink at all for over ten years. Then I started working in Hollywood. I drank there. You gotta. To stay sane.'

The doctor smiled.

'But it wasn't hard to stop. It caused my wife a deal of pain. We moved down to La Jolla to get away from all that. We always kept hooch in the house for guests, and my wife enjoyed a single sherry in the evening. But I drank nothing. My father was alcoholic and I have lived all my life in the fear of becoming one. But until my wife died I could always quit drinking. Until the last years of her life I was dry as a desert wind.'

He sighed, his hands still on his knees, and watched the goldfish circling in its bowl. He looked up with a sheen over his eyes.

'Then, as my wife's health deteriorated, I drank moderately. Regularly, but moderately. Some champagne at night. She died very slowly, and my intake increased as she declined. When she finally did die I started back on whisky and since then I haven't stopped. I've taken cures and spent weeks at a time in clinics such as this, and I've been hospitalised more times than I care to remember.'

He sighed.

'Something in my chemistry will no longer accept alcohol. There is some sort of chain reaction. I start off with a drink of white wine and end up drinking a bottle of Scotch a day. Then I stop eating. After four or five days of that I am ill. I have to quit and the withdrawal symptoms are simply awful. I shake so that I can't hold a glass of water. I can't stand up or walk without help. One day I vomited eighteen times. I wasn't sick at all, but something kept dropping down the back of my throat from my inflamed sinuses, and every time that happened I gagged my life out. For three days I could drink nothing but sips of ice water. But I always start again. I don't know why. Well, I do. There's no reason not to.'

don I will be crippled by taxes, and the reality ne of my girlfriends has her own life and I am each of their's. I have no emotional ties to much of the time I loathe the place. But I else to go. I'm stuck here. Alone. And drinking.'

Chandler stopped. The doctor shifted his weight, again uncrossing and recrossing his legs. He coughed.

'You're very honest with yourself. Thank you.'

Chandler's expression didn't change.

'Am I alcoholic, doctor?'

The doctor took a breath.

'Perhaps you are, perhaps you aren't. You've proved you can live without alcohol. You've given it up more than once in your life. But I do think that you can't live alone without alcohol. Morals are not my business, and you would not accept me telling you that they were. You're a lucky man in many respects. You're not divorced from your emotions, as many of us are. This, however, does make life difficult for you. You are sensitive, to put a word on it. You feel things that many of us do not. You aren't afraid of love. These are all reasons, I would guess, why women are attracted to you. You are not a usual man. However, you are in a bind. You are used to having someone to look after, and it is in that role, as protector and provider, that you feel most needed and hence most deserving of love. But now you don't have a person to live with and look after. I think you are realistic about love, and that also makes you unusual. You know, at your age, that you would be unlikely to love another person absolutely, as you did your wife. But such realistic beginnings are often the basis of very sound and satisfying mature-age relationships. I know you could give up drinking but the likelihood of it happening is minimal until you find a person to share your life. And, if not your life, then your home at least.'

The doctor raised his hands in the air.

'If that sounds too much like stating the obvious, I'm sorry. And I think a week or two in a doss house like this can best be regarded as a well-deserved rest from the rigours of your painful life. If, perhaps, a little overpriced.'

Chandler sat motionless, eyes split by his bifocals, chest heaving.

He slapped both knees and smiled.

'Well, doctor, you've given me hope for your profession. I don't think anyone has ever read me so well. I'll go away now and enjoy the rest of my holiday. Play some tennis. Practise on the six-foot board.'

He hauled himself to his feet.

'I have a girlfriend in Australia. She's at college in Armidale. In New South Wales.'

The doctor nodded as he stood.

'I come from Sydney. I was brought up at the beach. As you can tell.' He held his arm out, his skin white as a bone.

Crossing the room to the door he said, 'But I have an aunt in Armidale.'

He held the door open and extended his hand.

Chandler said, 'What's it like? Armidale?'

'You want the truth? Or the glossy brochure version?'

'You think I wouldn't know the difference?'

The two men stood at the door with hands gripped, as if they were involved in some ancient test of strength. The doctor looked over Chandler's shoulder as he spoke.

'Well, it's high up. It sometimes snows in winter, in spring the gardens are gorgeous, in summer it's so stinking hot you want to find a river and drown. Autumn's nice, but you know winter's coming so you can't relax. There's about a hundred churches and a dozen schools and the university college and, once you're out of town, nothing but sheep as far as the eye can see, except for maybe one tree on a distant horizon, and all in all it's about as exciting as standing in a queue to watch the tree grow. Except the tree's probably dead because trees take up valuable sheep space and they hate that out there. To be perfectly frank, I wouldn't mind if I never saw Armidale again. Oh, and one important thing – petrol. Gasoline. They rip you off blind. Never buy gas in Armidale.'

sunset strip on a saturday night

Gary Davis: I went down to collect him two weeks later. We drove back up the coast and he had colour in his cheeks and the sparkle back in his eye. He looked away out the window at the brown hills and said he had seen more colour in one afternoon at Kew Gardens in London than he had in forty years in California. 'It was like paradise,' he said. Then he breathed in deeply. 'But that smell, that sad smell of sage. Once you get it in your lungs, nowhere else in the world ever smells right again.'

I thought he was going downhill already. Then he laughed. 'And they can't make neon like we do. Every garden in London couldn't add up to one block of Sunset Strip on a Saturday night.'

The holiday had done him the world of good. He seemed positive and determined to make the most of what was left now Cissy was gone. Things seemed to be on a change.

Nita had the apartment opened up and had brought in some groceries, and I drove away with Ray waving from the front window, his jaw set.

Chandler watched Gary drive away down the street, then stepped back from the window and let down the shades. Without pausing, he went into the second bedroom where he stored his papers and books and took down a box from on top of the wardrobe. He carried it into the dining-room, set it on the table, and brought out a neatly-tied bundle of letters. He untied the ribbon and leafed through until he came to an apricot coloured envelope. This he set aside. He retied the ribbon, replaced the bundle in the box and took the box back into the bedroom.

He came back in, sat at the end of the table, and opened the letter.

I hope you don't mind me being so direct

Oakland CA
27 February 1955

Dear Raymond Chandler

I have just heard on the radio about your recent attempt at suicide. I hope you don't mind me being so direct. We have never met but your books are very dear to me and from them I feel you are a straightforward, if sensitive, man and you would prefer me to be straightforward too, rather than euphemistic. Of course I know nothing about the circumstances of your private life but I would like to offer my condolences, from one who has experienced the pain, for the loss of your wife. My husband died of cancer last spring. I know the agony of watching a loved one die.

What details I know of your life are garnered from dust jacket biographies. From these I gather that you were born in America but brought up in England; and that you now live in La Jolla. My husband and I drove through La Jolla several times on our journeys up and down the coast and even discussed the possibility of moving down there. The town seems to possess a gentility which California has little of. But at that point, six years ago now, my husband was chief librarian at the Berkeley campus of the University of California and there was no suggestion from either of us that he consider leaving that position. Of course by the time his cancer was detected it was too late to move. He died here among his family and that is the way we wanted it. My husband was a fine man and we all loved him totally.

It was therefore all the more cruel that he was taken from us so young. He was only fifty-five years old. I am now forty-nine, with the prospect of half my life ahead of me without the man I loved. And still love. You do not stop loving, as you know. I feel sure, from the comments you have made to the press, that this is the very sense of barrenness which led you to the incident with the pistol in your bathroom. I considered that option myself in the dark hours of many sleepless nights early after Paul's death and many more nights have passed when I wished that I had dug out his service revolver and used it. I knew where it was and could have done the job in a minute. He and I discussed the option more than once through his last months. I don't know what stopped me – perhaps the knowledge that they were early days and the pain would pass.

The pain hasn't passed, I have just become used to it. And I could not do the job now because of my two daughters and the two small children they have themselves. I have read that you are childless and so you will not have this reason to carry on. You will need, instead, extra reserves of strength and courage, and you will need friends. I have no doubt you were dealt much courage, but I would guess, like me, you do not have many close friends. Paul and I were best of friends and so, perhaps unwisely, shunned others. We didn't need other people. They detracted from what we had together. Yet because we were happy, others sought our friendship. I think when people see a couple very much in love they crowd around, hoping that some of the certainty will rub off. I am not boasting, I merely feel that this perhaps is the situation in which you found yourself with your wife.

And now she is gone and you are alone. No one can replace her but others can ease the pain of your loss. Please do not feel it insensitive of me to offer you my address, at the head of this letter. I will write my telephone number at the bottom. I ask nothing of you. If, however, you feel it would help you to reply to this letter, or if you should like to call me up, please do not feel, in these tender days of your mourning, that there is anything untoward in doing so. If you are in San Francisco and you would like to meet I should be honoured.

It was my husband, incidentally, who introduced your books into our house. He loved books, not surprisingly, and always said you would last long after the others were dust. He would very much have liked to meet you. We discussed, as one does, your likely qualities as a dinner guest. As long as you were seated beside a pretty and intelligent lady guest, we decided, you would discharge your obligations admirably.

This comes with my sincere best wishes.

Louise Delamotte

if you want to know me, my dear

Louise Delamotte: Later Ray told me that he had a box full of letters like mine. Letters from lady admirers that, he said, he kept for the odd wet weekend. Of course I was told this with a great deal of rakish bravado, which I am sure Ray did not intend to be completely believable. It made it all the more charming.

We had a very sudden friendship, one perhaps typical for Ray, but which, after his unpredictable withdrawal, left me reeling. He rang me out of the blue about eighteen months after I had written the letter – long, of course, after he had left my mind. He introduced himself and before I could regain my equilibrium, said that I had picked the only circumstances in which he could indeed be trusted to discharge his obligations as a dinner guest.

That's all he said. He didn't precede it by reminding me that I had mentioned this in my letter, and while I tried to understand what he was talking about I could hear his thick breathing down the phone. By then I think he realised he had embarrassed me, and he reminded me that he was referring to my letter and immediately, a bit too quickly, changed the subject and explained that he was planning to be in San Francisco in a day or two and asked if he could call. 'Of course,' I said, and scrabbled in my mind to arrange a time. I told him briefly which exit to take off the freeway. He said 'yes' twice and hung up.

It turned out, of course, that he wasn't coming to San Francisco for any other reason than to see me. I'd invited him to afternoon tea and he was early – he'd been driving around the neighbourhood for an hour to kill time. He was nervous, but it was still pleasant. He wore slacks and a sports coat and tie, and yellow gloves which he didn't take off, and explained were for his eczema. We chatted generally – about his life since his wife had died, about his new apartment, about La Jolla, about the differences between San Francisco and Los Angeles. He was very attentive and complimented me on the house, which he said was a wonderful change from the ghastly over-decorated places people lived in down where he came from. And he was very excited about the tea. He said he didn't particularly like tea, but did enjoy the ritual of taking it. He said he hadn't been offered afternoon tea since he left England, and that he and his wife used to take tea, but since she died he had stopped. He said this in such a way as to convey that the loss of his wife was still quite an open wound.

I took him on a tour of the house and he stopped briefly in front of the bookshelves in the study, which I think made both of us nervous. Me because, as much as I tried to not let it matter to me, I felt he was assessing us, and he because he knew that was what I was thinking.

He actually said, 'This is very rude, I know. Please forgive me.' Then suddenly he pulled a book from the shelves and said, 'Have you read this? I haven't seen this book in any other house in California.'

It was a book called *Mr Bowling Buys a Newspaper*, by an Englishman named Donald Henderson. 'Have you read it?' he asked again. I shook my head and admitted I hadn't. He leafed through it with obvious affection, and said, 'In no other book have I ever empathised so completely with the main character.' He looked up at me. 'If you want to know me, my dear, read this book. It is me.'

I did read it, of course. I picked it up and opened it about a minute after he had left. It was a terribly sad book about a middle-aged clerk in London who went to a good private school but had never amounted to anything in his life. To make up for this he commits a series of apparently senseless murders, is finally caught, and then sent to the gallows. The story shocked me. It was a bleak view of an unfulfilled and tragic life. Later, looking back, I understood what Ray had meant. It might not have been like him on the outside. But inside, perhaps, that was exactly how Ray felt.

He immediately started overwhelming me with attention. He came back up and stayed in a hotel the following week and I saw him every day. At the end of his visit he proposed that we spend a week up at Big Bear Lake. It was late summer and I agreed it would be a good break from the heat. But he was working too fast for me.

I was a widow, it's true, but since my husband died I had organised a busy and quite happy life for myself. I served on several charity committees in the Berkeley area, and I worked as a volunteer at the university's library. My daughter's children took up as much very pleasurable time as I chose to give them, and I read a lot and went to a yoga class run by a young Buddhist man in Oakland. I swam and I even sang in a barbershop quartet and wrote some poetry – which I showed no one, of course. Especially not Ray. It was not as if my life was empty.

But Ray seemed to assume that I was some sort of damsel in distress. He almost immediately wanted to know about my financial affairs, boasting that his years in offices had taught him 'more than how to sharpen pencils'. My son-in-law was already quite competently looking after my money and Ray's concern, I realised later, was simply an attempt to give his own life purpose. It was a classic case of transference. He felt aimless and lost and so, he decided, was I.

But this is the sort of thing you never see at the time. I agreed to go with him up to Big Bear. It was his and Cissy's favourite summer hideaway, he said. He was always utterly frank about how lost he still felt without her. Floundering with his nose barely above water, was how he put it. In retrospect, it was inappropriate for him to invite me up there. Big Bear was quite apparently a place that was full of memories for him. But at the time I felt honoured that he wanted to share it, and his past, with me.

I felt sorry for him, I suppose – that naive honesty does bring out the mothering in a woman. He was childlike, as if he had no interest in the usual armour a man builds up to protect his feelings. If he felt that something was good enough for him, he didn't care if it was socially acceptable or not. This, of course, could be exasperating, but, at the same time, also plugged in precisely to my motherly need to protect the defenceless – and, I suppose, to feel needed myself.

It was a lovely week. It's a steep climb into the mountains and then the road winds gently down through the trees and you're almost in the lake before you see it. It nestles there, deep and dark. 'Like a drop of dew caught in a curled leaf', Ray described it in one of his books. You rent little cabins set apart from each other, and when you sit on the deck in the afternoon sun you could be the only people in the world. We did a lot of that, sitting on the deck enjoying the sun and the view and chatting quietly about this and that. During the day we went hiking or canoeing. At night we lit a fire, and after dinner sat in front of it, not speaking a word.

One morning we woke up and the trees were dusted with snow. I insisted Ray come out for a walk before breakfast. He grumbled about it, but once he was out he became very excited, and the cold air and the exercise seemed to strip ten years off him. He said he hadn't been as physical since World War One, and that he felt so damned wholesome he was contemplating calling up Hemingway and getting him out to join us with his goddamn rucksack and sleeping bag. When he was relaxed Ray could be just as funny as his books. Funnier, because things just came out and you knew they were spontaneous.

That was the day he proposed to me. Well, that night. We were sharing a bed, although I must say we were very proper. We wore our pajamas, both of us with them buttoned to the neck, and although we fell asleep in each other's arms, that was all we did. There was something so considerate about Ray. He was not cheap, or rushed. You really sensed that he felt you were doing him an honour by allowing him to offer himself to you.

That night he was very nervous, coughing and clearing his throat, giving me strange looks. Eventually, when the lights were out and we were cuddled up, he made a speech.

He said he knew that we had only known each other a short time and we were both old and probably set in our ways – well, he was, anyway – but that we should seriously consider the possibility that, each in our widowed and single state, we could make the other happy. We could fashion 'a workable contentment', those were his words. He said that I seemed to know something about life which he had forgotten, or perhaps never learnt. I managed still to see everything with the fresh eyes of a child, he said, and for a 'sour old citizen' like him this was infectious and humbling. He didn't expect an answer right away. All he asked was that I go back to San Francisco and think about it.

When he finished his speech he took me in his arms and tried to kiss me as a young man might kiss a young woman. Or perhaps that was the way I experienced it, seeing as I had not been kissed that way since I was a young woman. I must say, I didn't like it, and pulled away. It felt just a little too rough, especially after his earlier gentleness.

This disturbed him. He was scared he had upset me, and apologised and started to retract his proposal. No, I said, that wasn't it at all. I simply needed a little time to get used to the idea. He accepted that and we cuddled up again, and both, I think, fell asleep almost immediately. And in the morning I woke up and said 'yes'. I accepted his proposal – and following that, well, as a man and a woman, we let nature take its course. And I must say, after such a lengthy ... unnatural period for me, it was touching, and really very pleasant.

At the time I knew nothing about Ray's drinking. He didn't drink with me because I don't drink. I certainly had no idea how anxious all this was making him. When he came to me he was often nervous, but that soon passed and our time together was easy and relaxed. It was a shock to realise, afterwards, that for Ray our association was so uncertain he had to drown his nerves in drink as soon as he was out of my company.

Only when he disappeared and I finally got on to Nita, his friend in La Jolla, did I realise the actual state of his life. She told me Ray had had another breakdown and was back in hospital.

'You probably don't know,' she said, 'how much Ray drinks. He probably doesn't drink in front of you.' She said she felt obliged to tell me, for both of our sakes. Because she could see what it was doing to Ray, and because she didn't want me to be harmed.

Ray was out of the hospital before I could drive down to see him. But after he came out I did drive down to La Jolla and brought him back up to stay with me – to recuperate, I suppose. And to keep an eye on him.

I was cautious to see what happened next. To see how he coped with not drinking, and if he did, in fact, drink on the sly. But he insisted he wasn't a sly drinker. He was brazen, quite cavalier about his drinking. He knew what it was doing to him, but that didn't stop him. It only made him more bullish. Of course, in this period, immediately after getting out of hospital, all this was talk. He wasn't drinking at all. His body simply wouldn't let him.

Then it all fell down. We went for another week up at Big Bear. It was November by this time, and the weather was cold, although no real snow had fallen yet. We had gone up to discuss our plans. Where we would live. How we would organise our lives. I wanted to stay in Oakland, and Ray was quite amenable to that. He said he'd be glad to get away from Southern California.

We did some more hiking that week, although we spent a lot of time inside around the fire, reading and drinking coffee. On Saturday night Ray cooked what he called his 'stupid steak', and on Sunday we lay in with our books. I remember I was reading a new book by the Australian,

Patrick White. *The Tree of Man.* Ray took one look at the first page and threw it down in disgust. It was exactly the sort of writing he hated. 'Sentences which no human being in his right mind could understand, let alone want to write,' he said. I didn't mind. I enjoyed the challenge.

Then we had this stupid row. About orange juice, of all things. Orange juice!

Ray made us juice and brought it back to bed to drink while the coffee was brewing. He liked doing that. Spoiling me. But that morning I took one taste of the orange juice and couldn't drink it. He'd cut the oranges on the garlic board. Or the night before chopped the garlic on the fruit board. It's one of my pet hates. In my house I'm very strict about the fruit board.

I said to him, 'Ray, this tastes of garlic. You must have chopped the garlic on the fruit board.'

No, he said, he hadn't. He'd made sure, because he knew it mattered to me. He tasted his juice and said it was fine. I must be imagining things, he said.

'Ray,' I said, 'I'm sorry. But I'm not imagining it. This juice tastes of garlic.'

'My darling,' said Ray, 'I did not chop the garlic on the fruit board. What more can I say?'

'Ray,' I said. 'I know the taste of garlic. It might be silly but it's one of the few things I put my foot down about. In our house chopping the garlic on the fruit board is an absolute no-no. I'm sorry, but it is.'

'Is that right?' he said softly. 'Is that so, Louise?'

He was looking at me without any expression, almost with hatred. His face had drained of colour and a small muscle under one eye was twitching. I can remember that look so clearly. It made my heart freeze. That and his lower lip jutted out for a fight.

We were at a watershed in our friendship, we both knew that. Our first argument. And although it was such a stupid, little thing, that somehow made it all the worse. That such a small thing could bring to the surface such venom, such determination. Such coldness! We didn't know each other, that was it. We had no past to temper the momentary hatred.

No real friendship to soften it. And I think we both realised then that what we were trying to do was not realistic. You can't just throw two people together, two people with two lifetimes behind them, and expect a sudden unity. No. We knew then we'd made a mistake.

It was shocking. We were both shocked. As if we'd both just witnessed something terribly unexpected and ugly. It silenced us. Sent us inside ourselves.

It was our last day. We were leaving later that morning, and Ray barely said another word.

We packed the car and got in and Ray started up the road to the rim of the mountain before the long wind down. He started slowly but before long he was driving too fast, speeding around the bends, spraying gravel over the edge, driving very dangerously. I was hanging on, afraid to say anything. Ray had his lip out, glowering, and I could see the sweat on his lip and on his brow.

Then he almost did drive us over the edge. He took one corner just too fast and lost control and we ended up literally within a foot of our lives. The tyres squealed and things crashed against each other in the back. I was petrified. The car came to a halt and suddenly, after what seemed an immense amount of noise, we were surrounded by silence. I just sat there, my knuckles white on the handle above the glovebox. I couldn't say a thing. I was too shaken to speak. And then I looked over at Ray and he was sitting just like me, clutching the steering wheel. But I could see his hands shaking and how scared he was.

'I'm sorry,' he said. 'I don't mean to kill you.'

And he started the car and we continued down the mountain at a reasonable pace. He drove me to the train station in LA as arranged and I never saw him again.

The next week I got a letter explaining that perhaps we'd both been too wishful and hasty. Or he had, anyway. He was sorry if he had inconvenienced me, he said, but he had had no intention of misleading me and had decided that under the circumstances the only option was to withdraw his offer of marriage.

And that was our last contact.

I went back into my life, to my grandaughters and charity work and yoga and tried to put the episode behind me. In due course I started seeing the widowed husband of an old friend of mine. We became very close but never did marry. Everyone comes into your life to teach you something, and I learnt from Ray, I think, that two lives made of different metals cannot be welded together by will alone. There has to be more.

Part four
trouble, brother, is something we is just fresh out of

two-word greeting

Market researchers have established that a two-word greeting allows an extra beat for their prey to ascertain that there is no threat on the end of the line. It is a small gesture of massage. A lubricant to push the foot that inch further in the door.

'Good morning, my name is ... '

I had a spiel prepared.

'I'm researching a book to do with the American writer Raymond Chandler and I'm trying to locate a woman called Deirdre Gartrell ... '

Pause.

'Chandler ... He wrote detective stories ... He was American ... C-H-A-N-D-L-E-R ... detective stories, crime novels ... No, he's dead, it's not him I'm looking for ... The woman I'm looking for is named Deirdre Gartrell ... Yes, Gartrell ... G-A-R-T-R-E-L-L ... That's right. That's why I'm ringing you. I'm going down the list in the telephone book. Deirdre ... She was a student at the university's college in Armidale in the late '50s. I know she was there in 1957. Yes, she'd be in her fifties now, I imagine. No, the family might not have lived in Armidale. Probably not, in fact. She lived in college, so probably ...

'I know she was in Armidale because in one of the letters ... Yes, she conducted a correspondence with Raymond

Chandler ... No, I don't have the letters. Extracts were published in a book of his letters ... No, she's Australian ... He was American ... She was in Armidale and he was in California ... Yes, it is fascinating ... No, they never met ... No, I don't have the letters ... I'm looking for the letters and I'm looking for Deirdre ... D-E-I-R-D-R-E ... Gartrell ... But she might have married. Probably she married, so her last name wouldn't be Gartrell any more ... Chandler ... C-H-A-N-D-L-E-R ... No, he's dead ... Look, thank you for your help. I'll keep trying. Thank you ... Yes, Deirdre ... Yes, it is fascinating ... '

I was exhausted just thinking about it.

There are over two inches of Gartrells in the Sydney telephone book. Over half of these live on the North Shore, one inch of Gartrells are spread in an arc from Chpdle to Crnla and out to Dhruk in the west, and the remaining fraction is taken up in large print by 'Gartrell White Cake & Pie Mfrs' at Ermgtn, well known for their packaged cake mixes.

I went straight to the D's. There was only one, in Crmr. I rang the number. I held the receiver against my ear and swivelled in my chair, looking out the window of the balcony over the rooftops towards the sea. Philip sat on the telephone book watching me, the tip of his tail slapping gently against the page.

The phone rang and kept ringing. I let it ring. It gave me thinking time. I couldn't believe it had taken me so long to get around to this, going through the Sydney phone book. Some sleuth. The woman from the university in Armidale had suggested months ago that this was the obvious place to look. But since then, excited to be sending off letters all around the world, I had simply forgotten about it. And what would I do anyway if D of Crmr was Deirdre? What would I say to her? 'Uh, hello, I believe you used to have something going with Raymond Chandler ... kind of.'

No one answered. Phew. I hung up.

I tried again.

Again no answer. It was the evening. Maybe D of Crmr was Denise and she was around at her boyfriend's watching *Married With Children*. Or maybe he was Denis and he was out the back under the car.

I went to the top of the list.

AC of Frnchs Frst knew of no one by that name in the family. He referred me to his aunt, BA of Whrnga.

BA took my number to give to a cousin.

BL of Try Hls had no idea what I was talking about.

CA of Whlr Hts, ditto.

D of Crmr was still at her boyfriend's.

FG of Nrmbrn said there wasn't any family he knew of in Armidale. I said that didn't matter. She might have come from somewhere else and boarded at a college. In fact, this was likely. FG agreed.

D of Crmr was still under the car.

FS of Lne Cve had an idea that there may have been a Deirdre in the branch of the family at Orange.

Orange, I scribbled on my sheet of paper.

FS suggested I make contact with a certain Aunt Gladys of Dolls Pt. Her name now was Funnell, but it used to be Gartrell. She was the woman to talk to, she knew everything there was to know about the Gartrell family. Everything. Yes, ring Aunt Glad, she was bound to know.

'Great, thank you,' I said.

'Yes, she's the one,' said FS.

'Great, thank you.'

'Aunt Glad, she's a walking history book.'

'Great, thank you.'

'Yep, she's your best bet,' said FS.

'Great, thank you. You wouldn't by any chance have her number?'

'Unfortunately, no, I haven't,' said FS. 'But look, I'll tell you who has, JC of Knthst. He'd know, for sure. He's Aunt Glad's nephew. Give JC a ring. You'll be set then.'

'Great, thank you. JC of Knthst. I've written that down.'

'Yep,' said FS. 'Glad's the one. She'll know. How old did you say she is? Eighteen? Yeah, Aunt Glad'd know.'

'No, she *was* eighteen,' I said. 'But look, thanks for your help, you've been great. I'll try JC.'

'Yep, try JC,' said FS. 'JC'll know Aunt Glad's number. I'd give it to you myself, but, well, hang on, I'll just duck out the back and have a look. You got a minute?'

I decided, thanks very much, but I didn't have a minute. JC of Knthst was at her boyfriend's too.

Maybe D of Crmr had gone on holidays.

I went out west to M at Dhruk.

'Good morning,' I said.

I spoke slowly and clearly and went through my spiel. Silence.

'Hello?' I said.

'Sorry,' a woman said. 'No English. No speak.'

A branch of the family from Croatia! Amazing.

D of Crmr had me worried. I hoped he/she had his/her cat in a cattery.

JC of Knthst was just dashing out. No, he didn't have Aunt Gladys's phone number. He wasn't actually her nephew. She was his cousin's aunt, not his aunt. JF of Brkvle, he was the cousin. He'd know. Give JF a ring.

D of Crmr must have won a world trip.

JF of Brkvle was alarmingly incautious. I could have been anybody. The tax department. A telephone evangelist. An extremely dangerous Gold Coast real estate salesman.

'Sure, no worries,' he said. 'Just hang on. And she's not in Dolls Pt. Aunt Glad lives in Sns Sci.'

'Sns Sci,' I repeated, and scribbled on my pad.

Philip's eyes opened, his ears pricked up.

(In *Farewell, My Lovely* Marlowe visits a hotel called the Sans Souci. 'Trouble, brother,' the Negro manager tells him, 'is something we is just fresh out of.')

'And look,' said JF, 'Glad's getting on. She's eighty-four this month. Speak slowly with her, speak clearly, be prepared to repeat yourself, and don't ring after eight o'clock at night.'

'Okay,' I said, 'thanks a lot.'

Aunt Glad sounded like the real thing. But I'd have to wait until morning. I gave old D of Crmr another tinkle, just to let him/her know I was worried. I let it ring. I went and put the kettle on. I came back. It was still ringing. I wondered about calling the police. I sat staring out the open window at the night sky. I hung up. I decided to give W of Chpdle a call, just to say hello, have a yarn, let him know how FS of Lne Cve was getting on. I tried D again, up at Crmr. D answered. His name was Douglas. He was ninety-one. He was just on his way to the loo and he'd noticed the phone ringing. He'd left his hearing aid beside the bed. But he thought he'd heard something.

I rang Aunt Glad at 8 a.m. I had my pencil ready. I leant my elbows on the hard wood of the desk. Philip sat on my notes in the centre of the desk. My heart raced. After trying to track Deirdre in and out of libraries and offices all around the world it looked like I would find her down a dead-end street only a few kilometres away.

The phone stopped ringing. A sprightly voice answered.

'Ah, hello, my name is . . . I'm hoping you can help me . . .'

'Yes, young man. I know all about you. Now, do you have a pen and paper? I don't have a phone number but I do have a postal address. The young woman I think you're looking for lives in Bathurst – although of course she's not young any more. She married a German. I'll spell her last name. Are you ready?'

to the superintendent of the post office, la jolla

La Jolla
13 August 1951

Dear Sir

Once in a while I get a special delivery letter. Sometimes they are put into my box, since it is my official address, and sometimes they are delivered to the house. Whoever does this lately seems to have developed a habit of arriving at 7.30 in the morning and trying to batter the front door down, thus arousing my wife from sleep which she badly needs. I don't criticise the man at all, since he is probably impelled by a strong sense of duty. But may I, in all courtesy and friendliness, point out: first, that a special delivery letter is hardly that urgent, as anything really urgent would come by wire or telephone; and second, that there is a mail slot in the side door of our house at ground level, and that simply dropping the letter in that slot would be my idea of a beautiful job accomplished with tact and consideration. If this should prove impossible to accomplish or should be in violation of any post office rule, then may I request that special delivery mail be deposited in my box, No 128, just like any other first-class mail. In my case at least it does not really require the red light and siren treatment. When this house was built the mail slot was put in the side door deliberately so that the mail man would not have to climb any steps. Usually whoever delivers special delivery mail does not know this, so he climbs to the front door, finds no mail slot and is thereby stung to fury.

Yours very sincerely
Raymond Chandler

a beautiful job accomplished with tact and consideration

I worked on the enclosed balcony overlooking the street. During the day Indian mynahs sighed in the pohutukawa tree out the front and pigeons poked along the red-tiled roofline of the flats next door. The mornings were silent and productive, punctuated only by the buses tearing down Bondi Road to get to the beach, and on the way back up pulling in to get their breath at the stop at the top of our street. The mornings were warm and sunny, but when the sun moved around in the middle of the day the balcony was as cold as a tomb. On Mondays the postman came late, when the day was turning on a pivot into cold afternoon and the sheet of fibro tacked over the southern end of the balcony started clattering coldly in the sea breeze. On other days I could expect him only a few minutes after eleven o'clock. Eleven o'clock – that difficult hour when your body tells you you've done a morning's work but convention insists that you haven't.

Our postman was about five-feet tall. He had thighs like hams and a Mike Tyson neck. He looked as if he had been squashed. A Walkman was grafted permanently into his crewcut. A ring glinted in his left ear. He wore shorts and running shoes in all seasons, especially winter. I was always ready for him. I'd hear him at the bikies' house two doors down, saying hello to Brucie.

Bruce was the bikies' Newfoundland. They'd got him as a puppy. A Newfoundland puppy. Despite growing to about the size of a Shetland pony in a year, Bruce stayed a puppy. While the bikies were at work, or wherever they went during the day, he paced sloppily back and forth in front of the house like a lion in his den, drooling and bored. The postman, who was about his height, had some sort of deal with him, but Brucie always terrorised strangers. One day I turned into the street and found a woman clutching her handbag on our low brick fence. At her feet Bruce paced the pavement slavering copiously, his huge slack tongue lolling from the side of his black, rubberised mouth.

'Oh, thank God,' said the woman. 'Will you get him off me?'

Bruce flung his tail from side to side and looked up at me with his great hanging eyes vacant and pleading.

Philip wasn't scared of Bruce. Philip sat on the windowsill, looking down on Bruce's territorial playfulness with tail-slapping immunity. If he ever actually ventured into Brucieville, it was only to carry out slinking feline sorties in the dead of night.

It's quiet in the suburbs at eleven in the morning. On every day but Monday, just when I was getting restless, I'd hear through the sighing and cooing silence the scrape of a dirty white running shoe, the shuffle of envelopes, and a soft ' 'Day Brucie'.

What happened next, I could say, was a leisurely stretch from my chair to the window. But I'd be lying. It was in fact the adrenaline swoop of a preying animal. In about the time it takes for one footfall to become the next, I'd be looking down on a large lonely Newfoundland standing dejectedly in the middle of the footpath as a stumpy man with a Walkman'd crewcut exited his territory into the dogless land of the flats next door. The flats between Bruce's place and ours.

I stood back in case he should look up. I watched him feed the letterboxes on the other side of our driveway. My heart raced. I waited, I watched.

He crossed the driveway to our boxes. His scalp was white through his thin hair. In his left hand was an almost unbearably fat clutch of letters which he fed one by one into our five slots. We lived in flat four. I watched his hand like a card player at a blackjack table. I knew the sounds of the cards falling. If there were several letters, or they were bulky, the gates of the letterboxes clanked dully as the letters were pushed through the slots. A single letter slipped gracefully in and disappeared. The days without letters were an empty, cruel disappointment.

Sometimes I couldn't wait until he reached our box, and I was across the living-room, through the kitchen, out the front door, down the cold tiled steps, two or three at a time, and out into the driveway before he had rounded the corner of our fence to head across the nature strip and over the road to his next drop. As casually as possible, but actually with almost uncontrollable anticipation, I took measured steps up the cracked concrete of the driveway and, as nonchalantly as I could make it look, lifted the gate of the box with the number 4 screwed onto it.

And one day there was a letter from a woman in Bathurst with a German surname.

yes, it's me!

Bathurst
March 1988

Dear Alan

Yes, it's me! You've found the Deirdre you're looking for.

Blue biro on ruled paper, quarto. Excited. Friendly. Welcoming.

On the cracked concrete driveway of a block of flats on the hill in Bondi, in the middle of the day, a man takes one thin letter from his letterbox. A large dog stands nearby with his head cocked, dribbling onto the pavement. An Australia Post knapsack on short, thick legs disappears around the corner. The man turns the letter to read the back and his face breaks into a wide grin. He punches a hand in the air. The dog slobbers up the pavement towards him, tail wagging.

I did 'conduct a correspondence with Raymond Chandler in the late 1950s'. But that sounds so formal! Even the name is wrong – I never called him Raymond Chandler. At first I called him 'Mr Chandler' but he quickly told me to call him 'Ray' and henceforth that was the only way I thought of him. The way I would say it was that we wrote letters to each other and became friends.

It is a coincidence that you should contact me now because, although I can't seem to find the letters, I have been coming across 'extras' from that time – a photo Ray sent me, a telegram he sent me. We are going through old papers and things in an attempt to simplify our possessions before moving to a smaller house next year – but don't panic! I would never throw such things away; they recall former times so powerfully. It's just that I haven't seen the letters for so long I can't remember when I last did.

I must admit that your interest in that period of my life rather amuses me. You seem to assume that my friendship with Ray was the centre of my life and not much has happened since. Nothing could be further from the truth. I was only seventeen when I first wrote to him. For two years I suppose he was my main emotional outlet. But after that I went on to other people, other things. I'd never read any of his books. (I did read one later and didn't like it.) I'd met my husband already (he is a German builder who came out 'for an adventure' in 1952 and stayed) and we started seeing each other seriously soon after I stopped writing to Ray. I was married when I was twenty-two and our first son was born when I was twenty-three. After three more children and nearly thirty years of married life I can honestly say I have wanted for nothing more. My life has been very quiet and, I suppose, conventional. No great dramas, but a great deal of domestic nourishment. It has turned out to be exactly the sort of life that I remember Ray railing at. But I haven't for one day regretted the decision I made to marry Walter, or the way things have turned out with our four children. We have lived in Bathurst all our married life, only fifty kms or so from where I was brought up at Orange.

What I am trying to say is that my relationship with Ray was a big part of my life then, but I grew past it very quickly. Ray and I had a father/daughter relationship, I suppose, but spiced with a sexual flirtatiousness, which came from both sides. Compassion prompted me to write to him initially – and boredom – but it was in such a naive, provocative way that Ray found it incredible, and hence intriguing. He answered rather cuttingly, so I replied in self-justification, and away we went!

I am sorry I didn't meet him in the flesh – but perhaps we would have both been disappointed. I was very simple and unsophisticated, but he may have found it fun to 'educate' me, Pygmalion style! I often became confused as to what Ray meant seriously, what was a joke, and, finally, what was the result of his drinking. He could be very hurtful, and I wasn't good at defending myself.

Then again, I was so introspective I gave him a false view of my life. He believed I was incarcerated in an all-girls' college and imagined some steamy relationship and frustrations that really didn't exist physically and was angry with me when I disillusioned him!

Anyway! To come to the point – would you like to come up and meet? Our house is very large, and the garden is too, and we want more free time, so we've decided to sell. But in the meantime we have plenty of room if you'd like to stay overnight.

Yours sincerely
Dee

PS This is what I call myself and what everyone has called me since I was a child. When people call me Deirdre I still wonder what I've done.

every box in the house

Bathurst
April 1988

Dear Alan

So! We have advanced a stage: you have been invited to visit, and you have accepted. Next question: when? We will be out at The Shack (a two-roomed hut we built by the river) at The Block (both are key family words) during Easter, or most of it. Wednesday mornings I teach English to a Japanese friend, Wednesday evenings I go to Tech to study Japanese. Sundays are usually family days. In other words the best time would be any days other than those.

    Walter and I are busy every day getting this house ready to sell. It's just too big for us now. We are going to build out at The Block with our chooks and vegies and the fish in the river and live there happily ever after. It's what we've been waiting for half our lives. When you raise children you love them, of course, and you would do anything for them, but after they're gone you realise that perhaps you've been living through them and you have a life of your own to lead and you'd better get on with it. We're getting on with it.

    Downstairs we have two big rooms full of cardboard boxes we are trying to sort out before we move. These are all the things we'd never throw out, the accumulation of almost thirty years of family life. It's kids' stuff mostly, old school exercise books and drawings from kindergarten (a German word, did you know that!), things like that. We've found receipts and bills and photos dating back to the very first years of our marriage, but I have to tell you again – I CAN'T FIND THE LETTERS ANYWHERE!

    I remember sending them off when that man did

the book of Ray's letters in America, and I remember going to the post office to pick up a certified parcel from overseas. But that might have been after the first book in 1960-something, not the American book, which I guess was only about 1980.

Best wishes
Dee

her arms opened

It was a cold day in May. A wind laden with grit eddied under the pylons of Central Station. Buses spewed clouds of exhaust and roared out of sight around the corner into Elizabeth Street, past the down-and-outs on the low wall who grumbled to themselves with their collars turned up. The train was one of the new XPT which continue past Bathurst on to Dubbo. It had tinted windows which didn't open. The passengers who wobbled down the aisle clutching their special non-spill State Rail cardboard trays from the servery in the middle carriage, spilt their State Rail coffee on people as they passed.

At the Flemington produce-markets forklift trucks moved noiselessly around the asphalt yards, carrying mounds of leafy green vegetables high in their outstretched arms. Past Penrith, the brown Nepean shimmered in the winter sun. We climbed into the mountains. On the railway platforms people in parkas clapped their hands together and peered coldly into the train windows. In the shopping centres, cars turned corners, exhausts steaming white.

We descended out of the mountains and continued west. Grazing land. Gnawed-short paddocks of dirty white sheep and eroded gullies. Grey gum skeletons contorted into the cold blue sky, crooked limbs cast down on the ground around their trunks. I was warm in the train and lost in thought, passing through this denatured landscape as if it was a film slipping by. Only in Bathurst, when I stepped down onto the platform, did the cold inland air hit me.

A tall woman with grey hair was waiting beside a four-wheel-drive diesel ute in front of Ben Chifley's memorial locomotive. She saw me and grinned, displaying a lot of tooth, and at the same time took her hands from her pockets, waved, and walked towards me, crunching gravel.

Her arms opened, like a mother welcoming a prodigal child.

'Give me a hug,' she said.

She led me to the ute, got in, and leant across to open the passenger door. On the seat was a large block of wood with a string through one corner and a key attached.

'Just throw that on the floor,' she said.

'What is it?'

She strained around to look over her shoulder as she pulled out. The indicator had a loud modern click.

'It's the key to The Block.'

She turned to the front, shifted into first, and drove into a broad street that led away from the station. Cars were angle parked into the kerbs but the street still appeared wide and empty. She turned to me. 'We still can't find the letters. Where does that leave us?'

I'm tall, I've got brown hair, and ...

Dee and Walter lived across the road from a golf course, and only a few hundred yards over the fairways from a jail, which, until the riots in the seventies, had an infamous reputation as a place of bashings and desperate escapes. Since then it had been rebuilt and was now utterly silent. Dee and Walter seemed oblivious to its presence, but once I knew it was there I was vaguely uneasy. I couldn't help imagining the tracks of escapees cutting across the dew on the fairways as early golfers teed off first thing in the morning. I kept thinking of young Pip being grabbed by the scruff of the neck in the rimy marshes at the start of *Great Expectations*. At the end of their road, down into a gully and up the other side, Ben Chifley's memorial stood at the highest point in the Catholic cemetery, a spire of weathered marble rising from a simple grave into the sky.

Wanting space and privacy, Dee and Walter had bought three house blocks on this street in the sixties. They wanted to be on the edge of town. They built a large brick house, put in a vegetable garden on one side, left the block vacant on the other side, and surrounded themselves with trees. They called their home Place Of The Trees. They had their space and they had their privacy. New housing estates had been built further out to the west, but their home was still, twenty years later, on the edge of the main town.

Walter designed the house to accommodate the family of six. Everything was on a large scale. Nothing was left to chance. The house was built on two levels with the top floor in the shape of a squared U. In one wing were the children's bedrooms. Walter and Dee had the other wing to themselves. The middle was family space, the kitchen, dining and living areas. The kitchen had a walk-in coolroom, as if it had been intended for a Chinese restaurant. The dining table was large and round with a rotating lazy Susan in the middle. There was a sunken area down several steps at the side of the room with a large open fireplace faced by a cushioned semi-circular bench seat. This was the 'conversation nook'. It had also, Dee said, been christened the 'sex pit'.

Deep in the bowels of the house was a wood boiler which provided hot water and central heating. Beside it was a double garage, rumpus and workrooms. Walter had a study, there were four toilets and a guest flat at the side. The walls were exposed brick. Lining the entrance foyer and stairwell were large photo portraits of each member of the family in idyllic leafy settings. The house was like a cross between Baulkham Hills and the Black Forest.

The youngest son still lived at home and kept his room upstairs. While they were getting the house ready for sale Dee and Walter lived in the small guest flat downstairs.

It was here, in the breakfast nook, that Dee prepared a German lunch. She set out three small wooden platters and, in the centre of the table, plates of black bread, ham, cheeses and pickles. She is tall and I am tall and the ceiling felt low as she made tea and we chatted. Dee talks as she writes letters, in exclamation marks and sighs and trailing questions aimed more at herself than whoever she is talking to.

Walter came home from work. He shook my hand. 'So you got here,' he said, smiling, studying me. His accent was still pronounced, although later Dee told me it is something she no longer notices. Walter was short and ruddy. Strong grip, tough hands. His body strained at his shirt buttons.

At lunch he sat opposite me and made open sandwiches by laying slices of cheese and ham on his black bread. He ate these with a knife and fork. He drank his tea black, explaining that he had learnt to do this after years of carting milk around to building sites, just for it to go off in the sun. He was silent through most of the meal, although I was aware of him listening and watching. I felt that I was being weighed up, assessed. We talked generally about Bathurst and Dee and Walter's family, and about my life in Sydney. Because of his years with power tools, Dee said later, Walter often misses a lot of what is said.

After lunch he excused himself, went through the door, and the house closed its silence around him.

it was the fifties!

'I was home for the summer holidays. I had the paper out on my knees and I was turning the pages without really reading them. I was almost drifting off, then I came to an article which attracted my attention. It was ... '

She removed her hands from around her mug of tea and made the motion of turning the pages of a newspaper – wide, airy arcs of her left hand, from the right side of her body to the left. She looked past me, focusing on her memory as she spoke.

'It was on the left side of the right-hand page. There was an advertisement beside it. It was a long article – it went to the bottom of the page – and there was a photo of him. He looked very sad. That's one reason I wrote.'

'And when was this? What year?'

She thought for a moment. '1956? 1957?'

'And what did the article say?'

'It was about how his wife had died and how it had been for him since.'

'He'd tried to kill himself. About a month after.'

'Did he?' she said. 'I don't remember that.'

She nodded and was silent, taking this in as if I'd told her some bad news about an old friend who was on hard times.

'How did he do it?'

'He tried to shoot himself. But the ammunition was old and the shots didn't go off properly.'

She nodded again.

'I only remember him seeming sad and being very honest about how he felt. And completely different from how I imagined detective writers to be.'

'So you wrote to him?'

'Yes. I wrote to him.'

'And you'd never heard of him?'

'No, I had no idea who he was. I didn't read detective stories. I thought detective stories were rubbish. Tough talk and bad writing.'

As she said this she fixed me with a gaze, almost combative, watching for my reaction. I smiled and shrugged. Nothing to go into combat over. Chandler made the point often enough that the reason mystery novels are generally regarded as trash is because most of them are. But in this respect, he would say to anyone who would listen, they're no different from any other writing. He hated the highbrows telling him that because he wrote well he should turn his back on mysteries and write a serious novel. In any book, he said, what mattered was the writing – and 'scarcely anything in literature is worth a damn except what is written between the lines'. 'The Insignificance of Significance' was one of Chandler's favourite themes.

'And did you write that same day?' I asked.

'Yes, I think I did. I don't see why I wouldn't have.'

'Did you type it?'

'Oh, no. I never typed letters. Ray did. He typed all of

his. I don't think I even had a typewriter then.'

'So, what did you write it on?'

She laughed. 'I can't remember. A page ripped out of an old exercise book, probably. Or a pad from uni.'

'In biro?'

'Perhaps. Or maybe with a fountain pen. Yes, I think it would have been a fountain pen.' She paused. 'Do you want to know what colour ink?'

'Yes. What colour?'

'I don't remember.'

'Do you remember what you said?'

'Well, not exactly. But it was only short. I probably said how sorry I was to hear about his sadness and how brave I thought he was to be so honest.'

She looked down into her tea and laughed.

'I tried to introduce myself. I was so naive. Honestly. I had no idea.'

'Go on. What did you say?'

She blushed.

I leant down towards the tape machine, smiling at her. 'Dee's blushing,' I said.

'I said, "I'm seventeen years old and I'm a student at New England University in Armidale, and I'm tall, and I've got brown hair." And then I gave him my measurements.'

'You gave him your measurements!'

'It was the fifties. That was the way we thought then.'

We were both laughing. I was thinking, God, wasn't life straightforward then. Dee was probably thinking, God, wasn't life awful then.

'Also, I think I'd just finished the Dorothy Dix column, whatever it was called. You know, where girls write in giving their measurements and say they want to meet someone who likes going to the movies and having fun. I suppose I had that sort of thing in my mind.'

I nodded.

'So you told him your measurements. Then what? Where did you send the letter?'

'Do you want to know what they were? My measurements.'

'Yes. If you want to tell me.'

'36C-28-38.'

'Thanks.'

'Not quite perfect.'

'Yeah? Why not?'

'Your bust and your hips were supposed to be the same. Also, I thought my waist was too big.'

She laughed, shaking her head. 'Crazy, isn't it? Summing yourself up like that.'

Her laughter dribbled away and she sighed. 'We've made some progress. I suppose.'

We looked at each other, wondering. But I was impatient to continue.

'Anyway. Where did you send the letter?'

'I don't know. I've been thinking about that. To the *Sun Herald*?'

'To Mr Raymond Chandler, care of the *Sun Herald*, Sydney?'

'Yes, I suppose so.'

'And did you expect to hear back?'

'Oh no. No, I think I forgot all about it.'

'Did you do that sort of thing a lot? Write off to strangers?'

'No, I don't think I'd ever done it before. It's just that Ray's story ... well, he seemed like a very special man.'

'Did you write a lot of letters? To friends and so forth?'

'No, not a lot. I had penfriends. At any one time I suppose I had one person I was writing to intensively. Letters filled a gap in my life. There wasn't anybody I knew who I felt I could really talk to. I did feel like a loner, an outsider. I used my letters to express my thoughts and feelings about the world. They were safe. You sealed them up and sent them off and then forgot about them. Until a reply came and then you did the same thing again. I was seventeen, very young and intense. It's a very introspective age.'

I nodded. 'But Ray did reply?'

'Yes, he did. A few weeks later. Maybe a month. I was still at home anyway, at Orange, because I remember his letter lying there on the dining-room table with all the other letters. I couldn't believe that he'd actually written back. I was so excited. Then I opened it.'

'And?'

'He'd written a nasty little letter.'

'What did he say?'

'That my measurements might have interested him once, but not any more.'

'No! He said that?'

Dee nodded and looked back down to her mug of tea, as if the memory still hurt.

'And I was upset, because all I had been trying to do was offer him my sympathy.'

'So what did you do?'

'I wrote him an angry letter saying I was just trying to be nice and there was no need to be so nasty.'

She paused and smiled at me. 'And that was probably on a page ripped out of an exercise book as well.'

'Because you were angry with him?'

'No. Just because that would have been the nearest paper to hand. But you're right. I didn't want him to get away with dismissing me like that. So I dashed off this angry little letter'. She smiled at me again. 'In fountain pen. And put it in an envelope and cycled with it into town. I must have been angry because it was two and a half miles into town and a hot ride. And then I certainly didn't expect to hear from him again.'

'But you did?'

'Yes. He wrote back. I don't know why.'

'Why, do you think? Why did he keep writing to you?'

'Why? Because ...'

She leant back and looked away out the window. Her chair creaked. Outside it was a cold autumn day. The sky was grey. Her hands rested around her mug of cold tea. She wore only one ring, her wedding ring. The cassette ground around, recording the silence.

'Because he needed something. And he thought he could get it from me.'

'What did he need?'

'What did he need?' She looked me straight in the eyes. 'What does anyone need? Love. To love someone and be loved back.'

hundreds of charming people

I spent the night in one of the kids' narrow little beds upstairs and caught the train back the next morning. I stared out the window at the skinny sheep and washed-away paddocks and thought about what I now knew.

I'd found Dee, but there were no letters – and I had no idea if either side of the correspondence even still existed. Or if so, where they were.

My guess that Dee had initially written to Chandler as a fan of his books had been completely wrong. She'd never even heard of him. And it was a miracle that he ever received the letter she sent him. What route must it have taken to arrive at Chandler's door? From the *Sun Herald* to his publisher in Australia? Who was that? Penguin Books? Then where? To the US? To Houghton Mifflin in New York? Or to Penguin in London?

If they remembered their own article earlier that month, the *Sun Herald* might have known that Chandler was in London at the time. Let's assume they did. Penguin were Chandler's paperback publishers. What would they have done with it? The right thing, it seems, seeing as he got it – sent it on to his English hardback publishers, Hamish Hamilton.

And Hamish Hamilton – where would they have sent it? Where was Chandler in January – or probably, by then, February – 1956? Still living at the Ritz? Or in the flat Natasha Spender organised for him at Carlton Hill in St John's Wood? The flat was just around the corner from the Spenders. The family, including the children, looked after him, bringing him meals and sitting with him when he didn't want to be alone. Chandler hated this 'beastly flat' and Natasha's attempts to incorporate him into her domestic life, when really what he wanted was her love alone. I could only imagine what Stephen Spender had thought of this, as it does not appear that Chandler tried to hide the feelings he had about Natasha. 'Dissimulation is too difficult and too wearing,' Chandler wrote at the time. 'That fine adjustment of behaviour which permits one to be in the same room with the woman you adore, others being present, and to be neither too

115

affectionate and familiar or not too quiet and remote to avoid the other, is just too subtle a decorum for me.'

In his memoirs Spender mentions Chandler only once. He arrived home late one night to find Chandler drunkenly holding forth to Natasha about the need for her to devote more time to her career. And presumably, before Spender walked in, on himself as well. Spender appears to have been thoroughly English about the matter, splendidly restrained, considering the attention Chandler was paying to his wife.

Anyway, by the time Deirdre's letter reached Chandler it must have been virtually indecipherable with redirection orders. And Chandler would have been reclining on the couch 'like a beached porpoise'. (Who said that? Ah. MacShane, in the 'Revenge'. 'He loved to lie on a couch or bed, looking like a beached porpoise'.) With a glass of Scotch at his elbow and the smoke of a Craven A coiling from the ashtray, he chose this envelope, probably one of many in that day's mail. Turning it from front to back, he hardened his lip in appreciation at the complicated route it had taken to reach him, slit the envelope open and read the short note scribbled on a page ripped from a university exercise book. And chortled. Or perhaps scowled.

It's no wonder he wrote back. Once.

But why did he keep writing back? Why did he keep responding to the letters this 'unknown girl in Australia' continued to send him?

'I have had thousands of letters, and I suppose I have written thousands ... Why should I take Deirdre into my heart when hundreds of charming people made no impression on me at all deeply?'

It was no great literary correspondence. For Dee it was 'two friends talking'. For Chandler, 'merely a rather kind attempt to resolve her problems'.

Chandler's version differed from Dee's. But still the question: Why? What drove him to get involved in the life of a girl a whole world away and fifty years his junior? A girl he'd never met. Who had never heard of him. And didn't even like detective novels.

Perhaps this was part of the attraction. And the mystery.

the big sleep!!!

In the old days the newspaper reading room of the State Library was an annex off the main reference library. It was a hushed place of quiet scholarship. You ordered your newspaper at the desk and waited for it to be brought up from the stacks by an ancient war-wounded attendant in a dark blue pure-wool uniform, complete with gold buttons and meaningless epaulets. He set it down on one of the long polished wooden tables and then stood behind you, breathing wheezily while you turned the cumbersome, disintegrating pages with respect. In the old library you learnt an awe for all things old. The past embraced you; you smelt it in the musty paper and it crumbled between your fingers while the strange type and out-of-date formality of the language transported you back. In those days you weren't just in the library to look up papers, you were enveloped in a complete historical experience.

Nowadays the State Library is a modern building, designed to blend with the extensions to the State Parliament House next door on Macquarie Street. You leave your belongings in a coin-return locker, are inspected by young, able-bodied security men dressed in mud-coloured viscose (they've still got the epaulets), and descend a wide curving stairway into a vast open-plan reading room lit to an homogenous fluorescent ambience and arrayed with touch-screen computers, video machines and plug-in audio information-retrieval systems. Around the walls are glassed booths with personal computers and electronic typewriters. Everyone in the room appears to be plugged into something – headphones, keyboards, or computer screens. The shelves of books look untidy and out of date. The library is no longer a gentle invitation to wade back into history but a harsh dunking in modern technology. Most of the students staying late into the night are Asian.

And no longer will you hear the hushed scrape of unwieldy yellowed pages. The major newspapers are now stored on microfilm. The *Sydney Morning Herald* and *Sun Herald*, from 1831 to the present, are lined up in little boxes on special narrow shelves at the back of the room. Each film contains three months of newspapers. Readers hunch in front of the microfilm viewers, faces lit by the dim glow in front of them, right hands on the winder knobs of the machines, the blood-warm recirculation of the air conditioning sending them slowly off to sleep.

I choose my box from the shelf, *SMH* and *Sun Herald* Jan-March 1956, find a machine, plug in and start winding.

In the Queen's New Year Honours list a London volunteer who subjected himself to the bites of 770 mosquitoes was awarded an MBE for services to malaria research. Thirty thousand people crowded on to Bondi Beach on New Year's Day. Two hundred and nine were rescued from the surf. Meteorologists blamed a southern ice pack for the rain which marred fourteen of Melbourne's fifteen-day Christmas break. Plans were unveiled to make Beirut the 'Honolulu of the Middle East'. *Rear Window* and *East of Eden* were packing the holiday cinemas. Grace Kelly announced her engagement to Prince Rainier of Monaco. A dress-circle seat for the new production of *The Summer of the Seventeenth Doll* cost 12/6. Attacks by gangs of bodgies created fear on Sydney streets. A 25-year-old surf skier attacked by a seven-foot shark at Maroubra swore revenge. 'I'm going back to get him,' he said. Experts advised restraint. At Melbourne Zoo a man picked a bad day to stick his finger in the lion's cage. A massive storm caused a jacaranda to fall on a car in Dobie Street, Grafton. Qantas launched their new 54-hour flight to London. An air ticket to Melbourne cost £8, £5/2/- to Wagga Wagga. Diego Rivera, en route to Moscow for cancer treatment, announced, 'I prefer Russia to any other country for necessary surgery.' Twenty-one acres of North Bondi were declared officially infested with Argentine ants.

Then this, *Sun Herald*, 22 January, page 27, left side, right-hand page:

A YEAR OF INSOMNIA FOR CHANDLER AFTER HE MARRIED... THE BIG SLEEP!!!

from Merrick Flynn in London

ABOUT A YEAR AGO RAYMOND CHANDLER, the writer of best-seller thrillers – remember *Farewell My Lovely* and *The Big Sleep*? – put a revolver to his temple and pulled the trigger.

Nothing happened, and so began what was to be the bitterest year he had known.

Now he can talk about it because the pain has eased and the year has ended.

He talked to me last week at London's Ritz Hotel in a room which, with a brass bedstead, meals and extras, costs £60 sterling a week.

It is an expensive way of getting along without a real home. But Chandler has been a little afraid of homely things. Because ... 'When you lose a home you've loved for thirty years it takes courage to start another.'

He sat legs asprawl, in shirt sleeves, homely in spite of himself. This is the man who created Philip Marlowe, the 'private eye', the toughest detective in modern fiction. And this is one of the gentlest men I have ever met.

He lost his home when he lost his wife, Cecily, just about a year ago. Cecily was his home. They were married thirty years, and for the last two Chandler nursed her through the illness that ended her life.

'But I wouldn't try again'

'I loved her very much.' It was a reflective statement, no longer emotional; it was a statement which looked back to that private drama when he tried to die.

He told me about that, too, this man who wrote in his last published book, *The Long Goodbye*: Suicides prepare themselves in all sorts of ways, some with liquor, some with elaborate champagne dinners, some in evening clothes, some in no clothes ...

For Chandler it was a bathroom, in an old dressing-gown, in the Californian home that was no longer a home without Cecily.

He pulled the trigger twice. It was old, faulty ammunition. And nothing happened. Chandler kept his life and lost his dignity. He had muffed the simple job of killing himself.

'I don't regret it. I don't think it was wicked. I believe every man has the right to end his life when it gets too much for him,' he said.

'But I wouldn't try it again. I can imagine only one circumstance in which I'd even want to. I'm afraid of poverty.'

He said that lightly, because he knows his fear is groundless. His first Philip Marlowe book, The Big Sleep, alone has made him nearly £30,000 sterling.

Has hatred of violence

Then he told about the weeks, the months, the year that came after his appointment with futility.

'I consider it takes two years to get over losing the person you love best – if you ever do completely. I've got through one.

'For the first week or two you're too numbed to feel anything. The pain starts. Then gradually it doesn't hurt so much, and that's the worst of all. It's hard to lose the woman you love. But it's harder still to face the fact that you can forget her at times.'

Raymond Chandler's life is still dominated by Cecily.

'I can't seem to write much now' he said. 'I don't know why; something seems to be missing.' He meant, of course, 'someone'.

He has written hardly anything in this last year. His typewriter stands open beside a pile of half-sheets of yellow paper. But the new Marlowe book he began nearly two years ago is still half-finished.

What kind of man is Raymond Chandler? Well, what kind of man is Philip Marlowe? For these two are head and tail of the same coin.

Take the tough, wise-cracking Marlowe and in reverse you have Chandler – tender, sensitive, hating all violence and cruelty.

Take Marlowe the never-doubting man of instant action, and you have again the tortured, self-doubting writer who could have been a poet, who tears up an entire chapter to begin again, who writes ten times more than is ever published.

'I suppose Marlowe really is a sort of secret me,' he said.

'But,' with a grin, 'I'm growing out of it. I used, like most people, to dramatise myself in all sorts of heroic situations.

'I'm very generous, and a psychiatrist would say that was because I was afraid of not being liked. I admit it.

'I'm afraid of loneliness, crowds, insomnia (I get it badly) and telling my age.'

Whither Chandler now?

'I've no ambition except to write one really good book. I must get working again properly. I'm beginning. I'm writing a bit in the mornings.

'I'll live mostly in Britain. I'm American, but I'm happier here.

'I've found a flat – it's time I had a home again. Alone. I don't think I'll ever remarry.'

It was then that I asked him, 'Are you glad now that you failed to die?'

It would have been easy for him, not wishing to shock, to answer 'yes'. He did not.

He thought for the answer. And it was a little while before he said: 'I think so, yes. This will be a better year than last year.'

red monaro dreaming

Yes!

I copied the article and took Merrick Flynn home to show him Bondi. He lay flat on my desk staring up at the sky. Philip lay on top of him, his head out on his paws, eyes closed. I stared out the window, running my hand lazily down Philip's back, in my mind ticking through the options of where to go next. A pool of cat saliva formed itself on the desk.

Indian mynahs squabbled in the pohutukawa. A couple of schoolgirls trailed down the path, sharing a bag of sweets and giggling. Brucie stood in the middle of the pavement watching them approach, tail wagging, head cocked. 'Brucie!' One of the girls dropped her school backpack and mounted him while the other embraced him in a bearhug. Across the street the coke dealer's curtains moved ever so slightly, his red Monaro gleaming expensively in the driveway.

My hand stopped moving on Philip's back. He opened one eye and looked at me archly. I'd had a thought. He let out one short mew. 'Waste of time, bud. Don't bother.'

I got him down and rolled him around, gave him a serious

tummy rub. He made a show of trying to bat me aside with his paws. But he was loving it. After a minute he jumped up and stalked away, his tail high in the air. Pretending to have had enough. But glancing back, giving himself away.

Fine by me. I slid typing paper out of the drawer and took up my pen.

in the beyond

Bondi
1989

Dear Julia

I found the article. It was just as Dee described, on the left side of the right-hand page, with an Ansett ad running down beside it ('Delicious Lobster and Champagne Supper', Sydney to Brisbane. Only £8/10/-!). I'll enclose a copy.

I'm wondering where to go from here. The thing is, it was never the dry dates-and-places of all this I was interested in – the historical necrophilia of Chandler and Dee's correspondence. I didn't read those extracts and think, Great, I won't stop until I find out exactly what the facts were here. Up-turn every clod.

No. What I've always wanted is the letters they wrote. And you know why. Because of these letters we write. I wanted to see how they did it, this business of writing without meeting. It's not the same as us, of course. Dee and Chandler really seemed to 'fall in love', in that impossible long-distance way. But I suppose it set my imagination working.

So this is where I stand. I've found Deirdre. She's told me her story. But I still don't know where the letters are, if they still even exist.

But then Dee did say something interesting, now I think of it. She remembered sending the letters away for 'the first book in 1960 something', and going to the post office to pick up a registered parcel, but she can't remember if that was then or twenty years later, 'after the American book'.

The 'first book' was *Raymond Chandler Speaking*, published in 1962. The 'American book' would have been the *Selected Letters*, edited by Frank MacShane, published in 1981. The Professor might still have Dee's letters. Although there's no reason why he should have kept them.

I've left a copy of the extracts from the *Selected Letters* with Dee to see if they jog any memories. It's funny, but I don't even know, really, why I'm doing this. It's just something which has taken possession of me. I'm in a river, enjoying the view as it takes me gently downstream, but I've got no idea where I'm going to end up.

Alan

these beautiful voices

Julia wrote back, enclosing a quote.

'I found this somewhere,' she wrote. 'Marina Tsvetaeva to Boris Pasternak in 1922:

My favourite form of communication is in the beyond: in dreams. To dream of someone. The second choice is correspondence. Letters are a form of communicating in the beyond, less perfect than dreams, but subject to the same laws.

'That's good, isn't it? It's what it's all about really, isn't it? This business of words on paper. It is only in our minds. Communicating in the beyond. Dreaming.

'But I did dream about you, you know. I had a dream that we finally met. You were living in a big house in the country, alone, and I came to visit. We sat on the verandah drinking gin and you brought out all this food, cheese and biscuits and stuff, which you ate, but I didn't touch. I wasn't hungry. I just drank and got drunk. Very drunk. And talked. Both of us just talked and talked. We'd never met and we had so much to say. Our conversation tumbled over itself as if we were wrestling. We laughed and grinned and nodded our heads in excitement at what the other was saying. I remember the feeling. It was very exciting, as if we were getting drunk on each other.

'We started in the late afternoon and by the time we couldn't talk any more it was late at night, absolutely dark. You had a tape of Mozart's *Requiem* that you played over and over. (This is my favourite piece of music at the moment.) These beautiful voices flowing out over the garden to the creek at the bottom. And finally it stopped and all we could hear in the silence was the sound of frogs. It was night, but still hot. It was the middle of summer, and the air was thick with jasmine. The silence seemed to make the smells even richer. We didn't say anything. We just listened to the frogs and felt our heads swooning through the thick sweet air.

'The only light was a bare bulb at the end of the verandah. You pointed to it. There was a swarm of gnats clustering around it. "Look," you said. "A black halo around the sun."

'Then we had to work out where we were going to sleep.'

god, I wish I'd kept those letters

I wrote back.

'How about this? Carolyn Cassidy remembering the letters from her husband Neal: "God, I wish I'd kept those letters. They were the love letters of the century, any century."

'Can't you just see her getting those letters? See her ripping open the envelopes, devouring them, her eyes scrambling along the lines, down the page, lip clenched between her teeth, forehead furrowed, a slight whimper, an anxious laugh as she turns the page. An exclamation. "Oh no!" Shake of the head, fingers to the mouth. Then silence, barely a breathing silence as she rushes to the end, hoping as she turns the last page for a kiss, an afterthought, one more line.

'The love letters of the century. Any century. Can't you just *feel* those letters arriving?'

a black halo around the sun

I wrote things to Julia I never even told Fiona. Things I didn't know myself until I wrote them. Things I dreamed and woke up from, sweating. This strange outlet. Letters to a stranger. Nothing is real until you write it down.

know that name from somewhere ...

University of California Library
13 June 1988

Dear Mr Close

Your letter of 3 June has been referred to me for reply.

I have checked our manuscripts catalog and could not find any reference to letters to or from Deirdre Gartrell in our Chandler collection.

Other than the Bodleian, I do not know of any other repositories with Chandler material.

Yours sincerely
Lilace Hatayama
Manuscripts Division

UCLA letterhead, white bond, electronic typewriter, no errors. And who is Lilace Hatayama when she's at home? I see her on the Santa Monica freeway, the top down, hair flying, black eyes glinting. I see her sitting on the balcony with a long cigarette between her fingers, a tall glass in front of her with a little paper umbrella in it, the sun setting gorgeously over the sharky black Pacific. Whoa! (Dr) Judith, where are you? I'll put the kettle on. A teabag, or Nescafé? Here, let me take your mac. That's right, sit yourself in front of the radiator. Hmm, nasty chest. How about some Vicks?

Columbia University
20 July 1988

Dear Mr Close

Thanks so much for your letter. I am naturally pleased that you have found Deirdre Gartrell.
    For the moment I can't recall whether I have copies of the letters you want or not, and all my papers are in storage at the Columbia Library. I hope, however, to take a look at them later this summer and will see what, if anything, I have. I haven't gone through them for years so off-hand cannot answer the questions you put to me.
    With all good wishes,

Yours sincerely
Frank MacShane

Yellow letter paper, typed by a secretary. Reference: FM:fc. Good old Frank. 'Gartrell? Gartrell? Know that name from somewhere ...'

Part five
the tug of a magnet

little bombs

Where do I start! Ray complained in one of the letters that I never told him anything other than my own thoughts. Anything about the university or what Australia was like, the birds or the flowers or the climate. Probably he was absolutely right, I was self obsessed. I know I was. All that mattered to me were my feelings. My ideas. I remember that very clearly.

But reading these extracts now, thirty years later, it's through the physical details that I remember the feelings. Then I wrote about my feelings without a thought to my surroundings. But reading them now, it's as if those few paragraphs are windows through which I can look back at the whole of my life at the time. The rooms I had in college, my friends, the lecture theatres I sat in, glimpses of what was said in those lectures, different leafy spots around the university, and moments I remember in them – it all comes back to me.

For instance, I just have to think 'Hut C' and a vista opens out across my whole emotional life at the time. The university had three old corrugated iron army huts that they used for student accommodation – A, B and C. In my first year I lived in Hut C. The uni also owned or rented houses in town and there was a distinct division between the students who lived in town and those on campus. You tended to make friends from the same group as you. That I lived on campus in the huts was an important part of my identity at university.

The rooms in the huts were tiny – just space for a bed – single, of course! – and a wardrobe and a little desk under the window. They were hot in summer and freezing in winter. Each of them had a smelly little gas heater which never seemed to work. The huts were cramped and uncomfortable, but the cameraderie and friendships made up for it.

In second year I was moved into another hut which wasn't as bad as the army ones, and in final year, 1958, I was in Mary White College, which was the first real residential college on campus. The rooms there weren't much bigger than the huts but they weren't as cold in winter – and, being in a proper building built of bricks and mortar, you felt a bit more like a real person instead of a refugee.

What's funny is that I can't remember for sure where I was living when I was writing to Ray. Only the dates tell me that. These are all dated 1957, and the *Sun Herald* article was January 1956, which means I was still in the huts. Which fits in, I suppose, because I've got a strong picture of sitting at that little desk in Hut C, staring out the window with my pen in my mouth while I tried to think what to say to him – just like I am now, staring out the window at the bare branches of the beech tree with my pen in my hand – sorry, my blue Bic pen (and this is a pad I bought for $2.95 at Woolworths) – trying to think what is most important to tell you from that time.

And I suppose it's this – just how much Ray's letters meant to me. No one else knew about them. Not one person. No one at home, no one at college. They were my secret, a part of my private world. I can remember so clearly getting those letters. They were islands of excitement in the tedium of study. I loved them. They were pep-pills, little bombs in the mail.

catching the train

You must remember that the university was tiny then. It had been operating as a part of Sydney University since the '30s but was only inaugurated under its own name in 1954. My first year, 1956, was when the first University of New England intake proper graduated, and in my time there were still only a few hundred students in each year. The campus was outside the town, on a property bequeathed by the White family, and it really was a small place, still a bit of a curiosity for the locals. As the years passed, however, the university bought up adjoining properties and now it's right on the edge of the town, just up the hill from the town centre. It's still leafy and quiet and rural, I suppose, but life then must have been like a holiday camp compared to what it is now.

I mention all this because I'm trying to give you an idea of what the layout was, the way we lived there. When the university college started taking students in the thirties everything happened in 'Bool' – Booloominbah – the old White family mansion. (The Whites were, incidentally, related to Patrick White's family at Belltrees in the Hunter Valley.) When I started, Bool was still the centre of the university, but that year the library was put out in a separate building and the union building was opened, and that's where the mail was held for collection, in little wooden alphabetical boxes on the left as you walked in the front door. This is where I picked up Ray's letters. It was an important part of each day, going down to check the mail. I didn't get mail every day, but it'd be a rare week I wouldn't get something. Everyone got letters from home on a regular basis in those days. People didn't use phones like they do now. My mother used to write at least once a week. I could always rely on her. I loved getting her letters – I loved getting any letters, let's face it (and still do) – and once I started writing to Ray, I was always hoping for something from him.

In a communal life like we had in the huts, I suppose everyone had their own little measures to ensure some privacy. One of mine was taking my mail back to my room before I opened it. I'd set myself up with a cup of tea and read the letters in peace, then – and this was the really delicious part – sit and stare out the window and let my mind wander over all the things I wanted to say in my reply.

This is what I really remember – writing to Ray, sitting alone in my room answering his letters. How well I remember those nights! I was so happy with just my pen in my hand and a blank sheet of paper (nothing special, just lined university notepads) and the night outside and my thoughts coursing through my head.

I can still see this so clearly, hunched alone over my desk with my pen rushing along the lines, bursting with the next thing I wanted to say. I remember the clamouring in my mind – my train of thought always disappearing around the bend before I was ready. Yet my thoughts were always so clear and vital and important. I remember feeling so safe and accepted when I was writing to Ray.

I'd write for hours! Huge, long letters about anything that was on my mind at the time – my friends, my family, what was going on at uni. It didn't matter how many pages I wrote, it didn't ever seem I'd said everything I'd wanted to. It was as if some things I wanted to say couldn't be said.

I'd write about my mother or my father, the subjects I was taking, the exams I had coming up, all the anxieties and triumphs I felt so keenly – and I think, looking back, I especially used Ray as a sounding board for a lot of those youthful insecurities and confusions which you feel at that age there must be some right answer to. You know, about love, and life, and the decisions which always seem so crucial at the time, but which later fade away into insignificance. I looked on Ray as a worldly, experienced person and I think I thought that if I could only find the right words to express myself I'd get wise advice and reassurance – and correct answers – in return.

And outside, beyond my reflection in the black window, were the noises of the night, possum scurryings and branch scrapings, a breath of music from an open window across the lawn, a laugh, a scrap of raised voices, sometimes the smell of a cigarette. Oh, I loved those nights. I think those nights were the happiest times I had at uni. They were complete, insular, solitary. I felt vulnerable with other people. I was never sure of myself. Sitting alone with a pen and a writing pad, insulated from the rest of the university by the lock on the door and the glass in the windows, travelling alone deep into my own thoughts – that's when I felt happy. The beauty of those nights with Ray was that I didn't need other people at all.

I think I always wrote more than him. But he complained so often about his massive correspondence that I don't think I ever expected him to devote himself to me as I did to him. Sometimes I didn't wait until a letter arrived. If I got impatient, or had something in particular to get off my chest, I'd just write. I *loved* getting his letters, but what mattered more was having him to write letters to, knowing I had that completely private outlet. It was – how can I describe it? – so *nourishing*. Those letters kept me alive during those years. They fed me. I lived off them. That Ray was famous had absolutely no bearing on our friendship. I didn't read his books and didn't care about the rest of his life. All I wanted him for were his letters, and the reassurance that he was there to receive mine.

some sort of magic

Thinking about all this now has made me wonder myself why I wrote to Ray – why I wanted to or needed to – and to understand this I think I'll have to tell you about my parents and about my childhood.

You know I was brought up on the orchard at Orange. It wasn't an old family orchard. I was born in Burwood, Sydney, in 1938 and our family moved up to Orange in 1942. Everyone was worried then about a Japanese invasion and a lot of people moved away from Sydney. My father bought the orchard with that in mind. He was from Orange and that was why he chose to buy up there.

I had a wonderful childhood. My parents each lost one of their parents when they were young. Because of this, because their childhoods were hard and they were forced by circumstances to grow up so young, I think they were determined to bring us up with as few cares as they could manage. They wanted us to have the 'real' childhood they missed out on. There were rules and discipline, but really we were left to our own devices as children. We were encouraged to find out about the world at our own pace, in our own style. Certainly I was. And because of the age differences in our family I spent my childhood essentially alone. My two sisters are nine and eleven years older than me, so when I was little they were teenagers, and they had both left home by the time I was ten.

I have one older brother, six years older than me, but when I was little he had his own games and his own friends and didn't want to be bothered by me. And by the time my two younger brothers came along – six and nine years after me – I was used to looking after myself. And, of course, they were boys. So really, I grew up alone. And because of the War Dad was away and Mum had more work around the orchard. That meant I was left even more to my own devices.

My father wasn't away for the whole war. He had been a telegraph officer for the post office before the the First World War, and during the Second World War he taught morse code to air force signalmen in Ballarat. But he wasn't away the whole time. I remember him being away a lot, but I also remember him coming home and how exciting the reunions were – especially between Mum and Dad. They really did miss each other. I remember during the War, Dad had an aerial up a gum tree beside the house and he'd decipher the morse code and tell us what was going on. The aerial stayed there after the War and he still picked up morse and translated it for us from places a long way away, like Fiji.

It was Gran who really looked after me. After Dad's father died, she lived with him – and with us – until she died, when I was thirteen. Because Mum and Dad, and Marcia and Lerida, had each other, and because Richard was off doing his boy's things, I formed my bond with Gran.

It really was an idyllic way to grow up. I had the run of the orchard and was allowed to do whatever I wanted, as long as it wasn't dangerous. And Gran was there whenever I needed her. When I was little I used to wake up very early, before dawn sometimes, and I'd be perfectly happy lying by myself and singing. I was always happy as a little girl. Completely carefree. I'd go into Gran, because she used to wake up early too, and get into bed and she'd read me the Bible. I had no idea what any of it meant, but I was perfectly happy lying there, snuggling up, watching the words on the page and hearing the sounds come out of Gran's mouth. She had a very soft, well-spoken voice and sometimes I'd look up and watch her lips form around the words and think it was some sort of magic. They were our private mornings together. Then Mum would come in at seven o'clock with bread and butter and tea, and the real day would begin.

I was very lucky. I never felt unloved as a child, I always felt cherished. I think grandparents are terribly important to little children. I never even had to think about love, it was just there, like air or water. I took it for granted. Its absence was inconceivable.

Because I spent so much time alone I became very introspective. I lived in my own world of goblins and fairies and golden-haired maidens who lived in tiny woodcutters' houses deep in the woods. My fantasy world was extremely benign. There weren't monsters or dangers lurking behind the woodshed. The things I noticed were pretty and beautiful, not ugly or frightening. It was the dappled sunlight in the trees I noticed, not the bogey men creeping around behind them, waiting to attack me. Cycling to school I'd avoid certain streets in Orange because I hated the feeling in them. They felt evil and menacing and I'd go out of my way just to avoid the feeling they gave me.

I grew up during the War. It didn't finish until I was seven, and it affected us in a hundred ways. Apart from Dad being away, it was around us every day. We had to be as self-sufficient as we could because so many things were rationed. We even made our own soap, from lye and lamb dripping. We were lucky because we lived on a farm. We had a milking cow (it was my job to separate the cream and churn the butter) and a big vegetable garden, and chooks, and geese for a while – not for very long because they were so stupid.

It's almost impossible to imagine now, when you can just

walk into a shop and buy whatever you like. We couldn't get chocolate, for instance, because sugar was rationed. That was definitely what I missed the most. And we had to save our dripping for the 'Fats for Britain' drive. Doesn't that sound ridiculous now? These great vats of lard being shipped halfway across the world to help the War effort. But it all counted. And every week the school had an Egg Day, when all the kids who had chooks had to bring one egg to give to the local hospital.

It's hard to believe, but that was the way we lived. And it may feel like yesterday – for me, at least – but it was fifty years ago. That's what I have to keep reminding myself. Fifty years! It's just impossible to understand, the passing of time.

happily ever after

Mum and Dad loved each other very much. They made it obvious every day in the way they deferred to one another, the way they respected each other. It was there for all of us to see, and we had no doubt it was normal. Dad was always hugging Mum, kissing her, touching her when they were talking. Often I'd wake up and hear them laughing in the bedroom in the middle of the night. I'd hear Mum giggling. At the time I suppose I thought they were just talking and making jokes, but that was before I knew anything about making love. After lunch on Sunday they always went up to their room for a rest and the whole house had to be quiet. It was wonderful. We ran amok, knowing that for those two hours we could go out and do what we liked and be totally safe.

Our parents showed us what was possible from a relationship and I never doubted that such a romance was waiting for me. I took it for granted. In one way I just assumed it would come, in another it was constantly on my mind, because I knew that was what I was searching for, and nothing less would suffice. It was an ideal I wouldn't compromise on. I wouldn't accept second-best, or the mundane and mediocre.

I suppose this is what attracted me to Ray – and to Walter. They were both unusual, both different, anything but mundane.

I read a huge amount as a child, and probably the books I read helped form my romantic view of the world. I spent a lot of time staring into space, dreaming. And I listened to programmes on the radio like 'The Argonauts', and wrote things. I was always writing. From the age of seven I wanted to be a writer.

I loved reading books like *Anne of Green Gables* where people found each other in the end and lived happily ever after. I always knew I'd fall in love with an interesting man and follow him wherever he wanted to go. Part of me did, anyway.

three hairs

My father was nothing like the average Australian farmer was supposed to be. He wasn't strong and sunburnt and broad shouldered. He wasn't even outdoorsy. As a person, he was much more brain than brawn. He had white arms and slim white hands, and long, sensitive fingers. And somehow he always smelt clean. He never seemed to get sweaty or dirty. And he had almost no body hair, except, I remember, three hairs on his chest which we used to pester him to show us as kids. Dad was nothing like the men around him. But he was strong-willed and confident and always had a joke to tell. He had the presence of a thinking man. He was popular in the community, and was always there in the middle of organisations and meetings.

He wasn't physically strong. He was rejected in the first AIF intake for World War One because of his bad health. He had a narrow chest and a 'hammer toe', and even at that age, because of his bad diet as a kid, and because his family couldn't afford dentists, false teeth. I suppose the army thought he wouldn't be able to cope with the tough food. It was lucky anyway, because this first intake was the men who went to Gallipoli, and most didn't come back. But he was determined to join up, and tried to build himself up for the next intake. He took on physical jobs and even cycled to Melbourne and back to get fit. In due course, I suppose when they lowered their entry requirements, he was accepted, and sent off to France. Luckily he survived, of course.

If Dad had been able to get a good education he probably could have done anything. I'm sure he would have gone into something where he could have used his mind. As it was, his father died when he was ten and he had to leave school to help run the little shop his mother had in Orange. So he never had the chance of working with his mind. He had to learn to live by his wits instead.

He'd done a hundred different jobs by the time he bought the orchard and tried to grow cherries. He'd driven trucks and buses and been a telegraph operator in the post office, and even had his own little store. He could turn his hand to anything. He was very smart, he had a good mind, and good entrepreneurial nous. After the First World War, he and his brother had the first trucking business in Grafton.

A lot of Dad's nous went into working out ways to make a living without breaking his back. He was in his forties when he bought the orchard, and it was only by good management that the place succeeded. He didn't have the body to succeed by physical labour alone.

Dad was quite strict. At the dinner table he had a rule that we weren't allowed to speak unless what we had to say was either educational or entertaining. This might sound authoritarian, but we accepted it and played the game. And it helped that he was a great listener. If one of us did tell a story, he would lean forward and listen carefully, waiting for the punchline or the reason for the story to come out. You'd always feel encouraged and valued. And he was a great story teller himself. He could turn the smallest incident into a good tale and have everyone hanging on for the end. We were always laughing at dinner. They were great family occasions.

It's no coincidence, I suppose, that Walter has many of Dad's qualities. He's not long and slim, but he is gentle, and always sweet smelling, even after he's been working, for some reason. He is strict but fair, and believes that there is always a right way to do things, and many ways you don't. And Walter is liked and respected in the community, as was my father.

the bright side!

My father's qualities were masculine. He was self-reliant and smart. He knew you had to work hard in order to survive. But he also trusted his own judgement. He was confident that he'd always think of something to get out of a scrape. He was always optimistic. You always felt safe with Dad.

Conversely, my mother, in her way, was the essence of motherhood. By that I mean she gave continually and, in the process, denied her own needs. When her mother died she chose to be the mother to her sisters and brothers. She started 'looking after', and 'looking after' was what she did for the rest of her life. She built her life around being there for others. Of course that style of motherhood is very out of fashion now.

Mum's father married again, but by then Mum was too old to go back to school. At least, luckily, she didn't have a nasty step-mother story. Her new mother really did love her and was very proud and protective of her. I can still remember going to see Grandma Weiley when I was sixteen, and her saying to me, very imperiously (but probably not meaning to be), 'Turn around, my dear. Let me look at you.'

I turned around, nervous because I knew I was being judged. And Grandma Weiley said, 'Hmmm, you aren't a patch on Dolly at the same age.'

I'm sure she had no idea how much that devastated me.

My mother also was always optimistic and positive. 'Life is full and interesting!' was her motto. She couldn't countenance the negative. She simply wouldn't hear it. She never felt her own life had been difficult. 'Look on the bright side!' she'd say if you were feeling grumbly. 'Think of all the poor people starving in Europe.' Or, 'You don't know how lucky you are, young lady. Some boys and girls don't have any shoes at all!'

Perhaps because she did have a hard life, she learnt early to focus on the good and it just became a part of her. It was a safety fence, I suppose, around her own feelings. By smiling all the time and working at being happy, she became happy. Whenever 'bad' appeared she turned away from it and found something 'good' to put in its place.

This was wonderful when I was young – but as I got older and wanted to talk about my real feelings I was frustrated because she didn't want to hear them. I could talk away at her but she wouldn't hear what she didn't want to. She'd keep cooking, or doing the ironing, anything to avoid eye contact, and then she'd tell you about the neighbour's cherry harvest or how many hankies she'd done that afternoon. Anything she didn't want to hear got blocked somewhere between her ears and her brain. You'd hear her version back and it'd be the cream skimmed off the top, an official version, the sort of stuff you'd read in a newsletter. I realise now that this was her own self-protection mechanism, but then it just felt like something was missing, and that I wasn't understood.

when enough isn't

Although I grew up blessed with great security and love, as I got older I knew I wanted more. I wanted more contact, I suppose, than I was getting. I wanted to talk, to tell people what I thought about things, and I wanted to hear their answers.

In their different ways my parents weren't available for this. For a start they had each other, and I remember from when I was little a strong sense of 'us and them'. I had my Gran, but she died when I was thirteen. And even if she had been there during those teenage years, perhaps I never would have wanted to talk about my growing-up things with her.

I think it was the same with my father. Although he probably would have been the best counsellor I could have had, I think I assumed that, merely because he was my father, he wouldn't understand my predicaments. It's what being a kid is all about, I suppose. When you're young, you're so sure you're different. It's only when you get older you realise everyone suffers the same problems in different clothes. Dad and I were close, he was supportive and gentle and we laughed a lot together and would often give each other a long hug to – what? – confirm our solidarity, but we didn't have heart-to-hearts. Perhaps, like Mum, there was a whole realm of emotional topics he didn't like to talk about. And, I would say, he believed it was better for us to try to work out the solutions to our problems ourselves. Whatever it was, I think it was as a salve to this that I took to writing.

I always wanted people to hear what I had to say. I always liked talking. I started talking when I was one and didn't stop. From as early as I can remember I always wanted to know things. I drove everyone mad with questions, asking 'why this?' or 'why that?' and they'd try to shut me up by saying things like, 'Because Y's a crooked letter and you can't straighten it.' And I'd throw myself on the floor and have a tantrum because I knew they weren't telling me the truth.

I'd talk to anyone. When someone came out to the orchard, I'd always try to get them to read to me. I'd corner them, and drag them off to the sofa, and open book after book in front of them until one of my parents came over and rescued them.

I was shameless, completely shameless. I latched onto whoever I could and bombarded them with conversation. One time I remember the refrigerator mechanic came out and my mother found me in the kitchen telling him all about our family, about her and Dad and my older sisters and brother, and the orchard and the cow and how Gran used to read me the Bible in the morning. I was telling him anything and everything. Mum said, 'That's enough Dee', and sent me outside. I could hear her apologising to the man.

'Sorry,' I heard her say. 'She just doesn't know when enough is enough.'

As a little girl I listened to 'Kindergarten of the Air' and when I grew out of that I joined 'The Argonauts'. I never missed it. From five to six every night I was glued to the radio. My Argonaut name was Chariton-39. We used to send our entries to Icarus. It was such a good show. It was the artistic lifeblood for whole generations of Australian kids. And you learnt so much. *The Muddle Headed Wombat* was written for 'The Argonauts', and first broadcast there. And they had a Science segment when everyone was encouraged to go off and collect insects, and try to squeeze boiled eggs into milk bottles and mix bi-carb and vinegar – things like that.

You wrote things and sent them in, and every week you'd listen to hear if you got mentioned on the radio. There was a hierarchy of awards. A Dragon's Tooth was the bottom prize, then a Golden Fleece, then a Golden Fleece with Bar, and you were sent certificates, blue or purple. Purple were worth twice as much as blue, and when you earned six certificates (for example, six blue or three purple, I can't remember which) you were sent a book – something worthy, in hardcover, from Everyman's Library. But the best thing was to have your poem or story read out on the show.

I got quite a few certificates, but I only ever had one thing read out. It was about when a bat got loose in our dining-room. You were encouraged to write stories from your own life, and this always frustrated me because I was sure everyone else had more interesting lives than mine. I thought my life was ordinary. So I used to make things up, but they'd never get mentioned on the radio. In those days I always looked for excitement outside my own life. I was sure some romantic future was waiting for me just over the horizon, just beyond my grasp. It took me well into adulthood to understand that every life is interesting. All you have to do is tell the truth and a story follows.

I wrote poems and stories. I sent them off everywhere. The *Sun Herald*, the *Daily Telegraph*, all the papers had kids' pages. Sometimes I won money in their puzzle competitions, and I remember they printed some of my stories, but I don't recall if my poems ever got published. I won the poetry prize in the Cherry Blossom Festival one year. All this added (marginally) to my pocket money. When I got to university, one year I even won the university poetry prize.

I also used to go in the eisteddfod, in the 'art of speech'

category, and I seemed to win there often, in 'reciting poetry' and 'impromptu reading', where we had to read aloud something we'd never seen before. I still love reading aloud. It's the actor in me, I suppose.

At school I was dux of my class from second to sixth grade and I was elected school captain. But that was in primary school. I got a shock in first form in high school when I only came third. But by the time I left, I'd climbed the ladder and I came first in my school in the leaving certificate. I wasn't a hopeless little dreamer, by any means, and I always knew I wanted to be a writer. When I was sixteen I entered a competition run by the ABC to have my say on radio in a series called 'Youth Speaks for Australia', and I went to the local studio, in Orange, and read an essay about how I wanted to be a journalist and change people's lives. But by the time I was old enough to do it, real life got in the way.

real world

My childhood might have been idyllic, but in retrospect I think that I grew up too sure that the world was an accommodating, benign place. When I got out there by myself I was equipped with few defences. I wasn't prepared for the realities of dealing with other people.

The problems started as soon as I went to school. At home I'd been allowed to run free. I'd spent most of my time alone, just toddling around the orchard, playing by myself, inventing stories and make-believe friends. But when I got to school I had to learn the rules of the schoolyard – and in some ways I don't know that I ever did.

One day I remember very well. I was new at school and we were playing follow-the-leader and we were caught climbing on the benches in the playground. There was a rule – probably in case you fell off – that you weren't allowed to stand on the benches. Perhaps the kids in the lead knew this and were just taking a risk, I don't know. But a teacher caught us and we were all carted off and punished – caned once on the palm of the hand with a ruler. I had no idea I was doing anything wrong and felt terribly humiliated that I'd been led into a trap without my knowing.

After that I would say I was never a blind follower again. It might sound melodramatic but I think I held back from that day on. I enjoyed school, but I never felt completely a part of it. I always felt outside, me against the rest. I knew I was different. And as I grew up and went into high school I knew then I was too tall and too bright – and too condescending – to really fit in. I knew I wasn't the sort of girl boys would choose as a girlfriend.

I think the kind of childhood I had – being left to my own devices, and being allowed to, or having to, make my own decisions – made me very capable as a teenager, and I knew exactly what I did and didn't like. I wasn't controlled or stifled. Mum and Dad didn't try to interfere in my life. I was made to be responsible for myself. When cherry season was on I used to cook lunch for everyone, for all the pickers – ten or a dozen people. I only did this because I hated picking. Mum would cook everyone breakfast then go down to the packing shed. She hated missing out on the action, whereas I preferred to be left alone to do things at my own pace. So I stayed back at the house and cleaned up and made the morning tea and lunch. The timing on both was crucial. They couldn't be late. Lunch was timed precisely. Everyone had to be washed up and sitting down by one o'clock. Why? So we could listen to 'Blue Hills' while we ate. 'Blue Hills' was a sacred institution.

the meaning of life

From about the age of fifteen I wanted to run away from home. I wasn't unhappy, just impatient. I wanted to get out and see what else there was to life. I used to sit on the end of my bed and count the pocket money I'd saved. Four shillings a week, I got. I think I knew I'd never do it. It was fantasy. But I would still sit there counting my money, dreaming about it.

By the time I left school I was very serious, and romantic at the same time. I wanted to go out and get a job as a waitress or in a shop, anything to get experience, to have something to write about.

But by the time it came around to making a decision about what I was going to do, reality came into play. Dad was sixty-two, and he'd already had two strokes. I wanted to go to university but I knew I couldn't impose any more financial burden on him and Mum. The only way of paying my own way through uni was on a teacher's college scholarship. It was the way lots of kids used to get out of home and get an education. The Department of Education paid your fees and in return you were put on a bond which meant you had to teach for four years after finishing or repay them for the tuition you'd received. So that's what I did, went to uni on a scholarship.

But I was still yearning to get out and experience life. I was sure there was more to life than I had in mine. And I didn't just dream about it. One holidays I advertised in the 'Casual Work Wanted' section in the *Sydney Morning Herald* and through this got a job in a service station at Gladesville. There were jobs everywhere in those days. You couldn't walk down the street without someone offering you a job, even if it was only three weeks in a servo.

What an adventure that was, scary and amazing at the same time. I stayed in a pub up the road from the service station. I'd never been in such a place. It was full of men who worked in the area, and I used to prop a chair up against the door at night because there was no lock. And I didn't feel safe with the window open so I used to lock that as well, which meant that every night I almost suffocated – and every morning I woke up exhausted and then had to go down and work in the service station. After ten days I rang Mum and Dad and asked them to come down and pick me up. And the room and meals cost almost as much as I was earning so I hadn't saved anything at all.

So much for adventure. Another time, instead of going straight home from uni (I used to come down to Sydney by train, and connect with another up to Orange), I decided I wanted to sort out the meaning of life – something like that – and so I checked into a pub on George Street, right down in the middle of town.

I was determined to taste city life, to do everything I couldn't do at home. I went to the movies and ate in restaurants and even went to the big musical running at the time, *The Pajama Game*. But I was miserable. I just wasn't, and still am not, a city girl. I hated the noise and crowds and bustle. I came down with the 'flu, stayed four or five nights, then went home. Still, I suppose I achieved what I set out to do. What can you learn about the meaning of life on George Street? Noise and bustle and crowds are about as close as you come.

As I got older, the conviction that there was more to experience than what was around me in Orange or Armidale increased. I never liked Orange. It was a small-minded sort of town. It was the way things were in the fifties. After the War we descended into a stultifying complacency. It was a time of prosperity and comfort and terrible narrow mindedness. The system was working well, and so to question it was to attack it. Everyone had jobs and money, and after the trauma and deprivation of the War, people just wanted to enjoy life. We grew fat on the spoils, I suppose you'd say.

You weren't allowed to be different. The slightest variation from the norm made people suspicious. Especially of the new immigrants from Europe. Even the names were aggressive. Balts. Refos. Wogs. Wops. Eyeties. If you wore suede shoes, you were a bohemian. If you were seen coming out of a pub with a bottle in a brown paper bag, everyone knew you were a plonko. If you carried one of those soft leather briefcases (called Baltbags), you were a wog or a Balt. This meant you were questioning the system which had brought the wealth under which you prospered. I knew there was more to life than this. I was hungry. I knew there had to be better food than what was on the table already.

I've got a picture in my mind of what the fifties were like. It's a family arriving for a Sunday afternoon tea. Everyone is scrubbed-up and neat. Hair slicked down, pink bows and pigtails. The little boy walks in and he is a scaled-down version of his father: little suit, short back and sides, black leather shoes. And the little girl walks in and she is just like her mother: pretty dress, neat little pumps. Not a hair out of place. That's what the fifties were like. Little kids being set up to be just like their parents.

I wasn't aggressively dismissive of the world I grew up in. I was just disappointed. I thought everything was so small-minded. If a boy liked you he'd scrawl swear words on your port. At school kids would come up and say, 'Do you collect stamps?' And if you said yes, they'd stamp on your foot. Things like that. Everything just seemed infantile and cruel.

I thought university would be different but all I found was that the little boys were bigger. It was very disappointing. It was supposed to be intellectual and challenging, but everyone played the same games. Except they were serious now because the people playing them weren't kids anymore. There were still little boys – and girls – stamping on your feet and scratching things on your port. University was even more childish than school because the people there weren't children any more.

body-generated heat

The point of all these stories is, I suppose, to help you see, in your words, 'the girl I was then'. The most important point is that I wouldn't have written to Ray if I hadn't been discontented with my life – or more exactly, the life around me. That is the crux of it. It's why I wrote to Ray in the first place, and why his letters back were so important, and how he became the only person I chose to talk to. He was outside my life, and I poured all these thoughts, these frustrations and fears and feelings, into my letters to him. They were a funnel, and I emptied myself into them.

I was searching for alternatives which suited me better. In this, Dee, aged fifty, is no different. We have led an earth-friendly life here in the Place of the Trees. Even twenty years ago we shunned plastics and processed foods. Our kids were brought up on oats and wholemeal bread. We have always grown our own vegetables. Since our TV went on the blink in about 1970 we haven't had another in the house. Out at The Block we allow no newspapers or radios. Our house here in town has a wood- or oil-fuelled boiler which provides central heating and hot water, and we have body-generated heat when collecting and sawing the fallen wood we use from The Block. It is a great way to spend a winter weekend – working up a sweat collecting and cutting wood.

I was using Ray to prise open a door to the world. I had such a thirst to know everything. In one of these letters Ray said, 'I am writing to a well-bred young lady and I don't want to offend her. I could go much further, but would it be right?' I remember so well wanting him to go further. Dying for him to go further.

That is probably what I loved about Ray. He stuck his neck out and spoke about those things most people prefer not to talk about. Perhaps he did hold himself back, out of a sense of propriety with a young girl, but given the world I lived in, I was grateful for every word he sent me.

I was terribly romantic. I was impatient for the great love affair I knew would engulf me – and I wanted it to be sooner rather than later. Sooner than sooner! I didn't imagine falling in love with Ray. That wasn't what I wanted from him. Well, maybe I did imagine it. But I knew it was impossible. More precisely, he was a substitute for the real thing. I needed to convince myself that my life could be different from that around me. I still wanted marriage and children, but they were to be on my romantic terms. They were to be special. And I didn't see specialness around me.

It was this feeling of frustration which also attracted me

to Walter. He was different from the people around me. He was European, and that gave him something which Australians didn't have. History, depth, resonance. He had some sort of internal quiet, and he still has it. I wanted something different, and I saw in Walter the possiblility for that difference. And looking back, I think we have achieved it. When I was seventeen he had for me the tug of a magnet. He's fifty-nine now and it's still the same.

his hands, his kiss

Yet, to tell the truth, I don't think I really cared about Ray much at all. I cared about what he meant to *me*, I cared very much for his ability to hurt or flatter me, but to be honest, I think for me, aged seventeen or eighteen, that is as far as my commitment to Ray went.

That might sound callous and selfish, but it is, on reflection, only logical. I'd never met him. I didn't have his hands to hold me or his kisses on my lips, or even the sight of him walking through the door. I had no real three-dimensional picture. He was in my life only as far as he was in my mind.

I was safe from him, is what I suppose I'm trying to say. We could never really reach each other, never really *touch*. There was always distance between us, the ocean separating us like a thick glass.

What I had with him was a fantasy relationship. A paper romance. Like looking through a one-way mirror; I could see what he was doing, or at least my version of it, and in turn he had his idea of me. But we were both wrong. They were only ideas. They weren't real. I only wanted him to fit a notion in my mind. If he'd shown me a reality that was too difficult to accept, I would have rejected it and him. Which is what, in the end, I did.

Ray and I agreed that if we ever met we might both be disappointed. Perhaps, yes, I would have been too normal for him and in all likelihood he would have been too unconventional for me. We'll never know. And I think, really, it's better this way. To have our dreams intact. Isn't that what letters are all about? Escaping? Living for an hour or two in an imaginary world of perfect friendship?

If we'd met, all this would have fallen to dust. He wrote to me: 'If you like a man's books, take care never to meet him.' And I didn't even like his books! I'd never read them. Does that mean I had to take twice the care not to meet him?

Especially as a writer, Ray knew that words on a page can approximate reality, they can substitute for reality – they can even, if you allow them, become reality. But they aren't reality. They are always in the end no more than an illusion.

the best defence

I did create a role for Ray. I gave him the persona I needed my correspondent to have, but in return I had little conception of Ray having his own agenda of emotional needs to satisfy. And one of those needs, I think now, was power. It was using words on paper that made Ray feel in control of his life. Because he was so good with words, writing made him feel powerful. I don't think that Ray would have written to me – or perhaps to anyone – if it had not made him feel better about his own life.

One of the hard things about reading these extracts is the memories they bring back of how much Ray could hurt me. Sometimes he would say something in a letter which would so cut me I couldn't answer. I'd leave his letter in my drawer and then in a week re-read it. By then my anger had usually subsided enough for me at least to reply.

He'd execute this hurt in the name of truth. By purporting to tell me things without the veil of tact, he knew he could cut me down like a flower. I was young and optimistic and inexperienced – and therefore vulnerable. He had so much less hope left to be punctured and he knew he could hurt me simply by being honest.

You see, I think his desire to feel needed was so great that when I – even unwittingly – stepped outside the box he had me in, I blurred the picture he had of me. By being or doing something he hadn't imagined for me, I unwittingly aroused his feelings of impotence and vulnerability – a state of mind which always spurred him on to defend himself with aggression. And this was when he could be terribly cruel.

It's logical, don't you think, that when you feel secure and competent in your own life, you don't need to win points at the expense of others. Ray, I would say, at that time of his life, felt little security in his own life, and so he tried to gain it through others. He felt most himself when writing, and so wrote a lot of letters and impulsively – when things were particularly bad for him, when his own defences were down – lashed out at whoever else presented themselves as an easy target. In this case, me. He would always regret it later, but that didn't stop him doing it again.

It is an indication of how lonely Ray must have felt and ... what? Panic-stricken, I suppose. Scared. Simply scared.

picture window

In one of the letters Ray mentions, almost in passing, that he has 'a serious anaemic condition'. It made me think two things. Firstly, that quite probably he was very sick during the time we were writing. And secondly, it made me realise how little he ever told me about his day-to-day life. Then in the next lines of the letter he seems to pump himself up with bravado and boasting. 'Once you have had to lead a platoon into direct machine gun fire, nothing is ever the same again.'

The overwhelming feeling these letters leave me with is how sad Ray was. He was old and drunk and dying – and he was lonely. Excruciatingly lonely. And yet, after my first letter responding to the newspaper article, I have no memory of that being my idea of him at the time.

This is how I thought of Ray then: I pictured him in a tiny apartment with a huge picture window looking out over a Californian beach, standing at the window muttering to himself how pea-brained it all was. Behind him the apartment was cluttered to the ceiling with dusty old furniture. And in my mind Ray was always dressed in a tie and white shirt and had a pipe in his mouth. Although in these letters he says he hadn't smoked a pipe since his wife died. So I suppose I just got hold of the idea of a pipe and shoved it into his mouth with no further thought about whether it might be true or not.

Another picture I have is from a letter he sent me. I remember – or I think I remember – he had a broken arm because he'd rushed outside one morning to get the paper and slipped on a rug and gone flying, knocking over the milk bottles as he fell. I remember that formed my image of him. I could see it so clearly – the bottles going everywhere, Ray splattered on the porch in his pajamas, his glasses twisted on his face. I feel sad even now, thinking about that. How lonely that picture is. No one there to even help him to his feet.

I suppose this is the illusion of letter writing. The fantasy of connection when connection is really the last thing possible. There's more connection in walking down the street and asking the butcher for a kilo of lamb chops. Sitting in my room at college, staring out the window with my pen in my mouth, I didn't want to know the reality of Ray's life at all.

This is why I got involved with Barry, I'm sure. He was real. He was flesh and bones and blood. He had hands to hold me. Ray was just pieces of paper in the bottom of my drawer.

mystery, romance ...

In the letter dated 25 July 1957, Ray talks about his feelings for me. I think it's a lovely description of friendship. 'In some mysterious way you have put me inside you.'

It reminded me of the real closeness there was between us – despite sounding so cynical about it now. I suppose, like any friendship, it was a mysterious thing. Why did we hit it off? You can get analytical and say simply that we each satisfied some need in the other, but that's very dry, isn't it? There's no mystery or romance in that. There's nothing of the soul. Nothing of the search for connection which is surely what propels people towards others – even if it is flawed, even if it is in the end an illusion.

... and lamb chops

Then things fell through with Ray.

I haven't written about this, have I? Why we stopped writing. Put simply, what happened was that reality came to bear on fantasy. As the months went by I gained an increasingly uncomfortable idea of Ray's life, and I didn't like it. I realised that he was often drunk and I had no emotional tools to cope with a drinker. I didn't know how to deal with the false emotion and drunken promises and empty silences afterwards. I had so much invested in the paper Ray that the real Ray could only disappoint me. I suppose, really, I simply didn't want to know who the real Ray was.

aged, cranky, will swap

What fascinates me now is that almost immediately, within a month or two of stopping my letters to Ray, I had another penpal, an East German boy named Helmut, a student of psychology at East Berlin University. Ray wasn't working out so I replaced him. Just like that! Traded him in like a used car. One slightly soiled writer, aged and cranky, will swap with younger model. How callous this feels now. What it means is that my connection wasn't with *Ray* at all. Ray could have been anybody. And when I got sick of him, or the reality of his life became clear to me, I replaced him.

I don't feel guilty about this, but I am intrigued. This was me, after all.

And the interesting thing is that Helmut and Ray were so very similar. When I told Helmut that I had a boyfriend here in Australia, he stopped writing immediately. Well, not immediately – long enough to lecture me that I had misled him, and his restraint on my behalf had apparently been misplaced. And to tell me that in the light of this he had decided to marry a girl whom he had known for many years and who, I gather, had been waiting patiently in the wings the whole time he and I had been corresponding.

From here my memory doesn't serve me well. Helmut and I must have remained on good enough terms to keep writing because I know that within months his girlfriend was pregnant. They escaped to West Berlin and got married there and had the baby. That was more than twenty years ago. They are still together as a family and Helmut is now a professor of psychology at West Berlin University.

So! How little I did really know of Helmut's life. He had been saving himself for me, seriously imagining some sort of romantic conclusion to our paper friendship. I might have imagined this, but never seriously. And this begged the question – if Helmut's idea of me was so wrong, how right was my idea of him?

a romantic conclusion

The point of this is that when I told Ray about Barry he acted as if I'd betrayed him as well. He lectured and bullied me. He was jealous and angry. He even rang me, and sent telegrams urging me to stop seeing Barry. Up until then I think he was secure in his image of me – a young girl segregated in an all-girls' college, panting over his every word. And when I told him I was seeing a boy, he got scared. Scared he'd lose me – a girl on the other side of the world young enough to be his granddaughter. This confused me, and in the end pushed a wedge between us. But I suppose, really, we were in the same situation. The reality of my life got in the way of his fantasy of me.

a strange instinct

Alcohol is like love. The first kiss is magic. The second is intimate.

The third is routine. After that you just take the girl's clothes off.
[*The Long Goodbye*]

Dee explained to me why she thought she wrote to Ray. But why did he write to her? What was in it for him?

I think the answer comes in two parts. Firstly, that Dee was a woman, and a woman more than young enough to be the daughter he never had. Secondly, because Chandler was a writer. Because, as Dee suggested, words on paper helped him feel control over his life.

Both aspects are primary to his character. Chandler's life was fused by these two elements – his relationships with women, and his identity as a writer. In one sense these elements created him, and in another he created them. And, I believe, they both grew around the cornerstone of his life – the absence of men in his childhood.

After his parents' separation when he was seven, young Ray was brought up almost solely in the company of women. His world was formed by the presence of women and an absence of men. And, more importantly, the absence of a man to model himself on. His father was an alcoholic, disinterested in family life, 'an utter swine'. When Florence took Ray back to live with her mother and sister in London, the family was provided for by her brother, Chandler's Uncle Ernest.

MacShane says that the family was not a happy one, and that Ernest 'despised the law but felt obliged to carry on the [family] firm, a mistaken attitude which led to much of the tension in the Thornton family'. In his own recollections, Chandler describes his Uncle Ernest as 'rich and tyrannical'. The two closest male relatives Chandler had could hardly be described as positive role models.

What effect would this have had on him?
Here's MacShane's answer:

Living in a matriarchal household, he could never fully relax. He was the man of the house. No one stood behind him; there was no one to guide him in the way that only fathers can. Forced into a position of responsibility long before he was capable of accepting it, he became aware of how alone he was. Abandoned by his father, he developed an extraordinary sense of loyalty to his mother, and a sense of justice that became a central part of his character and gave him the attitudes he was to express later through his character Philip Marlowe.

'I have lived my life on the edge of nothing', Chandler wrote late in his life. He knew that what he achieved he achieved alone, and when he fell he fell alone.

His isolation turned him into an observer, an outsider. Chandler acknowledged that from a young age he had experienced the desire to write. Even as a boy at Dulwich College he carried a small notebook 'in which he would jot down items of interest as they occurred to him'.

That's one side of it. But his upbringing also armed him with his particular knowledge of women, especially older women. Chandler thought he had some sort of special connection with women. To Dee he wrote, 'I do have a strange instinct for understanding people, especially women ... Often, when I was young and unmarried, I had to think for the girl too, to prevent her sometimes from doing something which I knew would shame her later.' Interestingly, only weeks later he wrote to Helga Greene, 'God, how little any man can know about women.' One wonders what insights those five weeks allowed him.

As the only son of a single mother in a household of women, this was probably the second-guessing role he learnt at a young age. In adulthood it became the over-developed sense of responsibility which he carried into all his relationships with women.

Chandler might have been comfortable around older women – his wife was eighteen years older than him – but the evidence is that he was anything but comfortable around young women. According to John Houseman, a producer who worked with Chandler in Hollywood and had also attended an English public school:

[Dulwich College] left its sexually devastating mark upon him. The presence of young women – secretaries and young women around the lot – disturbed and excited [Chandler]. His voice was normally muted; it was in a husky whisper that he uttered those juvenile obscenities at which he would have been the first to take offence, if they had been spoken by others.

The segregation of the public school system, and its prescriptive attitude towards its boys' feelings, leads to a sort of schizophrenic attitude towards women. Because girls are not part of a boy's everyday life, they are too easily idealised. Boys do not learn to interact with girls on a routine basis and hence the tendency is to see them as separate, living under different rules. This system encourages boys to see girls as sexual objects without preparing them to deal with women as individuals. Hence Chandler's smutty comments to others about the young women in Hollywood. He grew up aware of older women but did not know how to deal with the sexual feelings he experienced in the presence of young women.

When Chandler and Cissy met in Los Angeles before the First World War, Cissy was married to a composer and music teacher named Julian Pascal. The Pascals moved in the artistic circles into which another family, the Lloyds, had introduced Chandler soon after his arrival in Los Angeles. The Lloyds had a daughter some years younger than Chandler and when he came back from the War in 1919 as an eligible bachelor, it was hoped a romance might develop between them. Instead Chandler fell in love with Cissy.

What attracted him to her? To Dee he wrote that they 'just seemed to melt into each other's hearts without the need of words'. She was into her forties when they met, he was twenty-four, sheltered, quiet, more English than American; she was vivacious and worldly, already with much life behind her. Born in Cleveland in 1870, she had moved to New York

City when she was twenty in order to study music. She became a proficient pianist and, MacShane writes, 'photographs show her as an exceptionally beautiful woman with a delicate profile, soft hair, and a romantic look about her.' He notes that 'she seems to have been a model for painters and photographers', and that 'Chandler himself owned photographs of her taken in the nude when she was a girl'. Julian Pascal was not her first husband; she had been married in her twenties to a New York salesman named Leon Brown Porcher.

When Chandler met Cissy she was lively yet mature, and young for her age. She was sexual, and perhaps for Chandler the reassurance and companionship of an older woman was comforting; he did not have to decipher the disturbing sexual feelings that gathered around young women. And perhaps her intellectual maturity made her more of an equal than a younger woman. He certainly valued her intelligence and commented that her tastes in music and books were more esoteric than his own.

Chandler and Cissy did not marry immediately. Cissy sought a divorce from Julian Pascal but under Californian law they had to wait a year for it to become final. They could have driven across the desert for a one-hour divorce in Reno, Nevada, but they were too conventional for that.

Chandler's mother was living with him in Los Angeles. Through the War years the Chandlers and the Pascals were part of the same close circle of friends. When the US joined the War, Chandler and Julian's son, Gordon, had travelled up to Vancouver together to enlist in the Canadian Expeditionary Force. MacShane surmises that Florence may even have lived with the Pascals while they were away.

However, on the grounds of Cissy's greater age – closer to her own than her son's – Florence did not approve of Chandler and Cissy. This was enough for Chandler to postpone his marriage. He continued living with his mother, and after Cissy had left Julian, installed her in an apartment nearby.

The three lived this way until Florence's death, five years later. Chandler nursed her through a slow battle with cancer – not unlike the way Cissy died 'by half inches' of fibrosis of the lungs some forty years later. Florence died, finally, in January 1924, and Cissy and Chandler were married two weeks later.

In MacShane's words, theirs was 'a real marriage', but this did not prevent the tensions produced by Cissy's greater age having an effect. At Dabney Oil the presence of young, single women added to his feeling that life was passing him by and helped to generate the heavy drinking which brought about his dismissal in 1932. This in turn gave him the opportunity to rediscover the other legacy from his childhood – writing.

Despite his dissatisfactions in the marriage, Chandler had a stability with Cissy that provided the emotional safety net he needed to embark in middle age on a risky new career. This stability was formed in part by the highly developed sense of loyalty he had transferred from his mother to Cissy. He told himself she needed him and that gave him reason to change.

He stopped drinking, and with Cissy by then in her late sixties, they led a modest, quiet life. They didn't need a lot of money. Chandler could go about the solitary business of teaching himself to write fiction without having to provide a large income.

Chandler and Cissy had no children. Cissy was forty-seven when she left Julian Pascal. She had a stepson but no children of her own – and I would say that this helped determine the sort of writer he became. If the couple had had children it is unlikely Chandler would have been able to devote himself to detective stories. He could not have supported a family on the meagre fee that the pulp magazines paid. He might have tried to write for the 'slicks', as he called them, the women's glossies and popular magazines such as the *Saturday Evening Post*, but he disliked the shallowness he saw in those magazines. The tough writing in *Black Mask* resonated with the self-reliance and sense of justice he had learnt as a child.

By choosing detective stories Chandler could develop at his own pace. Out of the limelight, in the back alley of literature, he could learn the craft without interference, without attention. This befitted a shy and private man who, without the bravado of alcohol, was forced back upon his own 'beautiful if slightly tarnished character'. He trusted the gifts he had and quietly, in solitude, honed his skills.

How did Chandler become a writer? Did a particular temperament predispose him towards writing? Or, having taken up writing, were the conditions created for him to 'become a writer' – for certain predictable personality traits to take root and grow?

Was he always shy, reclusive, over-sensitive, paranoid, socially awkward, defensive, overly protective, arrogant, insecure, unhappy, deluded and alcoholic? Is this what made him a writer? Or is this what happened afterwards?

'If the good Lord had intended me to be an important writer He would not have allowed me to waste twenty years of my life in offices,' Chandler wrote to Hamish Hamilton in 1953. But perhaps Chandler had the good Lord wrong. He may have come to writing late, but he was prepared admirably for the career which made him famous. He was, from the earliest age, an observer, always an outsider looking in.

Consider his life. He was conceived in Laramie, Wyoming, deep in the mythical American Wild West. His first years were spent between Chicago and Florence's sister's home in Plattsmouth, Nebraska, in the heart of the raw American midwest. At the age of seven, having formed a fierce bond with his Irish mother against his American father, he was jolted from the wooden sidewalks and muddy streets of Plattsmouth to suburban London. There he was the only man in a house of women. He was sent to a stiff-collared English public school and educated, a frontier American, in classical Latin and Greek. After an early failed career as a second-rate Edwardian poet with an arcane interest in comparative philology, he returned to the country of his birth to spend thirteen years 'as the factotum of a corrupt millionaire' in the rough Los Angeles oil business.

All this was before he rolled a blank page into his typewriter and embarked on the new mid-life career that led him to become the most popular mystery writer of his generation. From birth to death his life was a painful accumulation of alienations.

It's no wonder he became a writer.

Always more at home in England than America, he lived in California for over four decades, rubbing up against its hard edges with fascinated revulsion. It was this abrasion that stimulated him to write. 'Half my life I've lived in California and made what use of it I could,' he wrote in 1949. 'But I could leave it tomorrow without a pang.'

According to Helga Greene, 'When he was relaxed [Chandler] could be the best company in the world.' But as a young man was Chandler relaxed? Was he a well-adjusted, likeable, loud, regular sort of guy? Or was he highly strung, neurotic, difficult, outspoken, and always sort of ... preoccupied? Even at school he was 'always jotting in a notebook'. His early essays, he said, were already 'quite nasty in tone'. He was restless, inquisitive, romantic, cynical. He didn't fit in. He had high expectations. He was doomed to disappointment, to self-criticism, to dissatisfaction – to an unbearable degree of unhappiness. He sought security away from a life in which he felt insecure. He was compelled to create a world of his own where he felt comfortable, where he knew his terrain and could control it.

And so he assumed the life of a man who sits alone at a desk. A man who lives life in his own head. He became a man who imagines, who trusts his intuition, who concocts stories, creates plots, has non-existent people talk to him, and answers them in the voices of other non-existent people. He became a man who lived by his wits, made decisions with the solar plexus, deferred to no one. Who stood alone. The personality which steered him towards writing became the personality of a writer.

The reclusive lifestyle which allowed him to hone his skills as a crime writer, however, was also directly responsible for the other side of his writing personality. Yearning for more human contact than this solitude provided, he became Raymond Chandler the correspondent, Raymond Chandler the letter writer. The two halves of his writing personality became inextricably entwined.

He became the man who could say, 'All of my best friends I have never met.'

And then Cissy died.

With Cissy gone, Chandler lost the stability that was vital to his survival. Describing her last months and the sacrifices he made for her, he wrote, 'Do you think I regret any of this? I'm proud of it. It was the supreme time of my life.'

By taking care of Cissy he was taking care of himself. It was fundamental to Chandler's equilibrium that he should feel needed. To Helga Greene he wrote, 'There is nothing predatory in me. I am much more of a giver than a receiver.'

Stripped of this role following Cissy's death, Chandler was adrift. His wife and his mother were gone, he was no longer a husband or son. He was not a father and therefore not a grandfather. At the age of sixty-six he became again the only other type of man he knew how to be – single. And he related to women the only way he knew how. His life until his death was a search to find another woman to take care of.

In London, the women Chandler met were twenty and thirty years younger than he, a new generation whose independence was created by the Second World War. Chandler had his work cut out with these new women. To create a role for himself, he imagined they were battling troubles which they needed a man to solve. This led him to behaviour which veered from the charmingly outdated to the simply pathetic. He may have been witty, gallant and generous, but he was also old and alcoholic. It was the women who looked after him, if only by allowing him to play his game. But this was a role he was not versed in. He had lost his identity as a man.

In these years, however, Chandler was forced not only to question his understanding of himself as a man; he also had to reassess his identity as a writer. He didn't know if he'd ever finish *Playback*. He wrote to Helga, 'I don't know how many times I have taken the Marlowe story out and looked at it and put it away with a sigh, knowing all too well that my heart was too sad to let me capture that mood of gusto and impudence which is essential to that sort of writing.'

He did eventually finish, but after Cissy's death he was not the same man or the same writer who had started the novel four years earlier. In his last years his 'heart was too sad' to write anything other than letters.

And by then he was famous. In London he was the celebrity he had never been in California. His role as a writer went through The Change. He had done his work and arrived. He was no longer the reclusive working writer he had been with Cissy in La Jolla. And perhaps because of this, his letters also underwent a change. Prior to Cissy's death, his correspondence, if always emotionally potent, had been concerned largely with intellectual matters. As he became less of a fiction writer his letters became centred on his emotional life – the life he had previously invested in Cissy and in his fiction. In these years he conducted even his intimate relationships by letter.

He never would have had his correspondence with Deirdre while Cissy was alive. Even had he the energy to involve himself in a life as distant as Deirdre's, out of loyalty to Cissy he would not have done so while she lay ill in the next room. After his initial reply to Deirdre, Chandler continued corresponding with her, I believe, out of the same behavioural imperatives that motivated him to choose the other women in his life. He had no reason to write to her. They had never met. But she made him feel needed – as a man and as a writer. Perhaps she also filled a role as a daughter – or a granddaughter – to be advised. Perhaps there was this as well.

But most importantly, she was out on the other side of the world, available only by mail. Living only on paper, a safe illusion. Using his favourite tool of seduction, his typewriter, Chandler's relationship with Deirdre might not have been what he most wanted, but at the time it was very much what he did need.

Part six
why do they do it? why do they always go off with lunkheads?

the hq at the end of the table

Gabrielle Mercy: 1957 came and still Ray couldn't come back to London because of his argument with the taxation people. It was terribly complicated. Letters back and forth between London and California. Masses of paperwork, lawyers and accountants. He loved all that legal manoeuvring, especially when he felt he was standing up for his rights. He had his attorney in California, and he was masterminding the operation from his dining-room table in La Jolla. He always said he would have preferred to have been a barrister or an actor, rather than a writer.

In the end, after all that fuss, he had to pay the grand sum of £646 to Inland Revenue – an amount which was dwarfed by all the legal and accountants' fees – and he was free to come back to London. But that wasn't until 1958.

philip marlowe floats

Gary Davis: He was also trying to set up a tax haven in the Bahamas. That piled another few inches of paperwork on the end of his desk. But that was the only enjoyment he got out of it in this life. The company was going to be called Philip Marlowe Ltd. It did come into operation, but not till after he died.

The name Philip Marlowe was actually Cissy's idea, from when she and Ray used to spitball ideas around in the early days with *Black Mask*. He had Johnny DeRuse and Sam Delaguerra and Pete Anglish and then from somewhere back in Grade Ten Eng Lit he came up with Marlowe Mallory, which he probably thought was real smart. Kind of indicates the attitude Ray had to the whole business. Not really all that reverent. Then somehow Cissy pegged him down with a name people might actually believe. You can understand why he missed her so much. He loved her mind.

it wasn't long before ...

Gabrielle Mercy: We pieced together over here, from dribs and drabs in letters, the story of Ray's drama with Louise Delamotte. He really was on an emotional roller coaster. It wasn't long after Louise that Natasha was in America on a concert tour. She was only performing in the eastern states but on Ray's insistence she made a special detour to visit him in California. I think he wanted to find out, once and for all, what there was between them. He knew that Natasha loved visiting new places, and he enticed her over to the west by proposing a motoring tour of Arizona.

the joke wore off

Gary Davis: Ray hated the sightseeing racket, but he went along with it for her. They went all over – 'mountains, desert and every other damn thing', and stayed at a little town outside of Phoenix called Chandler. What they did once the joke wore off, God knows. Stopped laughing, I guess, and moved on.

and every other damn thing

Gabrielle Mercy: Natasha left at the end of January, and Ray wrote soon after that he had accepted, finally, that the hopes he harboured for her were fantasy, that she would never leave Stephen and the boys for him. He wasn't angry about it, but he was defensive. He complained that he felt 'always available, never essential', but wrote to Helga, 'I do absolutely feel that I owe her an enormous gratitude for making life bearable to me again.' When he was recovering from Cissy's death, it was Natasha who reassured him that he still had feelings. Only, as it turned out, too many feelings. And not feelings which made anybody's life easy.

get sick soon

Gary Davis: I had a daily spot in the *San Diego Bugle* and whenever I was down with the 'flu or something, I had Ray fill in for me. He wouldn't take anything for it. It was a rare treat for the readers having prose as sparkling as Ray's dished up with their breakfast, and his columns always generated more response than any of mine. Especially from the lawyers. The lawyers at the *Bugle* went through everything Ray wrote. They knew he didn't give a damn. Which meant they better.

He did a column on cats – which came out pretty unscathed, seeing as cats can't litigate – and he did another on sex, which also was more or less libel-free. It broke your heart, though, that piece. Old Ray, so lonely and frank about it that even his memory of sex made you want to hurl yourself on the floor and weep.

But what got him most attention was a column he did on La Jolla. That needed a bit more fancy footwork through the sub-clauses. He said La Jolla was no better than 'a reluctant suburb of San Diego', and got stuck into the local necklace and boat-shoe brigade for having a consuming interest in cocktail parties, patio furniture, the fully automated kitchen, and not much else. This was a favourite theme of Ray's, Californian kitchens. Maybe it was a consequence of spending time in England, where I guess everyone cooks on gas rings on the dresser.

A sign appeared the next day at the southern limit of

town, just as you come over the hill from San Diego: YOU ARE NOW ENTERING RAYMOND CHANDLER'S RELUCTANT SUBURB OF SAN DIEGO. Errol Flynn, who was still on highway duty then, had it in the trunk of a patrol car about fifteen minutes later – but not before some crow-eye with a camera got a passing snap. It arrived on my desk that day and I ran it the next morning, which prompted the predictable flood of outraged letters. Five, maybe. Six, tops. All from La Jolla. Not one from 'Diego, surprise, surprise. You go over that hill into San Diego and the real estate drops ten thousand big ones. Not one home owner in Diego would mind being in La Jolla for a day – as long as it was sale day.

One letter in particular tickled Ray's fancy. Some joker suggested I should look after my health better – and maybe Ray should stand in for me more often. That letter cheered him up. And there weren't too many cheery days for Ray that year.

something smelly in the drawer

Gary Davis: He was trying to work. He had an old story he wanted to convert into a play for his big splash on to the English stage. That was his idea, to live in London and write plays. It wasn't a Marlowe story, more's the pity. It was called *English Summer*. It was dead before he took it out of the drawer – only by then Ray's nose wasn't working that well and he had to send it over to Helga and have her send it back before he realised. It was about an American in England who has to choose between two women and either way he loses – which was pretty much Ray's theme over those last years. 'Whatever you do, you lose.'

He was also trying to do a Marlowe story called *The Pencil*, about organised gang murders. But he said eventually that the story was 'too damned serious to be witty about' and threw it in the ocean as well.

drunk and naked

Dr Verringer Kurtz: I was Ray's physician in La Jolla until his death in 1959. He wasn't a well man. Emotionally, he wasn't well. This is what led to his drinking. He never recovered from the death of his wife. I would say that he lived through her to a degree that was harmful to his own health.

This is something most couples do to some extent. It's part of the interdependency of a marriage. But there are individuals who, so to speak, abuse the system. Individuals who never achieve the emotional maturity to best outfit them for a balanced life and hence rely on their spouse for their identity. Of course I must qualify this by adding that individuals who do achieve this level of emotional self knowledge are very much exceptions to the rule.

It is well known that creative individuals are often the least emotionally capable in our society. All artists are so because they are damaged. They bear scars. They are crippled, they can't walk straight. That said, as a society we would all be starving if we did not have our artists to feed us. They do the living we leave behind. They are our soul. As a society we delegate to these individuals the dark side of human nature which our day to day life cannot accommodate – the eyes and ears and sensitivity which most of us leave behind.

Of course, for the individuals concerned, the life of the artist is often difficult, regularly terrifying. Ray knew the darker side of himself to an extent that very few of us ever have the need to experience. Writers are perhaps the most introspective of artists. They must sit with their projects, and themselves, for a length of time which necessitates a kind of self knowledge which the artist can find frightening.

And, put simply, artistic individuals need regular relief from their own introspection. They want a break from their condition. They want time out. Just as a factory worker takes off his boilersuit and catches the bus home, in the way an office worker takes the elevator to the street and becomes another face in the crowd, so an artist wants to take off his boots and boilersuit and try, for a while at least, to put his feet up and become a regular human being.

But is this possible? Can an individual choose to become 'normal', at his discretion, if his very existence relies on his abnormality? Surely if he was normal he would cease to exist? I believe that Ray fell into a pattern common to many such individuals. Attempting to numb his sensitivity down a few notches, to anaesthetise himself a little, he resorted to alcohol. This is something probably most of us would understand. We use alcohol to relieve, temporarily, the difficulties of being human, of being whole. Of being more than our daily lives requires of us. Multiply this and you can start to appreciate the often unstoppable self-destruction many artists succumb to. It becomes apparent why so many artists are alcoholic.

There are also many practical reasons why an artistic individual might drink too much. Such persons often do not have the imposed structures which other workers can rely upon to ease the strain of daily life. An artist's time is often less ordered by outside forces. They must establish their own routines, their own discipline. They have only themselves to rely upon. This can be terribly stressful.

The sad reality is, however, that alcohol or other chemicals are often exactly what an artistic individual does not need. To achieve that 'humanness' which these individuals seek requires a deep subconcious relaxation. Prayer or prolonged and practised meditation might help open the pathways to such a state, but alcohol most certainly does not. Alcohol cannot reach those deep subconscious emotions which are the essence of the artistic temperament. Usually all alcohol does is irritate those concious emotions it does reach.

And this is exactly what it did for Ray. It was not even an efficient anaesthetic. It made him morose. It made him depressed, it brought to the surface his ancient reserves of self pity. All alcohol did for Ray was to substitute new bad feelings for old bad feelings.

Which isn't to mention the physical side of alcoholism. Physically alcohol was killing him. He didn't eat when he was drinking, and was soon suffering the early stages of malnutrition. His liver, his nerves, his heart and his brain were all suffering. Alcohol was attacking his body in a hundred ways.

In August 1957, for these reasons, I ordered Ray hospitalised. It seemed to be the only way to get decent food into him, to stop him drinking long enough for his body to regain some reserves. And he had a broken wrist from a fall. That sort of accident is very common amongst alcoholics. And even a broken wrist can kill a man in that condition.

scowl on legs

Gary Davis: He said he slipped on the rug while rushing out to get the paper. He was sloshed, no doubt. At any rate, Dr Kurtz figured it was enough to put him back in the La Jolla clinic. That and the fact that his blood carried about as much zing as three-day-old soda.

He was pretty low when he came out. They pumped him full of iron and he seemed to have a bit of colour back, but he was still pretty low. He still walked around like a scowl on legs.

And things weren't helped by the witch from Australia.

the personality of a piranha fish

Gary Davis: It happened like this. For years Ray had Juanita Messick as a secretary, but he let her go when Cissy started going downhill and he couldn't find enough work to justify keeping someone on full-time. Then he decided he needed a secretary again. He put a blind ad in the *Bugle*, keeping his name out of it. Betty saw the ad, 'Writer seeks part-time office assistant', thought, 'Here goes! On to this!', and telegrammed that day. This is a telegram a page long. God knows what she put in it. Her life story, I suppose. She was always very eloquent on that subject. And Ray was always a sucker for a difficult dame. Ray goes into a dating agency, looks around and says, 'Very nice, but like, you got any with a few more problems?'

So he gave her the job. One of his more inspired off-the-cuff decisions. Nita had been a gem. I think even Ray knew how lucky he was with her. She was the perfect secretary. She was smart, she was tolerant, she had common sense – and she wasn't so pretty as to irritate the wife. And she knew when to tell Ray to go to hell. Ray used to insist she practice telling him to go to hell, if that's what she felt like. 'If you want to go to San Diego for the afternoon, just say so and the hell with it.' That sort of thing. He used to leave messages like this on the dictaphone. He never said them to her personally.

But Betty Bluefields. I can't even use her real name for fear of her litigious nature. And seeing as how I can't really think of much good to say about her, I don't want to risk that sweet temperament getting the better of her. First thing Betty did when Ray died was go to the courts and see what she'd gotten out of it. She was a millstone around his neck from the minute they met to the day he died. It just goes to show what a state he was in that he kept her around and took on what he did with her and the kids. The kids were little jewels, considering. How they survived their mother is a miracle of human resilience. Mind you, I haven't kept track to find out what they carried into their own parenthood and dumped in their own kids' laps when the time came. And I'm glad. Some things hurt the human eye too much to see.

She was Australian, but she was married to an American. She was married, but she'd left him. Although God knows why he hadn't left her first. Anyway, that's why she needed the job. Two kids to feed and a divorce on the way. And I'd say, really, that's what got her the job. Ray's life was so empty he thought he'd fill it with some of hers. It must have been that. It certainly didn't sound like she was going to travel far on her secretarial skills alone.

I remember him dropping into the newsroom one day in desperation. He'd given Betty his car and she'd just had a wreck – on his insurance. He sat there sprawled in the hard-backed chair and took off his glasses and rubbed his eyes and said, 'She can't type, she can't file, she can't take shorthand, and she makes godawful coffee – apparently they don't drink it in Australia.' And here Ray put his glasses back on and looked straight at me. 'And she is not by temperament the type to make an efficient secretary.'

Which meant she had the personality of a piranha fish. On a good day.

Oh my God, and she wanted to be a writer! She wanted to be a goddamn writer. Soon as she had her feet up on Ray's desk she had him handcuffed and hogtied into an idea she had for a book exposing every case of medical fraud and malpractice since Hippocrates. Here's Ray having trouble finishing a goddamn short story and he's getting all worked up on an idea which promised to be bigger than the Bible and Ben Hur put together. A crowded cast of villains, admittedly, but hell, when Ray sits you down and tells you stories like that with a straight face you know he needs hospitalising.

He gave her his car, he paid her bills at the local stores, he set the kids up in school, he settled her into an apartment, he helped settle with her attorneys for her divorce. What was he thinking of! It's no wonder she thought she was home for the long haul. In due course he even signed his will over in her favour. If that's the business of a man with a sound mind then take me out the back and shoot me.

In '58 he even signed the royalties on *Playback* over to her for future pocket money. Thank God he had Helga. Soon as Helga got wind of what he'd done with *Playback* she called up Betty and bought the rights back for £2000, no discussions entered into.

Of course *Playback* wouldn't even exist without Helga.

without a pang

Gabrielle Mercy: We were getting terribly bleak letters from La Jolla. Ray couldn't come back to the UK because of the tax business, so he was trapped there, hating everything. 'Puce dinner jackets', 'meaningless chi-chi', 'dishwashers that do everything except sing *Tristan und Isolde*'. He could be very funny, but of course underneath you knew he was dreadfully lonely. He had a fall and broke his wrist. 'I'm typing this with one hand,' he would write, trying to impress us with his bravery.

Helga got so concerned, she decided to go over and see for herself what she could do.

seemed to suit him very well

Gary Davis: She was tall and very proper looking. Stern. She wore a brooch at the neck and gloves and one of those absurd British hats which look like embroidered dinner plates. She appeared very severe and aloof and seemed to boss Ray around, to mother him. And that seemed to suit Ray very well.

which counted most

Gary Davis: All year he'd been talking about 'the goddamned Marlowe book'. He'd written half of it before Cissy started getting bad, but after she died he just didn't seem able to face it again. For his type of writing, he said, you had to be firing on all twelve – and he wasn't. He was coughing along on about three. Not only that, the stuffing was out of the seats, the suspension was hard, the brakes were gone, the steering was loose, he was leaking oil, he had gudgeon knock and piston slap. He was headed for the scrapheap.

But Helga changed all that. The engine was fuelled with coffee and Scotch – but what the hell, it got *Playback* out of the repair shop and on the road. He finished the goddamned thing in six weeks. It might not have been *Crime and Punishment*, but he finished it, and that to him was what counted most.

he wrote

You know if it hadn't been for Helga, I'd never have finished the damn book. She arouses my mind and my ambition by some strange quality in her own mind ... there is some sort of chemistry between Helga and me that gives me a driving impulse. With Helga around I feel as though I could write anything – sonnets, love poems, idiocies, plays, novels, even cookbooks. What on earth happened between this rather cool, aloof woman and me?

a cookbook for idiots

Gabrielle Mercy: They even started a cookbook. It was going to be called *A Cookbook for Idiots*, which would have sold a million on the title alone. What a pity they never finished it. Ray boasted that he was the world's best cook as long as he was drunk enough. But as soon as he got drunk, of course, the first thing he lost was his appetite.

he wrote

My Swordfish Mascagni is famous for all of three blocks, and that's just in a light breeze. With a good stiff one off the ocean practically the whole of La Jolla is reeling. And my apples backed in cider are vociferously admired by practically everyone who owes me money.

gentle and decorous

Gabrielle Mercy: He was terribly excited to have Helga in California. It was as if a dream had come true. Not only did she have a mind he respected, but she was a woman he loved who loved him. She only stayed several weeks but it was long enough. Helga seemed to give Ray a new grasp on life. He finished *Playback* and was already planning the next Marlowe book, which he was calling *The Poodle Springs Story*.

They had a few days in Palm Springs before she left, and on their last night went to some 'swish place on the Strip' and, he said, spent the evening 'gently and decorously in each other's arms'. After that he seemed to became quite nutty about dancing. She put spring in his step in more ways than one.

dancing queen

Cindy Hernandez: He was old when I met him. But he looked good. He dressed up well. And he had manners. He was polite, in fact I could of swore he was English. He spoke like he was English. His lady friend was English, that's for a certainty. No way she could of been anything but English, you could see that in the way she looked, before she even opened her mouth.

I was working a joint called the Doll House, a pumped-up diner on the Strip, and Ray used to come in with his lady friend and have breakfast. Another reason I knowed she was English, she asked for breakfast special. No hash browns, no pancakes, just toast and tea and eggs sunny side up and bacon on the side barely cooked. And then she started talking nasty about the tea. Next day she brings in her own tea and asks for a pot of boiling water, straight, so she can make her own. 'I'll have to charge you,' I tell her, and she says, 'Don't matter, all I want is a decent cup of tea for breakfast.' Ray didn't say nothing through all this. He just sat there with his lip curled like he was laughing at it all. I realised after he always looked like that, a half-laugh on his lips. Ray didn't drink tea for his breakfast. He had coffee like everbody else.

Pretty soon his English friend was gone and Ray was in having breakfast by himself. Not that I knew nothing about him – he was just another patron, old, and probably stinking with money, from the look of him. Just like all the rest. And that day he stops me in my work and says would I like to go out dancing with him.

Well, if you knew how many of the old boys ask that, I almost laughed out loud. But then Ray said, real polite and proper, 'Of course, that's all I am asking – I have no ulterior motive. I've been watching you,' he says, 'and my suspicion is that you'd be a good dancer.'

Well, he was right. I love dancing. I'm a dancing nut. But seems no man wants to know about dancing these days, 'cept rock 'n' roll dancing, which ain't dancing, just running on the spot, if you ask me.

Course, I couldn't be sure about Ray. I mean he introduced himself and all, but his name didn't mean nothing to me. He's no movie star, or nothing. So I say I'll go away and think about it, meaning just that. I'll mull on it and keep my gaze on him and try and work out if I can trust him.

Also, I don't want Ormonde seeing nothing gonna make him angry. And I'm thinking over it and I'm thinking, yeah, I reckon a night dancing would please me something.

So next evening, after Ormonde has gone, I go to Ray's table and give him my number on a paper. And he's got that half-laugh again and says, 'Very discreet, my dear. But trust me, we won't be doing anything to upset him.'

Next day Ray rings and says, 'How about the Ranch Club on Saturday night?' And I say, 'The Ranch Club!', but stop myself and try to act cool, like I'm there every night, and say, 'Why sure Ray, the Ranch Club'd do me fine.'

The Ranch Club! I just gotta glance in that place from the other side of the street and the doorman gives me a dirty look.

'Sure, that'll do me,' I say, and I'm already thinking how I'll get out my white stole and long gloves, before I even get off the phone.

So, eighty-thirty Saturday night Ray calls by in a cab, and I know I'm looking like a million dollars because I've spent the best part of five goddamn hours banking it in front of the mirror. And Ray, being a gentleman, says, 'My dear, you look wonderful', and he's so polite and proper, and holds the cab door open for me, and gets out first at the Ranch Club and goes around the back to open it again, and I can't believe it, it's like the movies. Like the English movies. And I make sure I give that doorman a good long look before I move off, just so he remembers next time he raises his eyes across the street.

Well, we didn't get much dancing in, but we sure did a lot of eating and talking. Ray had us champagne and that sets my tongue off something fierce, and before long I'm telling him all about Bobby and the divorce and all that stuff I don't much talk about no more. And I ask Ray to tell me about himself and he starts on about what sort of books he writes and how his wife died and he's been so sad and can't seem to get settled again and most of his friends are in England and life there in La Jolla nearly ain't bearable for him no more. And he tells me his English lady friend was really his agent and she'd been out here helping him finish his book and they just had a few days in Palm Springs to unwind following. And, he says, he loves dancing, and I looked like I might be a dancer too, and so that's why he asked me out. Just to go dancing, no more. No strings, no big move afterwards. And I tell you, I'm more than a little sad about that by then. I was warming to Ray. Sure he was old enough to be my granddaddy, but he'd be such a gentleman like you just don't see nowhere any day now.

And anyway, we try to have us a dance but the floor's real crowded, being Saturday night and all, and Ray gets all worked up and sorry, angry almost, and I say, 'Ray, don't matter, it's been a lovely night.' And he takes me back to my apartment and drops me off from the cab, going around to open the door again, and takes my hand and just kisses me soft on the cheek once and don't try nothing and apologises again for nothing going right, and I say, 'Ray, everything went right. Don't matter about the dancing.' And then I get my courage up and say, 'Sure you wouldn't like something little for a nightcap?' And I can hear the air between us, real soft and warm and silent like, and the sound of traffic off on the Boulevarde, and there's the desert stars high up there twinkling like the roof of the Starlite Lounge, and I don't know if Ray's thinking what I'm thinking, but then the cab driver blows it anyway. He coughs some and shifts in his seat and suddenly Ray looks around and gets proper again and says, 'My dear, it's been a delightful evening, let's not spoil it now. I'll ring you in the morning.'

And that's it, he gets in the cab and off it goes and I'm standing there on the kerb, dressed up like a fairy princess in the middle of nowhere, and I turn around and go up the stairs and turn the key in the lock and switch on the light and close the door behind me and suddenly I'm back in my own life again, roaches scuttling behind the cupboards, the TV in the corner, the smell of coffee from the kitchen and Pine-O-Kleen from the bathroom, and I can't help it, I just sit down and cry.

And sure enough, Ray calls up in the morning, asks how I am, and I say, 'Fine, I guess.' And he says, 'My dear, what colour roses do you like?' And I say, 'What do you mean, what colour roses?' And he says, 'When a lady does me the honour of dining with me I always send roses.' And I can't help it, I just start bawling again. And he hears I'm crying and says, 'My dear, I'm sorry, have I upset you?' And I say, 'No Ray, you ain't upset me, I guess I just ain't used to being treated so kind. Usually ...' And then I say, 'Oh the hell with it. Ray, can we do it again? It was the best night of my life, really, it was.' And he says, 'My dear, I'm flattered, but I have to go back to La Jolla tomorrow, and I'm leaving for London shortly, so no, I'm afraid I won't be able to see you again.'

And that's all there was. The roses – red roses – arrived an hour later with a card saying 'From Ray, for my dancing queen', and that's all I ever heard of him. The Doll House weren't never the same after. Seemed I was always in tears until finally Ormonde says, 'Cindy, I can't have a waitress who starts weeping every time a customer orders coffee and eggs, I'm going to have to let you go.' And I understand. I know it's time to move on. So I say, 'Don't matter Ormonde,

I've been thinking it's time to see what's happening back home anyway.' And that's what I do, come back here to Witchita. And the rest, well, the rest's history. I opened this little place, Cindy's Nite'N'Day, and met Byron and had the girls, and well, I'm happy, I am, and probably I wouldn't have come back at all, none of this would've happened, except for Ray.

all day and tomorrow as well

Gary Davis: Ray wrote to dozens of people. He was always complaining about his overwhelming correspondence – not that he seemed to do anything about underwhelming it. He lived through letters, simple as that. He could spend all day writing letters, and then tomorrow as well. He had his girlfriends in London. He had his friends in the business – his English publisher, his American publisher, a few other writers, a librarian here and there, a mystery buff in Slackjaw, Wyoming. The list got long. People always wrote back to Ray because no one wrote letters like him. The letters he wrote me I've got to this day. I might sell them to some library somewhere if Penny and I feel like taking a cruise or a trip to China, but there's no way I'm throwing them out. I pick up those letters and Ray steps out and takes me right back to that view from the front window at Camino de la Costa the first day I saw it in 1946, when I sat down and felt tears come to my eyes it was so goddamned perfect. And there's Ray standing beside me, lighting his pipe, shrugging and saying, 'Well, we live here, so the hell with it.'

my girl in australia

Gary Davis: Stacked away in the middle of this pile, beside the Olivetti on the dining table, was the other girl from Australia. The one he'd never met. He didn't talk about her. He didn't talk about any of them. He used to pass on books the publishers sent him, mysteries mostly, which Penny would read and report back on. 'And what's the opposite sex got to say about this one?' he'd want to know, and I'd give him Penny's report when I returned the book, or sometimes he'd come down for supper and Penny'd tell him herself. He liked that. He liked sitting there having Penny rail at him about this writer or that book. He used to sit there at the table, or after supper on the couch, with that little smile on his lips, watching her rail. She could rail good and he liked it good.

Anyway, one day I called in and Ray flung open the door. He was furious, like a bull at a gate.

'For Christsakes, Ray,' I said. 'What's the matter?'

We went back into the main room. There was a letter wound into the typewriter. I'd interrupted him. He said, 'Nothing the matter with me, Gary. Nothing at all the matter with me. It's Deirdre. My girl in Australia.'

That's what he called her: my girl in Australia.

'Why?' I said. 'What's she done?'

I'd heard of her, but I didn't know anything about her. Ray had mentioned her, that was all. He liked that he had this girl he hadn't met. It tickled him. Flattered him.

'What's she done?' I said.

But the heat seemed to have gone out of him, and he slumped down on the couch and took off his glasses and rubbed his eyes.

'Why do they do it?' he said. What's wrong with them? They're smart, they're pretty, they've got more common sense in their little fingers than most men have in their whole goddamn bodies. They could do anything with their lives. And instead they go off with a lunkhead. A man a tenth their size. A man with a secure job, good looks perhaps, perhaps with the sexual agility of a lemur monkey – but with the emotions of a paling fence and a brain as tough as a soft-centred chocolate. I've seen it a hundred times. I've seen it in England. I've seen it here. And now it's happening in Australia. Why do they always go off with lunkheads?'

Part seven
if you marry this fellow your life'll be rooned

doghouse

We were at the table upstairs. We'd had lunch and were ready to start. Then I remembered something.

'Dee, you never told me which of Ray's books you read.'

She laughed. 'I don't remember. I might not even recognise the title. When I went into the bookshop at uni to look, that's how I chose. By the title.'

'*The Big Sleep; The Long Goodbye; Farewell, My Lovely.* Any of those?'

She shrugged. 'I don't know.'

'And that's where you bought it, the uni bookshop?'

'The Angus & Robertson bookshop. It was the only one on campus. The shop assistant was a man named David. I went out with him for a while later on.'

The bookshop in Armidale. A shop assistant stands with Deirdre in front of the shelves of Penguins.

'Orange are general fiction. Blue are non-fiction. Green are crime. Raymond Chandler writes crime.'

'Green.'

They cross to the shelf of green spines. The young man extracts a book and holds it out.

Deirdre takes it and turns it over.

'Yes, that's Ray. That's his photo.'

She reads the blurb on the back.
'Oh dear.'
'What?'
'Oh well, I suppose I'd better try one.'
'Have you never read any?'
'No. But I can imagine.'
'Really, you haven't? Oh, you'll love him. You'll come back and buy them all.'
'Will I?'
Deirdre opens the book she is holding and makes a face.
'What?'
'Doghouse Reilly.'
'Yes?'
'Are they all like that?'
'Like what?'
'You know – Doghouse Reilly.'
'What about Doghouse Reilly?'
'Have they all got names like that?'
'Doghouse Reilly was a joke. That was what Marlowe called himself when . . . Anyway, they're full of jokes. They're very funny.'
'Are they? Yes, I suppose they would be. Which is the best?'
'They're all good. *The Long Goodbye*. That's my favourite.'
'Is it?'
Deirdre turns her head to look through the titles.
'*Farewell, My Lovely*. That's a nice title. I'll try that.'
The young man nods, but looks at Deirdre quizzically.
'You called him Ray.'

too clever, too tough, too smart

'Is that more or less right?'
'More or less. A bit exaggerated. I don't think I've ever heard of Doghouse Reilly. And I don't know if David was a fan of Ray's. And I would never have let on that I knew Ray. I didn't tell anyone that. It was my secret.'
I nodded. 'Okay. Would you like to tell me about David?'

She barely had to think about it. 'No.'
'But you did you go out with him?'
'Yes. For a while.'
'And did you like the book? You don't remember which one it was? You did read it?'
'Yes, I remember reading it. Well. I don't remember not reading it. And no, I don't remember which one it was. But yes, I do remember not liking it.'
'Why?'
'Oh, too clever. Too tough and smart.'
'Did you finish it?'
'Yes, I would have finished it.'
'Do you still have it?'
'No.'
I paused. Her expression offered me nothing.
'And you don't remember when that was?'
'No. But he'd sent me the photo by then. And that was quite late in the piece. By then I was starting to wonder about him. Whether it was a good thing to be writing to him.'
'What do you mean?'
'We haven't talked about why Ray and I stopped writing, have we?'
'You've told me you realised he was a drinker and you didn't know how to deal with that.'
She nodded and turned away, thought for a few moments, then looked back.
'I suppose it's most honest to say that the letters simply petered out. We both moved on. When I realised he was alcoholic, or a heavy drinker at least, I started to pull away. I didn't want to offer him as much of myself because I knew how much he could hurt me. It was sad, but that was what happened.'
She took a deep breath.
'I was seeing a boy, and I told Ray and he got terribly jealous. And, I don't know how, but I knew he was over-reacting. I knew something wasn't right. And somehow I realised it was because he was drinking. And this set up a reaction in me so strong that it amazes me, thinking about it

now. My trust in him evaporated. I felt angry and used. And betrayed. He didn't mention alcohol to me once. If he'd been drunk the whole time we were writing, how could I believe anything he had said to me? Also, I was upset that there was this big part of his life which he was keeping from me.

'I remember going back to my room one night during this time and getting out all his letters and re-reading them. I'd read them all a hundred times. Parts of them I knew off by heart. But when I read them that night I felt like I was reading back over the love letters of a relationship that had finished. I was sad and I was angry – not just at what I read as his betrayal, but because now I understood this about him he wasn't the man I wanted any more. He was flawed and untrustworthy and I was left without the correspondent I wanted. That was what mattered to me more. It was quite a selfish response.'

he was a crocodile hunter and I met him at a dance

I sat with my hands folded over my exercise book, leaning forward like an interrogator.

Dee said, 'I don't mind talking about this, about Barry, up to a point. But I'm concerned – '

'Yes?'

'Look, what happened between Barry and me is my life. I'm concerned that I'm swamping you with facts. That you're learning too much of the true story and that there won't be enough left for you to invent. I'm concerned that whatever ideas you have for your book will be lost in the true story. And . . . ' She took a breath. 'And I'm concerned that you're hiding behind Ray. I think you're unsure of your own talents so you're riding on Ray's back.' She paused. 'And mine, too, I suppose.'

I said softly, 'You can stop talking any time you like, Dee.'

'Yes. I know that.' She looked down. 'So I'll give you the censored version.'

I waited, then shrugged. 'Good. Much better. Only as much as you want.'

She looked away out the window.

'His name was Barry and I met him at a dance.'

'When? Do you remember?'

She kept looking out the window. 'I was in second year. 1957.'

'Can you remember when in the year? At the start or the end?'

Dee had her eyes on something, thinking.

'Was it hot? Or cold? Winter or summer?'

'Yes, I remember. The dance was in April. So it was autumn. But it was still warm. It was a warm night, I remember that.'

I nodded. 'Warm autumn night. And what happened? What sort of dance was it? Was Barry a student?'

She shook her head. 'No, he wasn't. That's what I liked about him. He wasn't like the boys on campus. He was older, and worked for a living. I liked that. He was the sort of man I like. Strong and capable. That's how he was different to the boys at university. He was more grown up.'

I felt my hackles rise. I didn't know why.

'So what did he do?'

Crocodile hunter? Boundary rider? Horse breaker?

'He was a relief clerk in the railways.'

that's serious!

'It was one of the things Ray made most fun of. That Barry worked in the railways.' She laughed. 'He was right, of course. Not that Barry worked in the railways and was somehow beneath me because of that. But because, well, because I would have been sick of him in a month.'

'Sick of him in a month?'

'If we'd got married.'

'You were going to get married!'

'No. I never said yes. But he did ask me. He bought a ring.'

'He bought you a ring! An engagement ring? That's serious.'

Dee shrugged her shoulders. 'I suppose it is.'

She chuffled and looked away out the window. I watched her eyes. They followed the path of some wrens in the bare branches of the tree. She watched them for a long time, then shook her head and laughed again.

a memory loss at the inquisition

'And what do you remember about the dance? Was it a formal? Was it a student dance?'

'Yes, it was a student dance. But it wasn't formal. Just one of the Friday night dances at the student union. The local boys used to come to the uni to try to pick up a girl.'

'Is that why Barry was there?'

'Well, I'd say he was trying to meet someone, at least.'

'And can you describe what the dance was like?'

'It was just a union dance. Nothing special. It probably wasn't even organised beforehand. They just seemed to happen on a Friday night.'

'Was there a band?'

'Oh no. A record player. You only had bands for really big occasions.'

'And how many people?'

'A hundred. Perhaps. I can't remember.'

'Was there alcohol? Beer? Wine?'

'Not officially. But people would have had beer. And the boys from town would have brought some up.'

'And would you have drunk any?'

She shook her head. 'You don't stop, do you? No, I didn't drink any. I didn't start drinking until I went out with Walter. I tried to get drunk once.'

She smiled. 'But I won't go into that here.'

We met eyes and rested with that.

'Okay. Do you remember, then, how you actually met Barry? Did he ask you to dance?'

She twinkled. 'Sorry. I don't remember.'

the rules

I grinned. Okay. This was good.
'All right. So you met at the dance? Then what?'
'We went out a few times.'
'Where did you go? The movies?'
'Yes, probably. The movies. Probably another dance. We tried to have a picnic.'
She looked down. She was blushing.
'You tried to have a picnic?'
She moved the mug in her hands.
'I'm just remembering. It was raining so we didn't even get out of the car.'
She sighed.
'I must have been so naive in those days.'
'Why? Is that when you . . . ?'
Dee shook her head. 'No, not that.'
I waited.
'Well, you were only seventeen.'
'Eighteen.'
'Sorry. Eighteen. Ancient.'
She smiled into her mug. Her wedding ring clinked against the handle.
'So what happened? Or would you prefer not to talk about it?'
'No, I don't mind.'
She looked up, fixed me with her eyes.
'The thing is, by the time Ray got wind of it – by the time I told him, it was all over anyway. It only lasted about three weeks.'
'Three weeks!'
'Yes, exactly. I never saw Barry again after the picnic. But Ray exaggerated it out of all proportion. He assumed I was about to run off and go and live in Collarenebri or somewhere and ruin my life. But it was nothing like that. I'd just met this boy at a dance and liked him. I was eighteen. It didn't matter how many letters Ray wrote me, I was still hungry to find out about men. I was trying to learn the rules, to get out of my fantasy life, to get some experience in the real

187

world. I was trying to cure myself of Walter. I was trying to forget about him. Because he was unavailable, strangely enough I had him stuck in my mind as the only man for me. But I'd never had a man.'

She paused.

'I was still a virgin.'

I nodded.

'And I was afterwards, too.'

I nodded again.

'Well, yeah, so was I, at eighteen.'

'Were you? I would have thought that most people – boys, anyway – would have lost their virginity by then.'

I shrugged. 'Maybe they have.'

Dee suddenly seemed to be watching me with interest.

'You're embarrassed.'

'Yes, I suppose I am.'

'Why?' She leant forward, smiling. 'Talking about losing your virginity? Talking sex with a woman old enough to be your mother? Is that it?'

I shrugged. 'Yeah, probably.'

'Why? Mothers have sex lives too, you know. And they had them long before their children were born.'

'Yes, okay, Dee.'

'So? Why are you embarrassed?'

'I don't know.'

'We're just talking.'

'Yeah, okay. But can we, can we talk about Barry, instead?'

She laughed and leant across and gripped my wrist.

'Sorry. I was playing with you.' She clenched a bit harder. 'Sorry.'

I shrugged.

'Okay? Where were we?'

'The attempted picnic.'

She nodded. 'Yes, but that's rushing ahead. He wanted to take me home to meet his parents and everything.'

'You didn't go?'

'No. But I imagined what it would be like.'

hello, dear

The ute pulls up outside a weatherboard cottage in need of a coat of paint. It is autumn in Armidale. The trees are losing their leaves, the sky is high and cold. The driver's door opens and Barry gets out, dressed neatly in pleated trousers and a tweed jacket. His collar is open, he doesn't wear a tie. His hair is combed wet and flat. Dee sits in the passenger seat, looking out the window at the house. Her face shows no enthusiasm. The garden in front of the house is poorly tended. Sheets of newpaper are snared on the pigface in the scrappy bed in front of the rusty wire fence.

Barry holds the gate open for her. They walk slowly up the concrete path, his arm hovering behind her. She wears a heavy overcoat, her arms folded. She is taller than him. The screen door of the house squeals open, and an overweight country mother emerges, drying her hands on her apron. She smiles as the couple approach. Barry's hand rests at the small of Dee's back.

'Mum, this is Deirdre.'

Barry's mum holds out her hand. 'Hello, dear.'

Sunday roast. Fat Dad, Fat Mum, Dee and Barry. Silence. The clink of cutlery on china. Dee and Barry saw at their slices of lamb, Mum leans over to do Dad's. Dad has had a stroke. His face falls to one side, his right hand rests beneath the table. Dee tries not to stare.

Barry puts his knife and fork down on his plate and reaches his hand around his glass of beer.

'They reckon if I can stick out another year of G.A. at Uralla – that's Goods Assistant,' he explains to Dee and continues, 'then they'll put me up to A.S.M. – that's Assistant Station Master – for another year, and then I can apply for a transfer to Armidale, and, after a few years here, apply for Newcastle. And after there, who knows? Sydney.'

He lifts his glass to his mouth and his eyes rest on Dee, who is looking down at her meal. Mum and Dad are watching her. Dad puts down his fork, leans forward on his elbow and lets his giant hand rest around his glass of beer.

'You do the right thing by them, son, they'll do the right thing by you. They looked after us all right.'

He raises his glass. Dee watches a dribble of beer run down his chin. Barry leans towards her.

'When Dad was good enough to go back to work they found a place for him inside. In the office'

He smiles at Dee.

'It's full of old shunters. Hobbling around on one leg, trying to do everything with their left hands. So Dad feels right at home. Eh, Dad?'

He laughs. 'No one can understand a word they write.'

Dad looks up from his meal, his face grave. 'You stand by them, son, they stand by you. That's the way it goes.'

no dribbling

'How was that?'

She shook her head. 'I'm sorry. It's not the way I imagined them at all. I can't let you have that. I never thought they'd be that ... grotesque. And where you got the stroke from, I have no idea.'

'Nowhere. Just imagining.'

'Do you want to hear my idea of them?'

'Please.'

'For a start, Barry wasn't from Armidale. He was a relief clerk, filling in. I think he came from the coast – Newcastle or Wollongong. Perhaps even Sydney. I never imagined his parents would be as sad as you have them. I thought they'd be kind-hearted and welcoming, hard-working people. I imagined I'd quite like them but that we'd have no ... what? Intellectual connection. I knew it'd be uncomfortable with them. We'd all sense the gap between us, and it'd just be silent and awkward. Nothing menacing or ugly. Just awkward.'

'No stroke?'

'No. No stroke. And certainly no dribbling. Why did you have to have him dribbling?'

'No reason. Just atmosphere.'

'Will you take it out?'
'Can we talk about it later?'

rugs beside creeks

'You see, in those days, you didn't just move in together and have a casual relationship. You did everything by the rules. You went out. You held hands. You kissed, or you got kissed. You went out a few more times. You started cuddling – up the back of the pictures, usually. You went for drives in the country on Sundays, and had picnics on rugs beside creeks. And at night, after the pictures, you ended up at the lookout above town with all the other cars. If you were bad, or reckless at least, you had sex. If you were good, or careful, you didn't. Or didn't quite.'

'And you were good?'

'Well, not so much good, as unconvinced. My mind wasn't made up. It was more that nobody – Barry, or any other boy – knew the right way to ask. I wasn't a prude or anything. It's just that the opportunity hadn't presented itself. Don't forget that I had the model of Mum and Dad in front of me. They obviously had such a good love life. They were in love, but they were friends too. That's what I wanted. I didn't just want a man for sex. I could have had a hundred of them. I wanted the whole thing. Friend, lover, companion. And that was the problem with Barry. I realised he could never be the companion I dreamed about. That's why, in the end, I changed my mind. Why nothing happened with him.'

She looked at me.

'You understand?'

I nodded.

She kept looking at me.

'Yes, I think you do. You can't imagine, people your age. The strain was unbearable. You weren't supposed to even touch each other, but of course that's all you wanted to do. So almost as soon as you'd met, if he was a good boy, he was asking you to marry him. If he was a bad boy, and you were prepared to go along with him, you did it just like young people do these days. You just had to be more careful and secretive. And Barry was a good boy.'

'So he asked you to marry him?'

She nodded. 'Yes.'

'And what did you say?'

She shrugged. 'I didn't say no. And I didn't say yes. It was too quick. I barely knew him. I knew that much at least. And I suppose – I suppose somewhere about that time, because I was unsure and uncertain, I mentioned Barry to Ray. And then...'

'And then Ray got involved?'

'Yes.'

'What did he do?'

'He sent me a telegram, for a start. A forceful one, saying "Don't do anything until you hear from me". Then he wrote at length, as I remember.'

'Saying what?'

'Saying I'd be crazy to marry Barry. Saying I was too good for Barry. Saying I'd be bored and I'd be unhappy. And saying that all I wanted, really, was sex.'

'He said that!'

'Something like that. Then, well, I can't remember exactly, but that's when he started ringing me and sent me more telegrams. And the stupid thing is, it was over with Barry by then anyway.'

She sighed.

'Ray was completely overreacting, trying to protect me from a disaster of his own imagining, from a big mistake I wasn't making anyway. And in the process he was ... I don't know.'

She stared at me as she thought.

'He was undermining the idea I had of him as stable and wise and calm. Again, I was selfish. The more upset he got, the less he fitted my image of him. The more I questioned his worth to me. Not consciously. But that was the effect it had.'

I nodded.

'Okay. So by the time Ray got involved you'd already had your last picnic with Barry?'

Shaking her head, Dee looked away.

'Well, we'd tried to. But it was raining so we didn't even get out of the car.'

'So what happened instead? If you don't mind telling me.'

Dee looked at her hands crossed on the table in front of her.

'No, I don't mind.'

round the block a few times

Dee and Barry sit in Barry's car watching the rain pour down outside. They are parked overlooking a creek, a sodden paddock in front of them. Barry's arm is around Dee's shoulder. In her hands she holds a small blue box. Inside a diamond glints off a thin gold ring.

'Barry, it's lovely, but – '

'It wasn't really expensive, Dee. I'm careful with my money, I want you to know that. But I didn't want to skimp, either. It's a nice diamond, isn't it?'

Dee looks down. How can she tell? The diamond looks like any other.

'Barry.'

'It's de Beers. South African. The world's best, they reckon.'

'It's lovely, but – '

'You don't have to answer now. You can think about it.' A smile crosses his face and he nods to the ring. 'You can take it home. You know, test drive it. Run it round the block a few times.' He smiles.

'Barry.'

'Yeah, I know it's quick. But, well, you're special, Dee. I didn't want some other bloke to snaffle you up from under my nose.' He smiles again. 'What a mug I'd be then, eh?'

Barry moves in, closes the gap between them, reaches his face down to Dee's, kisses her. She makes a gesture of protest but he doesn't stop. After a few moments her hands relax, the ring falls into her lap, then she pulls away.

She says his name again and he puts his finger to her lips

and starts to disentangle himself from her as his right hand reaches down for the door handle.

'Sshh. I've just got to get something out of the boot.'

He opens the door and dashes out into the rain, banging the door behind him. A few drops splash onto Dee's face. She flinches and sighs and looks away out through the rain-running window at the sodden green scene in front of them. The ring's box hangs loose in her hands.

She jumps as the boot slams. Then Barry is back, tugging at the door. He can't get in, and bangs on the window.

'Dee! Open up.'

She reaches across and Barry is suddenly back in the car, wet and cursing.

'Bloody hell. You could farm fish out there.'

Dee turns to face him. 'Barry, I've got to say something.'

He doesn't answer, but waits expectantly. His open face derails her intentions. She glances down at the package in his hand.

'What is it? What was in the boot?'

Barry covers what is in his hand and slips it into his pocket.

'No, you first. What do you want to say?'

She looks away out the windscreen and sighs. 'Barry, I'm sorry. It's just all too fast.'

Barry puts his finger to her lips again. 'Sshh. It's okay. It's my fault. I was pushing you.' He reaches down and encloses the ring box in his hand, snapping it shut.

'This can wait. There's no hurry.'

He leans in and reaches his face against hers. But he is wet now and Dee draws back.

'Barry, no.'

Barry isn't giving in. He scrabbles in the pocket of his coat.

'It's all right, Dee. There's nothing to worry about.'

She looks down at the sodden packet in his hand.

'No, Barry, you've got it wrong.'

she shook her head

'Yes, that's not bad. I wasn't hurt, or upset. More, I was just angry that he was thinking so differently from me. That he was insensitive to my feelings. Or maybe he thought having condoms was the way to show me how considerate he was. Either way, he was wrong.'

'So what did you do?'

'I just said to him, "Barry, I'm sorry. You've got totally the wrong idea. I don't want this. I don't want to marry you. I don't want to have sex with you. I would have liked to be friends with you first. But I can't do it this way."'

'And what did he say?'

'He said ...' She paused and smiled. 'He said, "But Dee, we can still be friends."'

She shook her head.

'But you didn't want that?'

'No. I think then I realised he was the wrong person for me.'

She shrugged. 'He was a nice boy. But I wasn't broken-hearted.'

She went silent, and that seemed to be it.

'So that was the last time you saw him?'

She nodded. 'Yep. I got him to drive me back to college and when I got out of the car I never saw him again.'

the photographer's flash

She shrugged. 'So that was Barry.'

'Just like that?'

'In essence, yes.'

Suddenly she thought of something.

'I haven't shown you the photo, have I?'

She stood and left the room. A minute later she was back with a large envelope. She passed it across the table. I turned it to read the address.

'That's not the original envelope. I just put it in there last week.'

I nodded and up-ended the envelope, letting the photo fall onto the table. I recognised it.

'Huh. I know this.'

It was an 8x10 publicity shot of Chandler sitting in a high-backed floral upholstered armchair, holding his cat. The usual bemused smile slants his mouth and from it protrudes a straight-stemmed black pipe. His chin is cleft. He is looking down at the cat and the shadow of his glasses falls across his eyes. Behind him are shelves of books. The cat's eyes are round and scared from the photographer's flash.

The photo was taken by John Engstead in the early 1940s and has become one of the famous photos of Chandler. He didn't like most photos of himself ('there is no worse murderer than a newspaper flash gun artist'), but this one he approved of, and he had copies made to send to friends and admirers.

He wrote to Charles Morton: 'A man named Inkstead [sic] took some photos of me for *Harper's Bazaar* a while ago (I never quite found out why) and one of me holding my secretary in my lap came out very well indeed ... The secretary, I should perhaps add, is a black Persian cat, fourteen years old ... '

The photo might be well known, but this one was special. Across the top right-hand corner the words 'For Deirdre, of your RC' were inscribed in blue biro.

I held the photo by its edges, bringing it up close to examine the inscription and holding it away again to get a good look. I ran my fingers lightly over it, feeling its indentation. I was seized with a sudden excitement. Thirty years ago Chandler had scrawled these words. I tried to fathom this. Chandler's own hands had held what I was holding now! This wasn't a matter so much of star-struck awe, as simple incomprehension.

I pictured him in his apartment, at the long dining-room table where he wrote. I could see his crumpled white shirt and crooked bow tie. I imagined a bottle and glass at his elbow and the room stale with cigarette smoke. Unopened windows. The day bright behind the drawn shades. I could see his pen hovering over the photo and hear his shallow breathing. What should he write? Which words would best suit his most distant girlfriend – the girl he had never met who lived on the other side of the world?

I turned the photo over. On the back was taped a square

of thin typing paper. The original sticky tape was still in place down the sides but was now yellow and crisp, no longer sticky. On the paper was typed, in blue:

This was taken, I think, in 1946, just before we moved to La Jolla. I am holding the cat's tale [sic] to keep it from wagging. My hair is very much greyer now, but it is the best photograph I have had in a long time. Very much cut down, it has been used on the backs of Penguin books.

Ray

Underneath, in neat pencil, was written, 'Received 2nd May 1956'.

Then I realised where I had first seen the photo. Another piece of the jigsaw fell into place.

went straight, then didn't

My mother's green Penguins date from the years following the move to our second family home, a mile from the first in suburban Sydney. Both houses were on main roads. My eldest brother stood outside the first house waving a miniature Australian flag as Queen Elizabeth II sped by in a black Rolls Royce on her way from somewhere to somewhere else. It was December 1954, the month Cissy died in La Jolla. I was there too. My mother stood at the roadside, holding my brother's hand. It was a hot day, and my mother wanted the cars to come and be gone so she could go inside into the cool. She was feeling ill. She'd been feeling ill for weeks. It was six months before I was born.

We made the move to the second house when I was four years old, in 1960. From that time I remember summer. It was always summer. My mother painted the back bedroom in the new house, standing on a plank laid between two step-ladders to reach the high parts. She listened to the cricket on the radio. When the West Indies tied the Brisbane Test in 1961 we came crashing in from the backyard, sure she had fallen to the floor.

My mother was tall and pretty and wore her lips red. She smoked then, in the days before lung cancer, and her cigarettes lay in the ashtray with red kisses around them, their smoke rising straight then mysteriously going haywire. Her sisters and their husbands came around in the evenings and everyone smoked and drank beer, relieved temporarily of their kids. They could hear our shouts from the backyard, the reassuring sound of cousins playing.

The men wore open-necked shirts and pleated baggy trousers which they hitched up at the knees before sinking into low canvas deck chairs. The women wore sleeveless floral dresses tight at the waist, their arms bare and brown. Everyone was tall. The whole family was tall. My father flirted with his sisters-in-law, and white teeth flashed with laughter. Brown long-necked bottles stood sweating on the table. My aunts' glasses had red lips on the rims, and the smoke rose straight from the ashtray and then didn't. I wasn't tall. I was short and chubby. I stood at my mother's side waiting for a chance to sneak a cashew from the bowl.

These were the years of my mother's Penguins. There was always one beside her bed or on top of the TV. Raymond Chandler. Dorothy Sayers. Eric Ambler. She scrawled her name in blue biro across the top corner of the front pages. 1962 she wrote beneath her name. 1963. 1964.

Twenty years later, when I was the age my mother was then, I found those Penguins in a box in the back bathroom, their spines torn and yellow with aged sticky tape. They were waiting to be thrown out. I couldn't believe this. I grabbed them and rushed inside to upbraid my mother. These books! My first contact with Raymond Chandler. The start of all this. On the back covers above the bio of the author was the photo, very much cut down, that Ray sent Dee when I was still in nappies.

a bit on the side

I held the photo in my hands. 'Did he send this out of the blue? Did you know he was going to send you a photo?'

'Yes, I knew it was coming. He asked for a photo of me first, which I sent him.'

'One you had hanging around. You just sent him that?'

'Oh, no. Nothing like that. I had one taken especially, in a studio in Pitt Street. It cost me ten shillings. Which was a lot.'

Deirdre stands on the pavement in Pitt Street, Sydney. She looks down at a scrap of paper in her hand then up and down the street. She tries to peer above the awnings on the other side.

She is dressed in a light summer frock and sandals. She looks out of place. A country girl in the city. She is jostled roughly by office workers hurrying past. After a minute she wanders vaguely with the flow of people, still peering into shop doorways.

She climbs creaky wooden stairs and as she pushes open a frosted glass door a bell rings. On the glass is written Higginbottom and Bromide, Portrait Photographers.

Deirdre sits in a high swivel chair in front of a plain backdrop. A young man in a long, stained apron adjusts the bright lights which trap her in a semi circle. Another young man in shirtsleeves and bow tie hovers behind a cloaked camera.

'That's good,' the photographer is saying.

Deirdre says, 'I've only got ten shillings.'

'That'll be fine.'

'Is that okay?' asks the lights man.

'Yep, that's good.'

'What do you reckon, Kev?' asks the lights man again. 'No shadows?'

The photographer comes out from behind his camera. 'Killer, mate, it's good.'

He rolls his eyes at Deirdre, pointing at his ear. He grins. 'Deaf as a fence.'

The lights man looks at Dee and smiles. 'Kev's incredibly particular about shadows.'

He goes round behind the camera and his smile drops. 'Kev, what do you think about her hair? Think we should do something about that part? Are people still doing that? Parting like that? I don't think so. What do you think? Just turn your head for me, darling.'

He motions with his hand and Dee turns.

The photographer is standing with his hands on his hips. 'Since when did you know about hairstyles, Killer?'

He smiles at Dee.

'Killer's sister did three weeks of Hairdressing at Sydney Tech and ever since he's been the office expert on women's fashion.'

Dee smiles, slightly.

'I tell you, Kev. Parts are out now. You know that, darling? Parts are out. Parts went out last year sometime. Fringes are in.'

The photographer shakes his head. 'Killer, will you shut up? If the girl likes it parted, let her have it parted. What do you want, darling? A Killer perm, or a bit on the side?'

His face scrunches up into a wheezy laugh. 'Get it? A part? A bit on the side? Get it?'

Killer punches Kev in the arm. 'You said you wouldn't do that any more. It puts people off. You agreed.'

Kevin shrugs at Dee and his laughter gurgles to a stop.

'You're right. Sorry. You're right.' He looks at Dee. 'Sorry. Are you ready now? I think I like it, after all. I think it looks nice.'

the expression on my face

'You're not serious, are you? They weren't anything like that.'

'But there were two of them?'

'Yes, but that's about all you've got right. And the part. And the ten shillings. The photographers were just these two young blokes doing a boring job. Turn this way. Turn that way. It was over in ten minutes. They weren't funny at all.'

She shook her head at me and sighed.

'Anyway, the inevitable happened. Ray didn't like the photo. And he didn't hesitate to tell me so. He could be so cruel. And I'm sure he knew it.'

'Go on. What did he say?'

'Oh, everything. Your imaginary photographers were right. Ray didn't like the way I had my hair. And he thought the expression on my face was – well, he didn't like the expression on my face.'

I waited. Dee decided to keep that one to herself.

'And instead of sending me a photo of himself he sent one of another woman friend of his, a concert pianist he knew from London.'

'Natasha Spender.'

'Who?'

'She was the wife of Stephen Spender, the poet.'

Dee shrugged. 'I didn't care who she was. He assured me she was famous and had been to Australia and everything. But I didn't care about that. All I knew was that she was beautiful and obviously meant a lot to him. I wasn't particularly pleased about it. He said he didn't have a photo of himself on hand. That's why he sent one of ... what was her name? Natasha?'

I nodded. 'So what did you do?'

'I wrote and told him I was angry! I always told him when I was angry – not that it made much difference. He still seemed to say exactly what he felt like.'

'I'm sure he liked that, though. He said somewhere that Cissy used to get angry and throw pillows at him and he liked it. He liked her spirit.'

'Is that right?' Dee said.

She laughed. 'Anyway, he must have known it would upset me and it did. Remember that for me he wasn't Raymond Chandler, the famous writer. He was a man in California who I poured my heart out to. I wasn't writing to him to be a part of his life, I was writing to explore mine. That he was supposed to be such a good writer wasn't of importance to me, except inasmuch as he wrote me such good letters.'

I looked back down at the photo. The house creaked. Still I couldn't believe what I was holding in my hands.

'You can have that,' Dee said. 'A gift.'

I looked at her, wide eyed. 'Really? Are you sure?'

'It's yours. I've got memories. I don't need a photo.'

She paused.

'Look, it feels to me as if you really idolise Ray, and have a wrong, romantic idea of our relationship. But the reason I stopped writing was quite selfish. He was getting to be trouble. He wasn't easy anymore. It was becoming too difficult. And he was hurting me. He really could be hurtful. One of the things that he said about my photo was that I looked 'cowlike'. And about that time I started to work out that he was drinking and I think I just decided to go quiet, to stop writing.

'And then the phone calls started. And that's when I knew I had to stop.'

sprung metal

Chandler enters the open door of his apartment, breathing heavily. He closes the door and leans against it, catching his breath. He is in shirtsleeves and wears his favourite bow tie, yellow with black polka dots. Around his arms are sprung metal sleeve-raisers. He looks like an old-fashioned clerk, or a bookkeeper. In his hand is a bundle of letters. The room is bright with coastal light. It is the middle of the day.

He dumps the letters on the table in the middle of the room. It is a dining-room table, covered with books, papers, letters. His Olivetti stands on the placemat at the end of the table, a large black telephone is pushed away in front of an empty chair. Standing out among the papers is a tall bottle of whisky.

Chandler pours from the bottle into a waiting glass and takes the glass to the couch. He drops down, swings his feet up, lies back, takes a sip. He rests the glass on his chest and it moves with his breathing. After several minutes he drops his feet to the floor and sits up. 'The hell with her.'

He pushes himself to his feet and walks to the table, sits down and pulls the phone towards him, his mouth set. The shadow of his glasses obscures his eyes. He holds the receiver against his ear and waits.

He says, 'Yes, overseas operator please.'

The old green public phone in the vestibule of the college in Armidale. It is the middle of the night. The vestibule and the corridor leading off it are lit but the rest of the building is in darkness. All is quiet, there is no sound and no movement – until the phone makes a click and starts ringing. After the preceding silence it is terribly loud. A door is flung open and a girl clutching a dressing gown around her runs down the hall and lifts the receiver. 'Hello? Hello? Who is it you want?'

the tone changed

'No, it wasn't like that. The phones weren't in the corridor. They were outside, beside the front entrance to the college. Three red phone boxes in a row.'

'Okay. And were they the old green phones with the buttons?'

'Were they green, or black? I don't know now.'

'Green, I think.'

'No, I think they were black.'

'But they had buttons?'

'Yes. A and B. You pressed button B when the person answered. And button A was for getting the coin back in case something went wrong.'

I nodded. 'And they had that chrome slide at the top which held your penny until the phone answered. Then it rolled down into the machine when you pressed button B.'

'They sound ancient, don't they. They sound like a century ago.'

We paused.

'Okay. So the phone rang out in the box, and whoever was passing by picked it up, and what? The overseas operator said "I've got California on the line for Miss Deirdre Gartrell." Did that create a fuss?'

'Well, yes and no. It did create a fuss that someone had a call from America. It was unusual, certainly. But I deliberately didn't talk about it. I didn't want Ray to become public knowledge. He was my secret and I wanted to keep it that way. So if anyone asked me questions I just didn't answer them. Do you understand?'

She gave me the hard look I was starting to recognise. As if I was crossing that line myself.

I shrugged. 'Yes. I understand.'

'And it wasn't the international operator on the line. It was the university administration.'

'And they had the operator waiting?'

'Yes.'

'And they told whoever answered the phone that there was a phone call from America, for Deirdre Gartrell?'

'Yes.'

'And that person ran and got you? Or stood at the door to the college and yelled your name until you heard, or until someone heard who knew you?'

She laughed. 'Yes.'

'That must have taken hours. What time of day did he ring?'

'What time? Evening. Night-time. I think. It was dark, anyway.'

'So the cry went up, 'Deirdre! Phone call from America!' and you dropped everything and ran out into the dark to the phone box.'

'Yes, something like that.'

'Dropped your study, or whatever you were doing?'

'Yes.'

'And you knew who it was, obviously. You didn't have any other friends in America.'

'No. I knew who it was. And I knew what it was about too.'

'How?'

'Because he'd already written. And sent the telegram.'

'About Barry?'

'Yes.'

'So he really was upset about it? He might have had totally the wrong idea about it, but still, he was concerned for you?'

'Yes, he was.'

'And so what were the phone calls like? What was he like? How many times did he ring?'

'Not many. Three, maybe four times.'

'Uh huh. And what did he say? What was he like?'

'There were no pleasantries, no small talk, just straight into it. "Deirdre, if you marry this fellow you're a damned fool. Your life'll be rooned." That sort of thing.'

She smiled.

'And what did you think?'

'I thought he'd gone off the deep end. He'd totally got the wrong end of the stick. It was just this boy I'd been interested in, and Ray seemed to think I was about to run off and ... Anyway, I knew something was wrong. It made me wary of him.'

'And is that when you stopped writing?'

'No. I think I kept writing. But it changed the way I thought about him.'

'Then what? What about the other calls?'

'Well, until then no one, not one person, knew about Ray. Not even Jenny or Margaret, my closest friends. But when Ray rang the second time I think Margaret must have been in my room, because I think it was then I told her about him for the first time. About the letters, the phone calls, everything. And she couldn't believe it. She couldn't believe I'd been writing to Raymond Chandler, *the* Raymond Chandler, and never told her. She'd read his books. She thought he was wonderful.'

Dee laughed. 'She was much more excited about Raymond Chandler the writer than I ever was. Really, she would have made a much better correspondent for him than me.'

'Although maybe he wouldn't have thought that.'

She shrugged. 'No, maybe not.'

'So that was the second time?'
'Yes, I think so.'
'And what did he say that time?'
'What did he say?'
I nodded. She kept her eyes on me and moved the empty mug around in her hands.
'He said – he was drunk, of course, and so he probably didn't mean it, or didn't meant it the way it came out – he said that really all I wanted from Barry was sex, and therefore that was all the more reason not to marry him. And he said ...'
She kept her eyes on the table.
'He said if I was serious about learning about sex I should come over to visit him, and he'd teach me more in a month than I'd learn from Barry in a lifetime.'
I laughed out loud and Dee's face dropped. I clutched her arm.
'Sorry. I didn't mean to laugh. But it is funny.'
She shrugged, smiling. 'I suppose it is.'
I could just picture him saying it. Quite possibly he was right, but quite certainly it wasn't the right way to say it.
'So he offered for you to go over to California and be educated in sex.'
'Yes.'
'At his expense.'
'Yes.'
'And presumably to be educated by him?'
'Yes.'
'Were you tempted?'
She paused.
'Yes.'
'By the offer of personal education?'
'A bit, yes.'
'Or the free trip to America?'
'Well, I was flattered. Look, I was dying to find out about sex, and the thought of finding out with someone like Ray was wonderful. Yes, it was tempting. I mean, if I could have found a man, in the flesh, like Ray – not like Ray, but with Ray's qualities – I wouldn't have said no. But I knew with

Ray it would never happen. I knew it was all a dream. I couldn't have gone if I'd wanted to anyway.'

'Why?'

'For a start, because I was on a teacher's college bond. I was bound to them to finish my training. Then I had to work for five years or pay it off. Also, well, my father wasn't very impressed by Ray's offer. I don't know why exactly, but I decided then to tell him about Ray. I showed him a letter Ray wrote after the phone call, repeating his suggestion that I come over and be educated.'

'And what happened? What did your dad say?'

'Dad said Ray was nothing but a dirty old man.'

I suppressed another laugh. 'And what did you do?'

'I tried to defend him.'

'Why? I thought you said earlier that you were angry with him?'

'Oh, did I? I wasn't really though, not at that stage. I got angry later.'

'Doesn't matter. So what happened with your father?'

'We were sitting on the verandah, just the two of us. I suppose I told him about Ray then because Ray had offered to fly me over, and although I knew it was impossible, I wanted to make exactly sure. I remember Dad had Ray's letter in his hand. I think this must have been the first he really knew about Ray. He'd seen the letters from America, there's no doubt about that, but he believed too strongly that I should be able to run my own life and didn't try to find out who they were from. And so I took the free rein he offered me and kept Ray to myself. Until this time.

'I remember the view from the verandah. A really beautiful view, facing north, with orchards all around. And I remember Dad leaning on his elbows and staring out down the hill as I talked to him. And I think it was probably a Sunday again, when nothing was happening on the orchard and everyone else was asleep, or not there, anyway.

'See, we both knew it was out of the question, me going to California. I had to finish teacher's college, for a start. So really, it was more a matter of Dad just trying to protect me from myself, from my own feelings. From making a mistake and getting hurt. It was just what Ray tried to do with Barry. Except now it was Dad protecting me from Ray. I remember saying to him, "But Dad, he's in *America*, how careful do I have to be!" And Dad laughed and said, "I just don't want to see you go for a fall, Dee. I'm not telling you how to run your life. But he sounds like a dirty old man to me and I think you ought to be careful."

'That's really all I remember. That great view, and Dad handing me back my letter and kind of shrugging, "Well, it's your life, but he's old enough to be your grandfather."'

'And that was all?'

'Yes. That was all.'

'And that was after the phone calls?'

'Yes. Well, after two of them, I think.'

'Sorry, I'm still trying to get the chronology. Ray rang three times?'

'Yes, three times. I think.'

'And the second time he asked you to America?'

'Yes.'

'And that was when you finally told Margaret about him, and she was excited because she'd read his books and knew who he was.'

'Yes.'

'But by then you'd decided to stop writing?'

'Well, I didn't make a conscious decision to stop. But I was pulling back. Maybe I had stopped, or just sent him a note, or one letter. It was less than usual, anyway, because that's why he rang the third time.'

'He rang to see why you hadn't written?'

'Yes.'

'And what did he say this time?'

barely heard him

Late at night, Dee stands in one of the three red phone boxes outside the entrance to the college. It is winter, she is cold. She is trying not to shiver, despite the heavy coat over her pajamas. She stares down at the woollen slippers on her feet, the receiver pressed tight against her ear.

'Ray, I can't hear you properly. Yes, I'm sorry about what happened too. It was a misunderstanding. What? Yes, Ray, I know you're a lot older than me. No, I don't think you're interfering. Yes, you mean a lot to me too. Yes, I – '

She holds the phone away from her ear, looks at it, places it carefully in its cradle and wanders outside and back into the building.

chops okay?

'That's not bad. You're getting the hang of it. He said he was sorry about everything that had happened and that the offer of a visit still stood, and that he hoped he hadn't offended me irreparably, and then – he was quite drunk, I think – he said he loved me and hung up. It was all a bit sudden really. I just stood there holding the receiver, then put it back on the hook and went inside.'

Dee looked away at the squeaky chittering of the birds in the bare branches outside the window. The wind flurried the trees at the edge of the garden. We sat still. Finally I spoke.

'Do you remember how he said it? Was it: "Oh God, I love you! I need you, now!" Or was it: "I love you scrumpkins. I'll cook tonight. Chops okay?" Or: "I love you goddamn it, woman. Can't you see that!" Any of them?'

Dee smiled. 'No, none of them. More like: "This whole business is completely out of hand. I just don't know what I'm going to do with you. It's driving me crazy. But, well, I love you. I don't know why, but there it is. I'll go now."'

I laughed. 'Except he wasn't as polite as that.'

'No, he wasn't nearly as polite as that. That's what disturbed me. It was as if he was angry at me. I didn't know how to take it. And of course he was slurring – because he was drunk.'

I nodded, and leant forward.

'You know, you haven't told me what he sounded like. What his voice was like.'

She turned away to think.

'Well, the line was always bad, much worse than they are now. You really knew it was a long-distance call. Often I could barely hear him. He had a very soft voice. It was more English than American. He certainly didn't have one of those typical brash American voices. But he used American words and had a slight accent – and he was very wheezy. A lot of the time I couldn't understand what he was saying, and looking back I think that was because he was drunk. Often he kept fading away until finally I couldn't hear him at all. Then I had to ask him to speak up, and he'd get irritated and snap at me. "Why do I bother!" Something like that.'

I nodded, then grinned as I thought of something.

'You realise that probably you're the only person in Australia who has talked to Raymond Chandler on the telephone?'

boiled as a lobster, sober as a salmon

According to MacShane there is only one recording of Chandler's voice, a BBC radio talk he made with Ian Fleming in 1958. The talk was re-broadcast for the centenary of Chandler's birth in 1988. During the course of writing this book, via the surprising network of Chandler connections which emerged when his name started getting about, I was given a tape of this broadcast. Pieced together, the story goes something like this:

Ian Fleming: The BBC had me organised to do a talk with Ray. They did these things in those days – wheel a couple of old boys in and give them forty-five minutes of air-time to waffle on about, well, about whatever they wanted, really. It was in 1958. Ray's last book, *Playback*, was being released and the talk was timed to give it a bit of a shove.

We all knew Ray was drinking and had no idea if we could trust him not to turn up boiled as a lobster. Didn't matter that the damn thing was due to kick off at eleven in the morning, Ray often had Scotch with his kippers in those days. The producer chappie and I got to his hotel at about ten but he was well on the way to stinking already. We couldn't sober him up so instead we just propped the old dear behind his mike and hoped for the best. If you listen to the wretched thing you'll understand why I did most of the talking. I can't listen to it, of course. I sound like a retired major out of P.G. Wodehouse and Ray sounds, well, he sounds drunk and bored, which he was. That the cursed thing ever went to air is a triumph of audiophonic editing.

We were supposed to be talking about thrillers, but of course we waffled off on to any other subject we thought of. Ray gave a long description of how a gang killing might be organised in America, and blasted me again for forgetting that damned glass of water in Las Vegas. I had Bond eat in a Las Vegas restaurant but neglected to have the girl bring him a glass of water as soon as he sat down. Ray picked this up immediately and never let me forget it. The *Times*, or someone dreadfully well read like that, had him review *Diamonds are Forever*, so he'd already given me a serve about it in that. In *Playback* he sends his girl, Betty Mayfield, into a café, or restaurant, and he makes a point of her getting the inevitable glass of water as soon as she walks in. I'm sure the old boy blacked that in just for me.

Ray was in big demand for radio and television around that time, but his reputation with the bottle was getting about. On one occasion he was booked into a night talk show at BBC television. The producer, poor chap, went around warning everyone that Ray might turn up sloppo, and organised an emergency filler in case he did. He got himself in such a flap, this producer, that he ended up flat out on the floor himself even before Ray turned up. And, of course, then Ray waltzed in sober as a salmon. Very Ray. Very Chandler.

I might say also, that morning at the BBC was the last time I ever set eyes on Ray in my life.

the field marshal and the private

On the tape Chandler's voice is soft and nasal, his American accent curling the edges of good public school pronunciation. His condition is obvious. His voice often drops away, or is slurred and inaudible, and when he gathers himself to explain some point for the struggling Fleming, his manner seems laden with an unpleasant and bored belligerence.

Fleming later described Chandler as:

puffy and unkempt with drink... In talking he never ceased making ugly Hapsburg lip grimaces while his head stretched away from you, looking along his right or left shoulder as if you had bad breath. When he did look at you he saw everything and remembered days later to criticise the tie or the shirt you had been wearing.

The two first met when Chandler went to London in 1955. Both being popular writers 'outside the normal swim of things', they had a mutual distaste for the literary establishment, and they maintained, MacShane says, a 'chaffing friendship'. Fleming regarded Chandler as a superior writer. In one of his books he inscribed: 'To Field Marshal Chandler from Private Ian Fleming'. It was Fleming who organised this talk on the BBC.

During the talk this exchange takes place (Fleming speaks first):

- Yes, I agree there's too much violence in my books. Everyone says so. But [Bond] doesn't get hurt in the next book I've just written... much.
 - Have you?
 - Yes.
 - What's it called?
 - It's called *Goldfinger*.
 - Which?
 - *Goldfinger*.
 - How can you write so many books with all the other things you do?
 - Well, I sit down, and I have two months off in Jamaica every

year – it's in my contract with the *Sunday Times* – and I sit down and I write a book every year in those two months. And then I bring it back ...

- I couldn't write a book in two months.
- But then you write better books than I do.

after the phone calls

Dee shrugged and looked down, as if she was embarrassed.

'I didn't care about that sort of thing. I've told you that. I didn't care that he was famous. That's not why I was writing to him.'

'Yes, I know that. That's not what I'm saying. It just suddenly struck me that there is probably no one else in Australia who has talked to Raymond Chandler on the telephone.'

She shrugged again. I gave up.

'Okay. Let's go on. So what happened in the end?'

'After the phone calls?'

'Yes, after the phone calls. After he said you looked "cowlike" in your photos. Do you remember?'

She looked away again, into the winter afternoon outside the window.

'I think our letters just gradually dribbled away. I stopped writing and so did he.'

'Do you remember when? Do you remember how long you were writing for?'

'Well, I wrote first in January 1956. That was the start of First Year. And I went out with Barry in the middle of Second Year, 1957. And we would have gone on for a few months after that. But I wouldn't say past the end of that year, past the end of 1957.'

'You don't remember the last letter, or exactly how it ended?'

She smiled and shook her head. 'No. But it wasn't long before I was writing to Helmut.'

'And did you keep track of Ray at all?'

'No. Which isn't as callous as it sounds. He just passed out of my life and I got on with other things. I'm sure if I'd seen his name in the paper I would have been interested. I might have, I can't remember. And I didn't forget him. I thought about him a lot. Before you came along, I still thought about him. Remembered things he'd said. Laughed about his reaction to Barry. As time went by I suppose it became more amusing.'

'So you don't remember reading about him in the paper after you'd stopped writing?'

'No.'

'And do you remember how you found out he'd died? Did you read about that in the paper?'

She stopped to think, gazing out the window at the cold garden.

'That's interesting, isn't it? I wonder how I did find out he'd died.'

the knob turned

Dee was right. The more I found out, the more I wanted to find out, and the less I cared about the story I was supposed to be inventing. I sat in the train on the way back down to Sydney wondering where to go next. I went back through my mind, walking down the hallway, trying the doors. I walked past Deirdre, the door flung wide, light streaming out. None of the other doors would open. Bodleian. UCLA. MacShane.

MacShane. Hang on. I went back. I tried the knob again.

that big band sound

Columbia University
7 March 1989

Dear Mr Close

Thanks for your letter. I'll be delighted to see you when you come to New York. Perhaps you can find what you want in the Columbia Library where my papers are now stored.
 Anyhow, give me a ring when you arrive.
 With all good wishes,

Yours sincerely
Frank MacShane

Handwritten on Dodge Hall letterhead. A fine scrawl in black, very fine fountain pen. Alas, no airmail aeroplane stamp.

London
8 March 1989

Dear Mr Close

Your letter of 2 March has just arrived. I've looked up our correspondence in October 1987 and there is really nothing I can add to what I then said.
 Too bad your efforts in tracking down Deirdre Gartrell were unfruitful.
 There are, of course, copyright restrictions on the use of Chandler letters. The literary agent who now deals with this for the estate is:

Ed Victor Ltd
Literary Agency
162 Wardour Street
London W1V 3AT

Yours sincerely
Kathrine Sorley Walker
Literary Consultant to Helga Greene

Typewritten, manual on blue aerogramme, one error only – other than her misreading that I had, indeed, located Deirdre. And everyone keeps wanting to introduce me to Mr Ed Victor. Who is Ed Victor? With a name like that surely he should be out in front of a big band?

Bodleian Library
13 March 1989

Dear Alan Close

I have indeed finished cataloguing the Chandler collection, and there is some Gartrell material in it, about which I am now able to be more specific.

First let me say that we do not, in fact, have the original Chandler-Gartrell correspondence, which I think must have been returned to Mrs —, as she now is. What we do have is three sheets of copies of extracts from Chandler letters to Gartrell (made for Dorothy Gardiner at the time of *Raymond Chandler Speaking*), as well as letters about Chandler from Helga Greene to Gartrell, written in 1960, with a long letter from Ms Gartrell in reply. There is also a photograph of Gartrell (c.1957), and one letter – a carbon typescript – from Chandler, beginning 'Darling Deirdre' (30 Dec 1957), who is presumably Deirdre Gartrell.

You would be most welcome to come and look at

the papers in May. There will be no restriction on the Gartrell material, although a declaration form must be signed. You will need permission of the Ed Victor Literary Agency if you would like photocopies made, however.

You will also need a reader's ticket to enable you to use the library, and I am enclosing an application form. The 'Information for Applicants' should tell you everything you need to know about opening hours, charges, and so on. The form should be completed by a suitable recommender (academic or publisher) and you should bring it with you to the admissions office in the Old Library quadrangle, if you decide to come to Oxford in May.

Please do contact me again if you feel that I can be of further help.

Yours sincerely
Judith Priestman (Dr)

Unsigned! Why? Ref, JAP/JAS. Who is JAS? Cleanly typed on Bodleian letterhead. One error almost invisibly whited out. The utter professionalism here is knee-weakening. She's got the photo of Dee! And a letter. But I've got to get past Ed Victor first. I'm getting scared. All he has to do is say 'no' and the whole thing is off.

Part eight
a hindu at his own funeral

the future waiting to happen

Gary Davis: By the start of '58 the tax business was settled and Ray was free to go back to London. But he was still in all sorts of mess with Betty Bluefields. The doctor book had rolled on its back with its feet in the air, but by then Betty had convinced him that Australia was the future waiting to happen and he was all fired up to pack his pencils in his knapsack and find a pith helmet and go forth as if he was a man a third his age.

Ray didn't know what to do. Southern California had soured for him. He said La Jolla was like living in an old people's home. He had a hundred acquaintances but no friends. He wanted to be in England, where at least the degeneration was genteel and he could better stand the pace of his own decay.

He was in a trap with the Bluefields family. He gave them thousands of his own dollars for no other reason than he had concocted in his mind some sort of obligation to them. It was straight out of the psychology books. As if Ray suddenly felt the lack of a family and tried to take up with this one – guilt, obligation and all. He even let Betty wear Cissy's ring – it's no wonder she thought she had rights over him.

the great escape

Gabrielle Mercy: Ray arrived in London in February. He should have been happy to be back but it wasn't that easy – he had the Bluefields in tow. He got as far as New York then had a fit of conscience and rang them in La Jolla and organised for them to follow. He paid for their air tickets to New York and while they came over on a Cunard ship, Ray flew ahead to arrange for their arrival. When he got here he even announced he was going on with them to Australia. The whole thing was just unbelievable. He was acting as if Betty was his own wife and her children were his children. But they weren't.

In London Helga had organised a small flat for Ray at Swan Walk in Chelsea and when the Bluefields arrived Ray moved them in there. In the meantime he stayed at the Ritz. But Betty and the children didn't even seem to understand what they were doing in London. Betty was Australian, for a start, and the children had never been outside California. They were running wild with the upheaval, the boy terrorising the little girl, the girl hanging on to her mother like a two-year-old. And whenever Ray walked in all three of them clamoured around him with demands. Uncle Ray this, Uncle Ray that. Betty had no money of her own. Ray was her lifeline. He was responsible for them being here and she was going to make sure he didn't forget it. He couldn't have organised a better route straight back to the bottle. And the bottle couldn't have been counted on to be a better escape when he needed it.

He had booked them all to go to Australia on the *Orcades*, but by the time it sailed in May, Ray was simply too weak to go anywhere. Except hospital again – which, when the family left, is exactly where Helga sent him.

After he came out Helga set him up with a private nurse, a Texan by the name of Bruce Willis. He was a big man, over six feet tall and weighing probably sixteen stone. More like a wrestler than a nurse. He made no attempt to hide the fact that he was homosexual. He was a member of a club, the Knightsbridge Gentlemen's Club, where he used to go and 'lift weights'. We were all a bit nervous about this. Everyone knew that Ray had an unnatural loathing of homosexuality.

go ahead, wrestle me, ray

Bruce Willis: I let him know right from the start who I was. I said, 'You know I'm a queen, Ray. And I know I'm a goddamn queen. But I'm also a nurse. And that's why I'm here with you. No other reason. And I know you like me or you wouldn't have me here. And I kinda like something about you, so let's leave it at that and get on with business.' And we did.

unusual in a sixteen-stone texan

Gabrielle Mercy: What a strange pair they were! Despite his bulk Bruce was very gentle, and he developed an obvious affection for Ray. He refused to treat Ray as anything other than a friend in need, and that informality brought out the best in Ray's sense of humour. Often you'd see Bruce bent double, slapping his thigh, with his big fleshy face scrunched up so the eyes were totally closed, giggling that maniac giggle he had. I think Ray would tell jokes just to see Bruce in that condition. 'Ray,' I heard Bruce say one day, 'you keep them wisecracks coming, it'll be me who's gonna need the nurse. It'll be you putting me to bed, I guarantee.'

Bruce had those wonderful Southern manners. 'Yes, ma'am. No thank you, ma'am.' That sort of thing. There was another thing he used to say: 'Hell, t'ain't nothin'', and that became one of Ray's favourite sayings. He'd try to imitate Bruce's Southern accent, which sounded about as real as me trying to, and it seemed to give him great pleasure in itself. You'd hear him practising in his room, 'hell, t'ain't nothin'', over and again, almost choking on his laughter afterwards.

Ray liked to show Bruce off to his London friends as an example of what the English were not. Bruce didn't try to hide who he was. He was obviously queer, which wasn't anything rare in London in those days, but was unusual in a sixteen-stone Texan. I'd say most of us regarded Bruce as another of Ray's eccentricities, like his polka dot bow ties and the yellow gloves he wore for his skin.

something to start the day on

Bruce Willis: I just loved ol' England. The Queen, the Changing of the Guard, the Tower of London. I loved all the old stuff. I got a hold of Morris dancing and went to a group every week down in Battersea. On wet afternoons Ray used to get me dressed up in the white tights and bells and flounced dueller's shirts and the old joker's hat and have me dance a jig right there in the living-room at Chelsea. He used to love that. And I didn't mind. Hell, I learned to live with who I was years ago. Ain't no use fighting it.

I used to do Ray coddled eggs for breakfast. Ray loved coddled eggs and I loved cooking them. I'd cook him up coddled eggs in that little egg coddler I picked up at Harrods, and put in a big dob of butter, set up a mess of thick buttered toast and put up a pot of coffee strong enough to rot the jockstrap off a Bronx cab driver. It'd give Ray something to start the day on.

He needed food in him to get through those lunches at the clubs. They used to start their drinking there at eleven-thirty a.m. and there wouldn't be no food on the table till one-thirty. If he was on his feet after lunch and had a lie down in the afternoon, and had someone with him through till supper, you could be pretty sure he'd last out the night and then be good the following morning. I wasn't always there, but Helga or Gabrielle or one of the other girls always were. I had places to go at night Ray didn't ask no questions about and I didn't invite no questions about either. They're the reason I was in London and Ray knew it. He could make a pretty good guess why I chose London, England over Lubbock, Texas. We were both in England getting something we couldn't get back home. We had that understanding.

Then, when Ray's visa ran out and he had to go back to California, he said he wouldn't go without me. Fine by me. It was a good job. Ray and me got on. We respected each other's differences. That's the only way you get on with any folks in this world.

It was a godawful flight. We flew the new Scandinavian Airways 'Polar Bear' route. They take you over the top and say it's faster, but we had to put down in Canada someplace, and San Francisco, and by the time we got to LA Ray was threatening to ring his lawyers. Ray had a boiled egg over Canada which he said was probably laid on the Ark and kept him in the rest room for most of the way down the west coast.

three cheers for the pilot

Norbert Davis, businessman: I sell feeder troughs for pigs. I'd been in Belgium and I decided to try the new direct route home over the pole. I was seated across the aisle from an elderly party in the company of a large Southern gentleman. From the pitch of the big one's voice I had little doubt that he was of the other persuasion, if you know what I mean. And given that he seemed to be on rather intimate terms with the older gentleman, I figured they were some sort of companions. I assumed the young man's old friend was perhaps an actor or some sort of Hollywood attorney. Flamboyant, at any rate. Maybe the youngest son of a Boston family. If you know what I mean. His voice wasn't American, but neither was it English. And I got to hear quite some of his voice. The whole cabin got to.

Over Canada the captain announced that we were putting down in Winnipeg, and it seemed this displeased the old gentleman. I might say that by this time he had had a fair amount to drink. He stopped one of the hostesses and asked if he had heard correctly.

'You did, sir,' the young lady answered.

'And why, pray, are we stopping?' the old party asked. 'Is there something wrong with the plane?'

'Oh no, sir,' the girl answered. 'There's air turbulence ahead. So we're not taking any chances. We're just setting down until it passes.'

'And how long might that be?' asked the gentleman. 'Will you be handing out sleeping bags? Are they sending in huskies with more supplies? And why Winnipeg, for Christsake? Does the pilot's mother live there? Did he think it'd be a pity to pass so close and not call in and say hello? What, my dear, is in Winnipeg, for Christsake?'

'Well, there's an airport, sir,' the hostess said. Everyone around was listening well by now, which seemed to give the old gentleman considerable pleasure and was causing the poor young lady considerable discomfort. The old man's Southern friend was silent, watching out the window at the wing glistening in the sun.

'An airport!' the old gentleman said. 'That sounds like the first thing this goddamn company has got right since we came on board.'

He stood up in his seat and said loudly, 'You hear that, everybody? The pilot has ascertained that there is an airport at Winnipeg. Three cheers for the pilot.' Then he sat down and said under his breath, 'And let us pray he was looking at the right map.'

At which point the young lady retreated and the old gentleman seemed to retire into slumber. His Southern friend didn't turn his head but I could see a smile light his face, and I swear I saw him reach over and take the old party's hand in his and sit with it as if it was nothing strange at all to see one man holding on to another in a public place. I tell you the truth by God. And I must say it was really quite touching to see.

a shot of quietener

Bruce Willis: Things weren't going well. We took the local flight from LA down to San Diego and I knew we was in for a bad time. Ray couldn't hide nothing. You could read his face like a paperback novel. All the way down he glared out the window with his lip out. He'd warned me about Betty, but he hadn't warned me half enough. I hadn't met her but I sure as hell had heard about her. Ray'd put her on a boat to Australia, but she'd run out of cash, or credit, or both, and when she sussed out that Ray was coming back to California she decided she'd better too and she was there to meet us at the airport.

She started yapping as soon as we got outta the plane into the sweet clean air of San Diego, and didn't let up yapping until we got out of the cab at the hotel. I knew as soon as that door closed behind us, Ray'd have the cap off a fifth of Ballantines and I'd have my work cut out. But I was his nurse, not his jailer, and I couldn't tie him down in no straightjacket. I tell you, if I'd had my way I'd have gave that woman a shot of quietener and quieted her down but good. Six months or so woulda done me.

you oughta see him with bells on

San Diego Airport. Betty Bluefields and her two children wait behind the barrier while a Constellation taxis to a standstill and the steps are wheeled to the door of the plane. Betty is wearing lime-green slacks, a canary-yellow blouse and red-framed sunglasses, the glass so deep a green it appears black. She smokes a cigarette in a holder. Her hair is permed into blonde curls.

Ray and Bruce duck their heads as they emerge from the aeroplane. A hostess bares her teeth at them at the top of the steps. A woman's yells can be heard. 'Ray! Ray! Over here!' Ray's lip juts out. Bruce grits his teeth and says, 'Oh my Gawd.' Ray glances at him and doesn't smile.

At the barrier Betty bends down to her kids. The boy is thin and sullen, the girl is fat with glasses.

'Look James, look Colleen, it's Uncle Ray. Wave to him. Go on! Wave!'

The two men make towards the barrier. Chandler is walking with a cane, Bruce Willis carries a heavy overnight bag in each hand. The Bluefields are barely able to contain their excitement.

Out of the side of his mouth Ray mutters, 'Bruce, I'm afraid my memory is worse than I thought.'

Betty hugs Ray: 'Oh my Jesus Christ, mother of God, Ray, I didn't think I'd ever see you alive again.'

Ray attempts to extract himself, both arms down at his sides, one carrying his weight on his cane. 'My dear, the way I feel at the moment I'm not at all sure you are. Let me introduce you to Bruce. Bruce Willis, my trusted dancing nurse. You like the look of him now, you oughta see him with bells on.'

Ray crouches with difficulty to the children's level as they hug him with sticky hands: 'Hello my little Australian angels.'

Colleen says, 'Did you bring us presents?'

James says, 'I wanna gun.'

Betty says, 'James, you don't say things like that to your Uncle Ray.'

James says, 'I wanna Colt automatic.'

Colleen says, 'Um, Uncle Ray, my Belinda doll fell off the swing and her eyes fell out.'

Betty offers her hand to Bruce. 'Pleased to meet you, Mr Willis.'

'Call me Bruce, ma'am. Mr Willis, he's my pop.'

Chandler's vision shifts in and out of focus. He hears Bruce's voice. 'Here, Ray, hold out that arm, let me help you up there.'

Concerned faces appear and fade.

'Ray, you better take a seat here with Mis' Betty. I'll go search out them suitcases.' Bruce's voice again.

James pipes up. 'Are the presents in the suitcases?'

Cissy's hospital bed, Ray sitting with her. Cissy reaches her hand under the bottom of her oxygen tent. In her hand is a handkerchief. Ray takes her hand and holds it.

'No pills today, my darling. The doctor says it isn't wise.'

Cissy's eyes are rheumy and weak. They search her husband's face then look away.

'Is this the way you wanted it? Those pills are my only relief. Is this the way you want me to end?'

Ray sits in one of a row of airport chairs, Betty on one side, the children swinging their feet on the other. Bruce Willis lumbers away across the terminal floor. Ray takes off his glasses and mops his face with a white handkerchief. He is pale and exhausted. Betty leans towards him, keeping Bruce in her sights.

'Ray, is that fat Texan a goddamned queer? Is he a fairy?'

Ray keeps the handkerchief to his forehead.

'Yes Betty, that fat Texan is a fairy. And I trust him like a son.'

Betty Bluefields clucks her tongue, takes a drag of her cigarette and exhales noisily.

'Well Ray, I certainly wouldn't have one touching me. I hope you know what you're doing. Does he ... does he do intimate business for you?'

went to pieces

Bruce Willis: In London I managed to keep Ray healthy and more or less sober. In La Jolla all that went to pieces. The Australian woman had some grip on him. Personally I couldn't see much about her which wasn't worth turning and running right away from, but Ray seemed to feel he owed her something. Good lord, he gave her enough, there can't have been much left to owe her. He bought the kids presents, he took them out for meals, he paid the woman's bills, he helped them search for a house to live in, he listened to her on the phone for hours at a time, he put up with her coming around and bitching over coffee half the goddam day when he should have been writing.

I didn't have much time for that braying Australian bitch, you can tell. And all she did for Ray was get him so fussed up he reached straight for the bottle. Got so I figured the best place for him would be in hospital, so that's exactly where I sent him – kicking and screaming – to a fancy private place down in the desert past San Diego. Seems it was one of the few drying-out joints around about Ray hadn't been to yet.

the good lord provides

Mrs Margaret Munz: I owned a cottage located at 824 Prospect Street, near the centre of La Jolla, and the old gentleman who rented it passed away in June of problems associated with his smoking, which I never did approve of, but there was no telling him. Some folks are just determined to lie themselves down in their graves before the good Lord can do it for them, and filling your lungs with nicotine and tar, in my opinion, is the best way of doing it, short of holding a gun at your head. Well, I cleared old Mr Mitchell's belongings out and passed them on to the Ladies of Christ, and after giving the place a good airing I put it up again at the realtors in the village. My Darren didn't want me to let it, he wanted to keep it for one of his sister's grown sons who was entering college in the fall. But I never did take to Darren's sister, and anyway, I won't have Darren telling me how to run my affairs. That little cottage is all I own that he doesn't. And I know from my work with the church how many elderly gentlemen are out there in need of a place to live. Widowers, mostly. I like having a mature gentleman in the cottage. I like to feel I'm helping a soul that needs help.

When the nice Southern gentleman, the prospective tenant's male nurse, said the the prospective tenant was a famous author I had to rack my brains trying to find an answer for who it might be. John Steinbeck? Irwin Shaw? That Hemingway man? And I admit that when he told me the name Mr Raymond Chandler my heart did go flop just a little. I had no idea who Ray was. I'd never heard of him. Mind you, in this town we take pride in keeping ourselves to ourselves. 'Why don't you tell me the names of some of the books he's written,' I said to the young Southerner. 'I'm a great reader,' I said. And I am. The Rental Libraries live off me. Darren never lets me alone about it. But I believe in improving my mind, unlike him, Mr Golf Clubs.

Well, Mr Bruce did tell me the name of some of Ray's books and I hadn't heard of any of them. What sort of books are they? I asked. Detective novels, ma'am, he said straight off, and my heart sank again. And when I mentioned Ray's name to Darren, and the name Mr Philip Marlowe, he almost dropped his drink. I must admit this did give me just a few reservations about taking this Mr Chandler on as a tenant, that he wrote Darren's kind of book, but, well, when the young man brought Ray around and he was so genteel and well mannered I realised Darren must have made some sort of mistake as usual. He was a very good tenant, was Ray, and my only complaint of him is that he moved out and Darren's sister's son did move in and slouched around in there all the way until he flunked right out of college like I always knew he would. No one with Darren's sister's genes in their braincells ever made it past grade school. It must have been a rig from the word go that he ever got in in the first place.

the goddamnest thing

Bruce Willis: I tell you, Miz Munz was a happy accident just lying in wait for Ray and me to pass. She took a shine to Ray from first viewing. She even called him Pappy, which Ray thought was the goddamnest thing. We'd be sitting there in the front room looking out at the sea and the bikinis and beefcakes on the sidewalk, and ol' Miz Munz'd drive right up and we'd hear the handbrake go on and see her lean over to gather what she was bringing and Ray'd look over at me with that damned little smile of his and whisper, 'I wonder what the good Lord is about to provide us with today?'

Good Lord, and were we provided for! Cakes, pies, fruit, flowers, goddamn fruit jellies – Miz Munz didn't rest.

Started off she wouldn't call us nothing but Mr Chandler

and Mr Bruce, then one day Ray took her hand and held it in both of his and got old Miz Munz right there in his gaze and said, 'Miz Munz, I beseech you, the only people I allow to call me Mr Chandler are people I don't like, and you are not one of them. My name, please, is Ray.'

I was in the kitchen getting up some sandwiches for lunch and they were out the back in the little garden. I could see them through the window. They stood there for full on half a minute, I swear, Miz Munz staring right into Ray's eyes, until finally her legs started to shudder and shake and she took her hand away and brushed down her dress and said, 'Well, Ray, in that case you must call me Margaret. But don't you imagine for a second this alters our business relationship one little bit. Rent remains due on the first of the month as agreed.'

'Of course, Margaret,' Ray said, near choking with laughter. 'Rent in advance on the first of the month.'

Then Miz Munz got a grip of herself and started attending to a patch of flowers and said, 'Well then Ray, what you say we snip a few of these and vase 'em up for the sideboard?'

I turned away myself then and started laying things out on a tray, and when I looked back Ray was helping her with her snipping and they was muttering away to each other, bent over among the sprays so cute I felt the tears well in my eyes.

I don't know where Miz Munz got this Pappy business from, but once she'd dug it out she weren't putting it back. In later days she'd come in smelling and looking like a garden in bloom herself, her arms loaded with flowers and bowls of fruit as if Ray was on his back in hospital filling in his dying hours. 'And how's my Pappy this lovely morning?' she'd say, and Ray'd get hold of her hands and get those bifocals of his working on her and say back, 'Margaret, I thought it was a good morning until you arrived.' And he'd wait for her face to drop, then say, 'But now it's exquisite. A morning *par excellence!*'

I'd say for a certainty Ray would've said he shouldn't be called nobody's pappy. But I also saw for a certainty how it moved him to hear it said. As if it was something he didn't know how much he wanted to hear all his life.

it took me a while to work out what he meant

Mrs Margaret Munz: I said to Ray one day, 'Do you mind me calling you Pappy?' And he said, 'No, my dear, I don't mind. Only don't call me Papa, for Christsakes, or I'll be sued for false pretences.'

it must be good

Chandler had respect for Hemingway, but it was clear-eyed. One of the early pieces he kept from his days before *Black Mask* was a parody of Hemingway called 'The Sun Also Sneezes':

Hank went into the bathroom to brush his teeth.
'The hell with it,' he said. 'She shouldn't have done it.'
It was a good bathroom. It was small and the green enamel was peeling off the walls. But the hell with that, as Napoleon said when they told him Josephine was waiting without. The bathroom had a wide window through which Hank looked at the pines and the larches. They dripped with a faint rain. They looked smooth and comfortable.
'The hell with it,' Hank said. 'She shouldn't have done it.'
He opened the cabinet over the wash-basin and took out his toothpaste. He looked at his teeth in the mirror. They were large yellow teeth, but sound. Hank could still bite his way for a while.
Hank unscrewed the top of the toothpaste tube, thinking of the day when he had unscrewed the lid off the coffee jar, down on the Pukayuk River, when he was trout fishing. There had been larches there too. It was a damn good river, and the trout had been damn good trout. They liked being hooked. Everything had been good except the coffee, which had been lousy. He had made it Watson's way, boiling it for two hours and a half in his knapsack. It had tasted like the socks of the Forgotten Man.

In 1942 he spent some lines complaining to Blanche Knopf about his writing being compared to James M. Cain:

He is every kind of writer I detest, a *faux naïf*, a Proust in greasy overalls, a dirty little boy with a piece of chalk and a board fence when no one is looking. Such people are the offal of literature, not because they write about dirty things, but because they do it in a dirty way. Nothing hard and clean and cold and ventilated. A brothel with cheap scent in the front parlour and a bucket of slops at the back door. Do I, for God's sake, sound like that? Hemingway with his eternal sleeping bag got to be pretty damn tiresome, but at least Hemingway sees it all, not just the flies on the garbage can.

In 1946, however, his opinion had soured. Again to Blanche Knopf:

Even Hemingway has let me down. I've been re-reading a lot of his stuff. I would have said here is one guy who writes like himself, and I would have been right, but not the way I meant it. Ninety per cent of it is the goddamnest self-imitation. He never really wrote but one story. All the rest is the same thing in different pants – or without different pants ... This man has only one subject and he makes that ridiculous. I suppose the man's epitaph, if he had the choosing of it, would be: Here Lies A Man Who Was Bloody Good In Bed. Too Bad He's Alone Here. But the point is I begin to doubt whether he ever was. You don't have to work so hard at things you are really good at – or do you?

However by 1950, discussing the critical savaging that had been given to *Across the River and in to the Trees*, Chandler was back onside:

Obviously he was not trying to write a masterpiece; but in a character not too unlike his own, trying to sum up the attitude of a man who is finished and knows it, and is bitter and angry about it. Apparently Hemingway had been very sick and he was not sure that he was going to get well, and he put down on paper in a rather cursory way how that made him feel to the things in life he had most valued. I suppose these primping second-guessers who call themselves critics think he shouldn't have written the book at all. Most men wouldn't have. Feeling the way that he felt, they wouldn't have had the guts to write anything. I'm damn sure I wouldn't.

That's the difference between a champ and a knife thrower. The champ may have lost his stuff temporarily or permanently, he can't be sure. But when he can no longer throw the high hard one, he throws his heart instead. He throws something. He doesn't just walk off the mound and weep.

Chandler respected Hemingway but could also see his failings. Both men were formed by the values of the late nineteenth century – Hemingway by the tough American frontier spirit, Chandler by the emotional strictures of the English public school system. Both men relied on an armour of machismo to protect their public selves from the vulnerabilities and uncertainties of their private selves. But by the time they had reached their sixties these values, the cornerstones of their characters, had become redundant. Neither could cope. Within years Chandler would drink himself to death, and Hemingway would put a gun to his head and blow his brains out.

In *Farewell, My Lovely* Marlowe nicknames a dumb cop Hemingway. The cop gets frustrated with this and finally asks of Marlowe: 'Who is this Hemingway person at all?'

Chandler has Marlowe reply, 'A guy that keeps saying the same thing over and over until you begin to believe it must be good.'

the only person awake in la jolla

What do I do with myself day to day? I write when I can and don't write when I can't ... I'm always seeing little pieces by writers about how they don't ever wait for inspiration; they just sit down at their little desks every morning at eight, rain or shine, hangover and broken arm and all, and bang out their little stint. However blank their minds or dull their wits, no nonsense about inspiration from them. I offer them my admiration and take care to avoid their books.

Me, I wait for inspiration, although I don't necessarily call it by that name. I believe that all writing that has any life in it is done with the solar plexus. It's hard work in the sense that it may leave you tired, even exhausted. In the sense of conscious effort it is not work at all. The important thing is that there should be a space of time, say four hours a day at least, when a professional writer doesn't do anything else but write. He doesn't have to write, and if he doesn't feel like it, he shouldn't try. He can look out the window or stand on his head, or writhe on the floor. But he is not to do any other positive thing, not read, write letters, glance at magazines, or write checks. Either write or nothing. It's the same principle as keeping order in a school. If you make the pupils behave, they will learn something just to keep from being bored. I find it works. Two very simple rules. A) You don't have to write. B) You can't do anything else. The rest comes of itself.

Bruce Willis: He got up about five in the a.m., sometimes four, and that's when he worked. The first morning I think he just couldn't sleep, and then he couldn't sleep again and started liking it, that time of day, being the only person awake in La Jolla, and I suppose he figured he might as well be making the most of it. So after that, every morning about that time I'd hear the tea kettle boiling, then there'd be some silence, then the clack-clacking would start. It's a good sound, the sound of a typewriter, from the other end of the house at any rate. It's an industrious sound, and from Ray it was a healthy sound.

Ray liked to say he never got hangovers, and to that I'd say back that the reason Ray never got no hangovers was because he kept drinking instead. But he didn't get hangovers at Miz Munz's because he was fresh out of the drying-out clinic and wasn't drinking in the first place.

It was only small, just a cottage, but perfect for Ray because there was a study for him to work in and perfect for me because the study was at the front and the bedrooms were at the back. I like the sound of typing, but at four in the morning I like to sleep better.

hogs in shit

Bruce Willis: He'd come out around nine or ten and I'd cook us both breakfast, a good breakfast – ham and eggs, and coffee to kick your teeth in. I had Ray type out those lines from *The Long Goodbye* and had them up on the wall above the stove: 'I went out to the kitchen to make coffee – yards of coffee. Rich, strong, bitter, boiling hot, ruthless, depraved. The life-blood of tired men.'

Ray'd get there after a morning balling the jack, and while the eggs cooked and the pot brewed I'd put my arm around his shoulder and we'd stand in front of the stove and recite those lines like a prayer. Ray wasn't so modest he didn't know the sound of good words when he heard them. Even if he did put them together in the first place. They were good moments. Close. I carry them in my memory, those mornings.

Most days he was in a good mood, whistling even, which was something to hear, and cracking wise. He reckoned he wasn't born to live alone, and said he'd be in the gutter if not in the goddamn mortuary without me, but I think it was just a relief for him to be on the level again and, especially, writing again. Other days, of course, he'd come out and you could see just by the angle of his tie, he'd had a bad morning. 'Ray,' I'd say, 'if it was bad today it'll be better tomorrow. You know that.' And he'd stick out that goddamn lip and grunt and take his seat at the breakfast nook with his arms out either side of the *Bugle* or the *LA Times* and find something to curse in every goddamn article on every goddamn page.

We'd eat our breakfast together. While he was working I'd go out the back and do my yoga in the little garden. Sometimes Ray'd stop early and I'd open my eyes and he'd be leaning there against the doorway, watching me with his lip curled up in that little smile he put on. One time he knew I'd seen him and he said, 'It looks good Bruce, but I wouldn't say it's doing a helluva lot of good for your figure.' Then he turned and went inside, leaving that hanging in the air.

Ray was the best job I ever had. Hell, beat even a thousand

a month with one of those diamond-toothed rich bitches you can't never please.

After breakfast Ray liked us to walk downtown together and do errands, and if he'd had a bad morning this is when he'd cheer right up. Everyone knew him and he'd have words to say with all the shopkeepers. He couldn't buy nothing without haggling it was bruised, or tough, or raw, or broke, and from the pleasure on his face when he got back out on the street with a dime off the price of his tomatoes, you knew that was what he liked most about shopping. He'd shuffle from shop to shop with his nylon shopping bags, happy as a hog in shit.

Then we'd come back and he'd sit down with his mail and I'd put up the sandwiches for lunch. Sometimes he had a dozen letters, sometimes more. Books, magazines. You put a name to it, Ray got it through the mail. He wrote to Helga near every damn day. And all his other women friends, he was always clacking off letters to them. He didn't have real friends, like you or me has real friends. He had names and addresses on envelopes.

Afternoons were quiet, and that's the way I like them. Sometimes we'd both lay ourselves down for a little siesta, other times Betty'd come around with her goddamn brats, other times Ray'd lie on the couch turning the pages of a book. If he had the choice, Ray'd always lie down. He was more a horizontal man than a standing man.

About six I'd do us dinner. Steak, tournedos, fish cutlets. One time Ray made a big deal putting up spaghetti with a meatball sauce he said the chef at some Italian joint in Soho swore him to secrecy over. He put on one of Miz Munz's aprons and made a big mess and had us all drink red wine while he cooked. The thing about Ray, he could drink hard liquor for weeks at a stretch and still be standing, but two glasses of wine and he'd be out on the couch. It was one hell of a night, him dropping things, cussing the stove, smashing two glasses. When he started chopping for the green salad I sat him down and took over for fear he'd lose the fingers that made me a living. That was the only meal he offered to cook. And I sure didn't make no fuss holding him to any further effort.

Nine o'clock would see Ray in bed. Sometimes we sat up with the chessboard between us. That was a late night for Ray. He liked to win and I always let him win – it got him into bed earlier and I could get into my travelling pants and get downtown.

the life blood of tired men

Bruce Willis: Everyone said what a genteel town La Jolla was. No billboards. No through traffic. Only the rich and quiet. But I tell you, I ain't visited a town nowhere where there wasn't some place to meet men of my own kind. In La Jolla it was down an alley right behind the main shops where Ray spent the mornings arguing over rump and over-priced vegetables. I never told Ray it was there and perhaps he made a point of not asking. Some of the men I met there at midnight I'd see with wives and children the next day, and neither them nor Ray was any the wiser about where we'd been the night before. I didn't like to disturb Ray with my night-time preferences, and anyway it weren't his business and he knew it weren't. But I tell you, some nights I couldn't for all the words in English tell you how I ever got home, and on the mornings after those nights I sure never heard Ray's tea kettle blow, or no clack-clacking of nobody's typewriter. I was further away than the back of any house. And some mornings, and this is God's truth, it was Ray who made my breakfast and poured my coffee, and he never said one word, and I reckon those words he never said says more about a man than any other words he might of spilt the other way.

I'll take texas, and I'll take men

Bruce Willis: I always told Ray I weren't going to stay forever, and I didn't. I flew back to London in October. Ray was scared. He knew he couldn't live alone. He knew he needed someone to keep him in line. He needed a reason to stay on the straight and narrow. And I think he talked himself into believing that Betty was it. Well, if she was, that was his business. But I couldn't stand her another day. She never stopped. She whined and wailed and wore everybody down. And she loved nothing more than to get Ray alone and dig the knives into me behind my back. I tell you, if all Australian women are like her, I'll take Texas, and I'll take men. Which was the real reason I was heading back to London. I had a man I had to see about a couple of things: one was mine, the other was his.

fronted up to an adventure

Gabrielle Mercy: Ray stayed at the cottage after Bruce left, but wrote immediately to Helga asking her to come over. He was terrified of having to live alone again. He knew he'd go downhill without company. He feared what would happen. He was like a man who has known madness and lives in fear of knowing it again. Helga was ill herself and suggested that I go over instead. I was just starting a new job. So I suggested Hiliary.

Hiliary had the house next door to Ray's in Swan Walk, where he had lived earlier in the year. She was in her sixties. Her husband had been Roger West, the detective writer, and I'm sure Ray was grateful he was long dead by the time he met her. He wrote the type of English detective story Ray loved to hate. 'The body in the attic, the butler with the cast-iron face, big fires in the drawing-room, brandy balloons, much leaning on the mantelpiece and smoking of pipes, plump parsons and euchre, and above all lots of long invigorating walks in the damned countryside whenever the plot gets too thick to pull a spoon out of.' I can hear Ray holding forth on this even now.

Unfortunately for Ray, these sorts of stories sold by the lorry load, but fortunately for him, Roger was no longer around to get in the way of his friendship with Hiliary, whose vigour in all things was truly extraordinary. Hiliary,

Ray used to say, was one of those women whom widowhood was invented for.

At first the prospect of Hiliary coming over scared him. 'I love Hiliary,' he wrote, 'but I don't think I've got the energy for her. I'm old and I am tired. She is old but I have never seen her tired.'

He was right – neither had I ever seen her tired. Hiliary did everything, was a member of everything, and was always keen to try anything new. She was a mad walker, and was always trying to drag Ray off with her.

'Come on,' she'd say. 'Off the couch. Hampstead Heath while you can still put one foot in front of the other.'

She never drank, ate oats for breakfast, didn't touch red meat and was a birdwatcher and member of the Thames Clean River Committee. Her saving grace, in Ray's eyes, was her sense of humour and 'go to hell' attitude. She even played the bagpipes – badly – while Bruce Willis did his Morris dancing in the living-room. I remember her another day in the living-room at Swan Walk. She was standing in front of Ray in her riding breeches and boots with her hands on her hips, Vita Sackville-West style, while he lay reclining on the couch like a pasha, his shoes kicked off, wriggling his toes in his socks. She was giving him one of her pep talks.

'I estimate, Ray, that you've got no more than six months to change your ways. Cut out the drinking completely, stop eating dead animals, get that fat Texan to cease murdering you with coddled eggs, start every day with a pint of pure mountain water to clean the system, go for a long ventilating walk along the river, come back for porridge and a cup of dandelion tea, eat nothing but fresh fruit between meals, buy only Hovis bread, get yourself a few pounds of raw almonds and walnuts from a delicatessen in Greek Street, stop reading the newspapers – especially that organ of class oppression the *Times* – take only camomile or valerian tea in the evenings, be in bed by nine p.m., get up at five, have Bruce show you a few yoga positions, never so much as smell a cup of coffee again – do all that and you may – you may – just live to see seventy.'

By this time she was pacing back and forth in front of

him. He hadn't moved. He was lying back watching the whisky swirl around the ice in his glass. You could see him composing his response.

'Hiliary,' he said, 'if seventy needs all that, I don't need seventy.' He raised his glass towards her, smiled, and lifted it to his lips. 'You can have it, Hiliary. You have seventy and take mine as well. Hell, take Bruce's too. He won't be needing his, I'm sure.'

For all this, Ray and Hiliary had formed what I suppose you'd call a friendship of opposites, and Helga agreed that her presence in California might be just what Ray needed. We both knew how much Hiliary fronted up to an adventure, and she had never been to America. Helga made it clear that she would pay all expenses. Hilary took no convincing. She flew over in October and moved into the room where Bruce had been.

90 degrees and getting hotter

Hiliary Easton: I caught the local Constellation down to San Diego. It was 90 degrees the day we arrived. Ray was there with Betty and the two children. Helga of course had warned me all about them.

hold my hand, I'm scared

Behind the barrier Ray holds the hand of Betty's daughter Colleen. The other hand is up over his eyes, his cane is dangling from his wrist on its leather strap. Betty smokes a cigarette, the little boy sits on the floor at her feet. SAN DIEGO WELCOMES YOU is lit in red neon across the top of the terminal building. It is the same scene as Ray's arrival with Bruce Willis. The same airport, the same flight, the same plane, the same smile glued on to the same hostess, the heat shimmering off the tarmac, again the nausea rising in Ray's stomach.

Hiliary emerges from the plane, shielding her eyes from

the blast of heat. The hostess smiles. The propellers wind down to a slow halt.

'Is she there, Uncle Ray? Which one is she? Is she old like you?'

'Colleen, don't say things like that to Uncle Ray.'

'Like what, Mummy?'

'You know what, young lady.'

'It doesn't matter, Betty.'

'Yes, it does, Ray. She's got to learn some manners. It's her father's family. Now apologise to Uncle Ray, Colleen.'

'I didn't do anything wrong, Mummy. What'd I do wrong? What'd I do wrong, Uncle Ray?'

'You didn't do anything wrong, Colleen.'

'She called you old, Ray.'

'I am old, Betty.'

'That doesn't matter. Little girls don't go round telling people they're old. Not in my family, they don't. Now apologise to Uncle Ray, Colleen.'

Hiliary approaches down the entrance-way. She is wearing white slacks and a royal purple blouse. She raises her arm. Her teeth are white in her smile. Her ring finger flashes in the sun. Suddenly there is a commotion in the crowd and people bend down. The smile drops from Hiliary's face. She increases her speed.

Faces. Hiliary's face. Betty's face. James, Colleen, two men in white tunics. A hard bench. A cool dim room. Raised voices. A door slamming. A gruff man's voice, calling in two syllables: 'Ray-mond!' His mother's lap, his head in her bosom, her hand stroking his hair. 'Will we be all right, Mummy?' 'Yes darling. We'll be all right. We've got each other, haven't we?'

Cissy's voice. 'I'm scared, Raymio. Hold my hand, I'm scared.'

Ray looks up, sees Hiliary hovering over him, her hand on his brow. Her cool hand, his brain throbbing, throat burning with hard ice. His own voice as a child, moaning. His mother in a dark room, cooling his forehead with a damp cloth. Her soft voice. 'Darling Raymio. My little Raymio. You'll be all right, my darling. You'll be all right.'

Hiliary's voice. Her cool hand. 'Don't move, Ray. We're all here. Don't worry about anything. You've collapsed, but you're all right. It was the heat. Stay still. You're all right.'

everything

Gabrielle Mercy: Ray wrote, saying she was marvellous. Washing dishes, making the beds, doing the breakfasts. Mending, taking letters. Even cleaning his old military brushes, he said. I could just see her. Buzzing all over the place, doing everything. She was just what Ray needed. She did all the housework, and when they didn't eat out, all the cooking too.

hawaiian porridge

Hiliary Easton: In the afternoon Ray and I went shopping together. It was a good way of getting him out of the house and onto his feet. He had given the Bluefields woman his car so we had to walk down to the village instead. We had those nylon bags and each carried a load home. It was good exercise, even if we were usually arguing on the way back.

In Dutch Smith's store, La Jolla, Ray and Hiliary, looking like an elderly English couple on vacation, pick up cans and inspect them. Ray peers down through his bifocals to read the labels. Satisfied, Hiliary drops a can into her shopping bag and moves on down the aisle. Ray, two paces behind her, catches up.
'What was that you just put in your bag?'
Hiliary looks startled. 'What was it? It was pineapple, Ray. Australian pineapple rings. They're one of my weaknesses.'
'Canned pineapple? From Australia! For Christsakes, Hiliary, we're in California. We're almost hemmed in by goddamn pineapples. They arrive from Cuba by the boatload. They'd crawl into our goddamn beds if we let them.'

'Yes, but I like canned pineapple, Ray. That's all you can buy in London. Unless you're prepared to pay five pounds at Harrods for a little green spiky thing grown by indentured ten year olds on some feudal estate in Nicaragua. And I refuse to support that sort of thing. And the Cubans are just as bad.'

'All right. No lecture. What are you going to do with it?'

'The pineapple? I'm going to open the can very carefully so as not to get any blood in the syrup. I'm then going to pour the syrup off into a cup and probably take one sip and one sip only. Then, when my porridge is cooked, I'm going to lay one ring – one ring each day – on top of it in the bowl, pour on just a little of the syrup, and then, outside in the morning sun, I'll eat the contents of the bowl very slowly, chewing each mouthful thoroughly, enjoying the sweet good health it gives me, grain by succulent grain.'

She stands defiantly as Ray stares at her.

'My god, Hiliary. You're not going to try to get me on to that, are you? What do you call it? Hawaiian porridge?'

the pleasure

Gabrielle Mercy: We were all hoping Ray and Hiliary might come to some arrangement about their private life. They obviously got on very well and were no doubt quite clearheaded about the pleasure they could give each other in their old age. Perhaps they even discussed this themselves. Ray wrote to Helga that he was changing his will in Hiliary's favour.

the lamp on and a tumbler ready

Hiliary Easton: Betty seemed to have some sort of hold over Ray, and Ray was powerless against it. It seemed that fulfilling an imagined obligation to her made him feel needed, gave his life meaning. When she got wind that Ray was changing his will she was impossible.

It's hard to believe she wasn't on a deliberate policy of destabilising Ray. She was already on the phone at all times of day and night with the most petty complaints. She could find any excuse to bother him. The neighbours kept her up all night having a party, the car made a funny noise going up a hill, the store had put its prices up on bath soap, the little girl got in a fight at school, her mother was ill in Australia, the lawn needed cutting and there was no one to do it, the meat they bought was too tough to eat, the dog escaped and didn't come back until morning, the little boy swore at her, she was lonely, she needed money for a dress, she was bored, she was bored, she was bored.

Then the phone started ringing in the dead of night. We had no idea who it was. Whoever it was would hang up, or stay on the line breathing.

But Ray wasn't going to be intimidated. He took to sleeping with the lamp on and a tumbler of whisky ready by his bed.

you can't scare me

Night-time. The bedroom lit by the bedside lamp. Ray is holding the phone, pajamas buttoned to the collar. He twists to reach for the whisky on the bedside table.

'I can wait. I'm not hanging up this time. I'll sit here until you say something. I'm not scared of you.'

He takes a sip of the whisky. No voice comes from the phone.

'I don't know who you are but the longer you stay on the line the better chance the police have of tracking you down. I know the cops in La Jolla. They're friends of mine. They know about these calls. You can't scare me that easy.'

He takes more of the whisky.

'Ray?'

'Who is it? Who's there? Name yourself. You can't scare me. Name yourself.'

'Ray, it's me Ray. Betty.'

'Betty! Betty, for God's sake. What the hell's going on?'

to the point of stupidity

Daytime. Betty is sitting at Ray's dining table, smoking nervously. Ray is pacing back and forth with a glass in his hand.

'You know I've helped you out a lot over the past year, and not just financially. You know I've been generous. God knows, generous to the point of stupidity, I often think. And I can't be expected to support you for the remainder of your living days – or mine. I have other friends and other commitments and, frankly, my money is my money and I'll do with it as I choose. And I won't be blackmailed into changing my mind.'

Betty weeps. 'But Ray, what about the kids? How will I pay for their school, and earn a living, and keep house? What am I supposed to do? You can't just dump us.'

so he drank

Hiliary Easton: Once he'd had that first whisky he couldn't stop. Betty's behaviour was upsetting him terribly. He didn't know what to do. So he drank.

Dusk. Through the big window the sky is yellow and green and the sea black. Ray is snoring on the couch, a bottle empty on the floor beside him. The radio is on softly, the tubes at its back lighting the corner of the room.

A key turns in a lock. A door opens. A person bustles in. The door closes. Hiliary's voice moves from room to room.

'Ray? Ray?'

She enters the lounge-room and sees Ray. She is wearing slacks and sensible shoes. She has been for a 'long invigorating walk'.

'Oh, bloody hell.'

A doctor removes a stethoscope from his ears and stands.

Ray is still out cold on the couch. Hiliary stands beside him.
'He's all right. But he can't keep doing this. If he stops now he's got a good chance of enjoying a vigorous old age. If he doesn't, I give him four or five months at the most.'

Ray stirs and tries to focus his eyes. 'That's a lie. I'll live forever and you know it.' Having said this he slumps back down into sleep.

The doctor checks his pulse against his watch. After a minute or so he lays Ray's hand on his chest.

'I'll sign him in to the observation ward. Maybe a rest, a week or two, will do you both good.'

the devil

Gabrielle Mercy: Hiliary was tough, but still old, and still human, and all this was getting to her. She knew she was watching Ray die. The day Ray got out of hospital, she rang Helga in tears. 'That woman,' she said, 'Ray gave her his car so she offered to bring him home from the hospital. She drove up, and do you know what her first words were? "Let's have a drink to celebrate!"'

then he snapped

Gary Davis: One morning he rang just as I was getting ready to leave for work. I was late. Penny was yelling at Jackie, and Gary Jnr was harassing Pedro the little chihuahua. The house was in mayhem. I picked up the phone and almost bit it off yelling hello. Ray was so faint I had to ask him twice to say his name, and the second time he yelled into the phone, 'For Christsakes Gary, it's Chandler. The man with a date on his forehead.'

He was on the bottle, I could tell that easy enough. And it would only have been eight in the morning. He was breathing heavily, wheezing away, not saying anything. I tried to shush everyone else up.

'Go ahead Ray,' I said. 'How're you doing? Is Hiliary

settled in? Is she putting weight back on you?'

He didn't answer, just wheezed away on the end of the phone. I had eye contact with Penny, you know how you do on the phone, and she was trying to quiet the kids.

'Ray,' I said, 'I'm just heading out to the office. Can I call you from there? Is there anything special you wanted?'

Then he started crying, sobbing on the end of the phone, and it was as if Penny and Jackie and Gary Jnr heard him at the same time, and they all went quiet and suddenly the whole place was silent, just me holding the phone staring Pen in the eyes, the taste of coffee and eggs still in my mouth, and Ray sobbing over the phone.

'Ray?' I said.

Then he snapped. 'No, goddamn it, nothing's the matter. You go off to work. I've just wet my bed, is all. I wet the goddamn bed. I haven't wet the bed since I was five years old, for Christsakes. Since I was five, Gary.'

I said, 'Hell, Ray don't worry about that. That'll happen to all of us. That's nothing. How about I call in on the way home this afternoon and we take a walk on the beach. The three of us. You, me and Hiliary. One of Hiliary's walks. I'll tie her feet together so we can keep up. How about we do that?'

I was looking at Pen as I said it. It wasn't the first time this sort of thing had happened. Another late supper. I shrugged my shoulders at her. I saw her sigh. What could I do? I wasn't going to hang up on the guy 'cause he wet his bed. I think we all knew his time was close.

He kept sobbing on the end of the line.

'I wet the bed, Gary. Chandler wet the goddamn bed.'

calm

Gabrielle Mercy: Helga's plan was to fly over, try to calm everyone down, and if necessary bring Ray back to London, where he could get some peace. Everyone seemed to sense that it was a matter of life and death this time. Helga wasn't well, she was just out of hospital herself. But we all knew this wasn't something to put off.

the doctor and the nurse

Hiliary Easton: I met Helga at San Diego Airport. Ray was too drunk to come. She took one look at me and said, 'Oh, you poor thing.'

It was mid-afternoon when we got back to the cottage. Ray was asleep in his room. She went to his door, looked in, muttered something to herself, came over, put down her bag, and said, 'What's his doctor's number?'

like no other person

Gary Davis: Helga insisted Dr Kurtz admit both of them to La Jolla Convalescent that afternoon, no discussion entered into. She figured Hiliary needed the rest as well. She gave orders that she and I were the only people allowed in to see Ray. Helga knew he'd never gain ground if she didn't keep Betty out of his hair. I called in a couple of times through the week. He was low, exhausted and weak. But alive.

Helga spent most of her time in there, sitting with him, holding his hand. He could be completely lucid for periods and then drift off to sleep for hours at a time. Helga talked quietly to him, filling him in with news of friends, and what was going on in London. She had an effect on him like no other person. She gave him hope, that was it.

They talked a lot about old times. I caught them one time arguing about the route they took to get to Oxford when they hired a Rolls for a day. Whether they went through Hemel Hempstead or High Wycombe, for Christsake. Another time Ray had his colour up slandering a few other writers. I hadn't seen him as happy in years.

with considerable good humour

Hiliary Easton: Whenever Ray drifted off Helga came in to see me. We talked about what we were going to do with him now. She was determined to get him away from California. She knew the beneficial effect she had on him. Ray was positive again with Helga around. He talked about what he was going to do, not what he couldn't do any more. Helga was probably the one person who could save his life. It was no secret he'd been asking her to marry him for some time – although of course in Ray's eyes it was Helga, the lonely divorcée, who needed him. She bore this with considerable good humour. I think she saw this as part of his old-fashioned and somehow comforting chivalry.

Then one day she came to my room. Ray was asleep, she said. 'How is he?' I said. 'Well, he's had a bit of excitement,' she said. 'Is he all right?' I said. 'What's happened?' And she smiled like a schoolgirl and said they were going to get married.

old men on walking sticks

Hiliary Easton: When Ray came out of hospital we drove into La Jolla to pick out a wedding ring. The three of us. What an absurd outing it was. Ray needed our help just to cross the pavement from the car to the jewellers'. What can they have thought? That I was Helga's sister and Ray was our father? Certainly not that he was the one getting married. Although perhaps in California this was nothing new. Perhaps they had seen this a hundred times. Old men on walking sticks coming in to get engaged.

It was Ray's insistence that Helga have a ring, despite her utter disinterest in wearing one. Ray also wanted to formally ask her father's permission for her hand in marriage. It didn't matter to him that Helga was over forty, a mother of two grown sons, and running a very successful business. To Ray, she was his bride. She had chosen him to protect her and provide for her.

He also changed his will to make Helga the sole beneficiary. Ray had fiddled about with his will a great deal over the previous months. When I arrived, everything was left to Betty Bluefields. Then he decided he should leave his estate to me. I tried to talk him out of this. But for him it was a gesture of appreciation, and an attempt at this late stage to commit himself to one person, to one course. And although Helga was independently well-off, it was important to him that the will be changed in her favour. Such a preoccupation with wills! He must have known how frail he really was.

the new life

Gary Davis: He called to thank me for everything I had done for him over the years. He said he and Helga were going to live in London and he would be leaving La Jolla in a few weeks, for good. This was fair enough – he had always wanted to go back to London, and to be with Helga for that matter – but the way he was speaking it wasn't that he was crossing the Atlantic, but preparing himself for the big journey – crossing the Styx to the Other Side.

He asked if I wanted any of his books. He said he was going to have to be ruthless about his 'vast accumulation of personal documentation'.

more permanent storage

Hiliary Easton: Most of Ray's books were still in storage, along with the furniture from his house with Cissy. But his papers had long been a concern to him. His letters and files were all in boxes in the spare bedroom at Mrs Munz's. He knew he had to do something with them.

Helga offered to take care of them, planning to organise them into more permanent storage. She hoped he'd forget about them and that they'd be left for the literary scholars. But on the first of March, the first day of spring – which

I'm sure wasn't lost on him – he took matters into his own hands.

Billy Lee Munz: My auntie called and said the old man who was renting her cottage was moving out and would I come around to lend a hand. It was a Saturday. I wasn't at classes so I agreed to help. I thought it'd be moving boxes and books and things out into a van or something, but the old man – Ray – didn't have that in mind at all.

valuable promises

Hiliary Easton: His idea was to burn the lot. Helga implored him to wait. But Ray was determined. 'I've made promises,' he said. 'These papers were my private life and I intend it to stay private.' As a friend, I think Helga knew he was right. But as a literary person and agent, the last thing she wanted was to watch years of his personal history go up in smoke. She knew how valuable his letters were. So instead she suggested he only burn the most personal material and store his manuscripts and business correspondence until they could get back to London and decide what to do with it. He agreed to this, and many boxes of files ended up in Gary Davis's garage. After Ray died, Helga paid for Gary to send them all by sea mail to her in London.

Mrs Munz had a drum in the backyard where she burnt her garden clippings. We lit the fire in that. There was a young man helping us. He was a nephew, I think, of Mrs Munz's. He did all the heavy lifting. Ray sat in a chair pointing out which boxes were to be burnt and which ones were to be packed.

whole lotta shaking going on

Billy Lee Munz: The spare bedroom was full of boxes. The old man had a cane and he sat there pointing at which box he wanted me to take next. I was taking them out and piling them beside the incinerator in the yard. He seemed to be in a good mood, even if he was wheezing and coughing a lot. He kept singing and humming to himself. One time, coming back in, he held his cane out and stopped me, and asked if I knew what song he was singing. I said, no, I didn't. He said it was called 'English Rose'. Then he said, 'All the irrigation in California, my boy, cannot produce a single rose like an English rose.'

I carted all the boxes out, then he asked me to carry his chair out. He went in front of me leaning on his cane. He was shaking a lot. He had on a white shirt and bow tie, old-fashioned style.

and then he kissed me

Mrs Munz: I knew it wasn't going to be an easy job finding another tenant as genteel and charming as Ray. That day when I had Billy Lee round helping was one of the saddest days of my life. I didn't want Ray to leave. He was a good tenant, despite his drinking. He was always charming. He kissed my hand every single time I called around.

shadow over the yard

Hiliary Easton: It was late afternoon by the time Ray had finished sorting the boxes. The cottage cast its shadow over the backyard, and even there, in California in spring, there was a chill in the air. Ray sat in his chair, and Helga and I stood about clutching our cardigans close to us. Ray gave the young man orders. 'That one first, then this one.' He tapped the boxes with his cane. The young fellow lifted the cartons into the incinerator and poured kerosene over them, and Ray threw on a match. They went up with a gust of orange flames and black smoke. Helga and I and Mrs Munz all stepped back, but Ray didn't move. He sat with a stony face, watching in silence.

'I feel like I should be in there too, burning to ashes,' he said. He looked up at the paper ash disappearing into the sky. He lived so much through his letters. Then he said, 'I suppose in a way I am.'

Helga went and stood beside him and took his hand. The light of the flames played on their faces, reflecting in their glasses. It was the only time I ever saw Helga wearing Ray's ring.

The first two boxes he burnt were his letters to Cissy, and his to her. Then their personal diaries. Then other letters which Ray regarded as personal. Everything he'd ever received from Natasha Spender he burnt. And the letters from the girl in Australia. They went on last.

forever

Gary Davis: Helga and Ray and Hiliary all left La Jolla together in early March '59. They took a cab down to San Diego Airport and I drove the luggage down in my Olds'. There were a lot of tears. Margaret – Mrs Munz – had gotten terribly fond of Ray. And Betty knew she was watching her meal ticket get on a plane and leave her life – forever. We all knew he wouldn't be back. None of us thought we'd ever see him again. He'd aged something bad, those last months. And I got to admit I felt something in my heart for Betty that day. She was sad as the rest of us. She had feelings too. Just they came out upside down, dumped on everybody.

Ray was a big name by then – if you moved in those circles – and a measure of this esteem was that he had just been elected president of the Mystery Writers of America. It was probably pretty much of a sympathy vote – they all knew that Ray was on the downhill. But I guess they also knew that when it came to crime writing, without him they'd all be stuck back in the thirties, running around with guns for months.

Anyway, Ray was going to accept the MWA presidency at a big dinner in New York. So the three of them caught the local flight up to Los Angeles together, then Hiliary got on a 'Polar' flight straight back to London, and Helga and Ray went on to New York.

I may go out when it isn't raining

Sheila MacGregor: I worked in New York with Guinness Mahon, Helga's father's bank, and had met Ray on the *Mauretania* when we were both sailing to London in 1955. Subsequently I introduced him to Helga. When they came to New York I put them in rooms at my hotel, the Beaux Arts, on East 44th Street.

Those days were very close. Ray's health was still precarious. He was very weak, unable to go anywhere without his cane, and without one of us at his arm as well. The weather was miserable, and we spent most of the time indoors, talking quietly about mutual memories and Ray and Helga's plans for the future. It was an extremely strange time, infused with unreal optimism, and tainted with the sadness of Ray's decline, which was so apparent to everyone – including, I'd say, Ray himself.

Nonetheless, he was excited about returning to London, he wasn't drinking, and for a few hours a day, until he tired, he was very witty. At the Mystery Writers' dinner he made a speech sitting in a chair with his cane at his side and he had all of us laughing, but mostly, I'd say, to relieve the sadness. Everyone in the room knew it was likely to be the last speech they'd hear him give. But his humour hadn't left him and he still had great presence. He said he didn't know what he was going to do in England – perhaps go out when it wasn't raining. He ended his speech by thanking everyone for their kindness and reassuring them that 'however much love I may have inside me, I have no more words that need be said'.

Ray's other business in New York was to ask Helga's father, who happened to be in town at that time, for his daughter's hand in marriage. Helga, of course, thought this was preposterous. At her age and with her financial and emotional independence, her father's endorsement may have been pleasant but it certainly wasn't necessary. She went along with Ray's old-fashioned suggestion mainly to get him out of La Jolla and on the road to his new life.

They had dinner with Helga's father, and by then Ray's chill had really taken hold. He did appear on his last legs, and not surprisingly Mr Guinness objected to the marriage. He said to Ray's face that he was too old, almost his own age, and Ray, of course, took it as a personal rebuttal. It is ironic that Ray's mother had objected to him marrying Cissy for exactly the same reason.

The weather was getting everyone down. Ray knew that in London he would be facing more of the same – rain and drizzle – and being used to the permanent sun of California, he grew very depressed. Meanwhile several letters had arrived from the woman in La Jolla, Betty Bluefields, describing her difficulties since he had left and this, together with his ill health, decided him to return to California to convalesce. Helga carried on to London, and Ray planned to join her there after a few weeks.

With the benefit of hindsight what transpired instead was understandable, indeed predictable, but we all felt terribly guilty and sad for Ray that we hadn't the prescience to try and change the outcome. But by then perhaps it was out of our hands.

making the speech

Gary Davis: I got a call from Ray. He was back in La Jolla, at Mrs Munz's cottage. He said things hadn't gone well in New York. Helga's old man had poured water on the wedding plans, the weather was the pits, and, he said, he'd come down with something. He said he'd stay there at Mrs Munz's until he was better, then go on to London as planned. I called in to see him and I knew as soon as I walked in how low he was. He was stinking, for a start. There was no food in the house except coffee, and he was all alone. 'Come stay with us for a while, for Christsakes,' I said. 'Penny won't mind.' But he wouldn't do it. He said he'd be better in a few days.

Before I could start arguing with him, Betty arrived with a sack of food and I left, figuring at least that he wasn't alone and I could argue with him another day.

The next I heard was on Friday, March 23. Ray had pneumonia and was in La Jolla Convalescent. It was the nurse, or someone on the desk. I said I'd be right down. I was at the office. I rang Pen to tell her and she said stay as long as you need, and I knew what she meant.

When I got there they had him in an oxygen tent. He was conscious, but only just. One minute he knew who I was, the next minute he thought I was Cissy and he was talking to her. He reached his hand out under the tent and I took it. It was cold and if it had any strength at all I couldn't feel it. He turned his head from side to side, saying something. 'Is this the way you wanted it? Is this the way you wanted it?'

I stayed till dark and then went home to Pen. I rang the following day, Saturday, and on Sunday, and they said Betty and Mrs Munz had been in and there was no change in his condition. The next day, Monday, in the morning, they called me to say he'd been transferred to the Scripps Clinic, which is only five minutes away from us down here in 'Diego. I said I'd drop down at lunch as soon as I'd finished my column and see how he was going.

The column was a real bitch that day – it always is on a Monday – and I didn't get out of the building until about three, three-thirty. I grabbed a sandwich and went straight down to the clinic. Which was just as well. When I got there I said who I was there to see and the nurse took me straight into his room. They'd taken the oxygen tent away and Ray was lying there, wheezing and rattling for breath. A doctor had his stethoscope out on his chest, and two nurses stood on either side of the bed looking grave. If you ever see a nurse looking grave, you know it's no practice run. They looked up at me as I came in. 'Relative?' the doctor said. 'No,' I said. 'Friend.'

'Has he got any relatives down here?'

'No,' I said. 'And not many friends either.'

The doctor nodded. 'Okay, we don't know how long he's got.'

I went and sat in the chair beside the bed and took his hand from where it lay on the covers. It wasn't just cold any more, it was icy. I sat there watching him straining for each breath, gasping it in, letting it out – so long between breaths you wondered if there was going to be another. We all just watched, willing him on to the next, or praying for it to end quickly. A bit of both I suppose. They had his glasses off, and each breath seemed to drain his face of a bit more life. His skin was yellow and waxy. And cold. So cold you wondered it hadn't happened already.

Then it did happen. Without warning, without drama, the death rattle stopped and with one long sigh his chest sunk and there was no more breath. He just seemed to run down, like a machine runs out of fuel.

The doctor had a final listen with his stethoscope, making sure, I suppose, then pulled the tubes from his ears and nodded and left the room. The nurses closed his eyes, propped up his jaw with a towel and folded his hands across his chest. I sat watching them. They were fast and efficient. You could see they'd done it a hundred times before. But one of them, the younger one, was sniffing back tears. 'I'm sorry,' she said. 'My father died fast and none of us were with him. Thank God Mr Chandler had you.'

That was nice. I took her hand and thanked her. 'Can I have ten minutes?' I said, and she nodded and opened the door, and left.

I sat there for a while with both his hands in mine trying to work out what to say. I knew there was something I ought to say. But instead I just sat looking at his sunken cheeks and propped-closed mouth and tried to understand that a death had just taken place. I couldn't. There was a body in front of me but I couldn't understand that it was the Ray I knew, and that this body wouldn't be walking around grizzling and glaring at me over the top of those bifocals and making sour little jokes any more. Who can understand death? All you've known is life, how can you imagine death? I felt a few tears roll down my cheeks, and leant forward and kissed him on the forehead. 'I'll see you there, Ray,' I heard myself say. And then I got up and left.

the big sleep

Gabrielle Mercy: Ray's funeral was held at St James Episcopal Church in La Jolla four days after he died. The service was conducted by the same rector, by then retired, who had buried Cissy. On that occasion Ray had insisted on using the main church, and this had added to the despair of her passing, as only eight people were present. Fortunately someone thought to have Ray's funeral in the small chapel at the side.

There were seventeen mourners. Among them were his lawyer in San Diego, his accountant, someone from the Mystery Writers of America. Gary Davis and his wife. Juanita Messick, Betty Bluefields, her children. Perhaps Mrs Munz dressed up her golf-playing husband and brought him along for the numbers.

After the service, the casket was taken to the Mount Hope Cemetery in San Diego and he was buried. No one thought to have his remains cremated, to be set beside Cissy's as he had wished. Gary Davis wrote and told us it was a clear Southern Californian spring day. There was no smog and the horizon was a clean line across the ocean in the distance.

But it was a Bank Holiday in England and none of his friends over here could even find a florist to send a wreath.

DEATH OF WRITER
New York March 27 (AAP)
Author Raymond Thornton Chandler, 70, died at La Jolla, California, yesterday of bronchial pneumonia.

He was a member of the Mystery Writers of America which selected his *The Long Goodbye* as the best book of 1954.

His other books included *The Big Sleep, Farewell, My Lovely, The Simple Art of Murder,* and *The Lady in the Lake.*

Chandler began writing fiction in 1933. His 'private eye' hero, Philip Marlowe, set a trend in detective-story writing which featured short clipped writing, strong verbs and eye-arresting similes.

Sydney Morning Herald 28 March 1959

today's shoes

It was my twenty-first birthday, 6 June 1959. We didn't have a proper party, just an At Home over the weekend. Friday, Saturday, Sunday. I'd barely seen Walter since that first meeting after I finished school in 1954. That is, I'd seen him around, when I was out with my sister with the baby in the stroller. We went past his house and saw him, things like that. And one time he invited me to come and listen to a new record he had. That must have been 1956, first year of uni.

I can't remember how it happened. We must have run into each other somewhere. He said, "You like music, don't you? I've got a new record, would you like to come and hear it?" And of course I was round there in a flash. It was Schubert's *Trout Quintet*. We were sitting in the living-room listening and Karl came home, one of the other boys. He was seeing a girl called Eva, a Hungarian girl. Very young, she was still at school. And he sat on the couch and fell asleep while the music was playing. He'd had a hard day at work and been out seeing Eva and he was exhausted. Yes, I remember that. And, you know, they're still together, Karl and Eva, almost forty years later. Germans are very loyal. Once they make up their mind about something they stick with it.

I didn't see Walter again for a long time. Certainly not alone like that, by invitation or anything. I probably ran into him in the street. And I'd say the reason he asked me over that day was to have another look at me, to see if his first impression was right. He was interested in me too, but I was young and he wanted to wait a few years and see how I turned out. He's nine years older than me. Which meant then, when I was seventeen, he was twenty-six. That's a big difference at that age. He didn't want to make a mistake.

Anyway, we'd organised this At Home for my twenty-first. The idea was that people could just drop in, stay as long as they wanted, have tea in the afternoon, or a drink if they came in the evening. I had some girlfriends coming up from teacher's college and I'd invited a lot of old school friends, and Mum and Dad had some of their friends coming. And I'd asked the

German boys, all of them, so as not to expose my interest in Walter. Of course the only one I really wanted to see was Walter. He was the one I really cared about.

And he came! He was the only one to come. The others each had reasons. Perhaps they were just excuses so Walter could come alone. I don't know. I didn't care. I was so excited. It made the weekend worthwhile. It was as if I'd been holding my breath for four years, and I had it in my mind that this was my last chance. I'd decided that if I didn't make contact with him now it'd never happen.

You can imagine, I was so happy. He stayed the whole afternoon, and he brought me a present, a Brahms record, because Brahms is from Hamburg, which is the city near where Walter was brought up. We walked in the garden and sat on the verandah talking. It was June, so it was pretty cold. I've got a photo of the two of us on the path in the garden, and I'm holding my little nephew's hand and looking down trying to hide my huge smile. It continued all the next day. I just couldn't stop smiling.

But he was still very careful. He had a job renovating a shop, a newsagent's in Rockdale. I was living in teacher's college in Sydney, and he said we could maybe get together sometime. I was so excited. I remember I scribbled the address on a page ripped from one of those day-by-day desk calendars.

That was in June. I came back down to Sydney, and Walter did ring me and we did go out together, and then once more, and then again. The first night we went to the movies at a place on George Street, up near the Great Southern Hotel. It was a European double bill, and one of the films was *La Strada*, which I'd heard of because Ray had mentioned it to me in a letter. The other was *One Summer of Happiness*, a Swedish film which was shocking everyone then because it had bare breasts and a love-making scene. I remember the whole cinema going quiet when it came on. I suppose it was very adult and risqué for me then, and I thought all the more of Walter for taking me there.

During this time my heart was so full of Walter that other parts of my life necessarily got left behind. I didn't stop thinking about Ray when we stopped writing but he had certainly ceased to matter to me in a day-to-day way. I didn't even know he had died. It wasn't until I got Helga's letter a year or something later that I found out about Ray's death. And that was so strange. All that time I was still having conversations with him in my head, mentally writing him letters and receiving them – and he wasn't even alive. It was a huge shock. It was sad, of course, but I remember feeling betrayed again, somehow, as if the energy I'd expended had been wasted, abused.

But that was later. In the meantime all my dreams of Walter were coming true. By the end of the year we were assuming we would be married soon. It was just a matter of organising the other parts of our life. I probably would have happily married him then, but it was Walter who insisted I finish my 'apprenticeship' and teach for at least one year. He thought it was important I put my theoretical training into practice. So the next year, 1960, I went up to Canowindra and taught in the local intermediate high school. I boarded with a family in the town and came down to visit my family in Orange and Walter in Bathurst. As the months progressed we planned our wedding, and we were married in December. But my father didn't live to see us married. He died that September of a stroke. So it was a real transition period. Starting a new life, an old one ending. I suppose I was lucky I had Walter and the excitement of marriage that year, or it probably would have been dreadfully sad for me.

I know you'd like me to say I read about Ray's death in the newspaper, and knew that period of my life was over as I headed into the next. But it wasn't like that. It wasn't so neat. I didn't know he'd died. I didn't look down into the mud and see the notice in an abandoned newspaper or anything like that. I didn't sit there in shock with memories racing through me. That time of my life was simply over without me knowing it.

I'd thought about him many times, of course, but it was always with some regret – and confusion, I suppose – about the way things had ended between us. I thought about what might have happened if things had worked out differently, especially after that first meeting with Walter in 1955. If we'd become involved then would I have ever written to Ray? Would I have needed to?

I think it scared me how much Walter was exactly the sort of man I wanted. He was, and still is, a lovely, gentle, strong man. He's shy but with a strong centre. He chooses his words carefully, and doesn't rush into things. But once he has made up his mind he sticks to it. He had something then, and still has it, which made him stand out from the Australian men I knew, and I think this is what has always attracted me to him. It was his German background perhaps, the culture and history of his country. It seemed to feed some yearning I had then which I could barely put a name to, the need for something different, the knowledge that there was more to life than the life I saw around me.

Of course this was what made me write to Ray, and keep writing to him. He filled that gap between my real life and the life I dreamt about. If I had already been with Walter I doubt I would have wanted to, or needed to, write to Ray.

This is all ifs and maybes, of course, and who is to say the advice and reassurance Ray gave me didn't rub off? I'll never know. But no doubt there is truth in it. We're all just the sum total of everything that's happened to us, after all – the past, walking around in today's shoes.

Part nine
trout fishing in america

nothing fits

How do you write about your own life? It's complicated. Nothing fits properly. It never sounds the way you'd like it to sound. You write it down and it is clumsy, incompetent, even cruel.

I decided to go to America. Initially I wanted to see if Professor MacShane had the letters. Fiona and I made a plan. She would fly over and go travelling in Central America. I would stay and finish the book I was writing and follow several months later, after earning some money to travel with. I would do the Chandler business and we would have a holiday at the same time. But by the time I went Chandler had become a secondary consideration in the back of my mind. By then I was going because Fiona was there and I wanted to see what was left of our life together after the months apart, after what had happened, after ... all this.

I never thought I'd be attracted to Julia. The nature of our correspondence made it possible for me to create a fantasy of her, but the impression I had from her letters of the real woman created no such romantic anticipation in me. She was simply someone I enjoyed writing letters to. I might have played with the idea of her, but I had little doubt that the reality would prove quite resistable.

I was wrong.

How we met doesn't matter. I was on the north coast. We met. In a bush hut, by a creek with frogs. And she wasn't at all the person I expected. That afternoon our lives changed. Forever.

'Surely you realise,' wrote Chandler to Dee, 'that when you write so frankly to me, it is because I am far away and because we may never meet. I rather hope we shall, unless it destroys an illusion. You need the illusion.'

Julia was married. Fiona was somewhere in Central America. Perhaps this is why it all happened. Anyway, it happened, and it went on happening.

The illusion, for us, was over. The story now was very different.

I told Fiona. I wrote to her. I told her this thing had happened while she was away. I told her who it was. I told her I still wanted to come over to Los Angeles, as arranged. I needed to see her. I couldn't just walk away without an end. And anyway, I didn't regard what had happened with Julia as the finish of Fiona and me. Fiona might, but for my part, I needed to see her, to see.

Fiona wrote back, we had phonecalls, long Pacific Ocean silences.

'Okay,' she said, 'come over. We'll see what happens.'

Fiona was the real reason I went to America. Not Chandler, or the letters.

l.a. story

Fiona met me at LAX as planned. It'd been months; it felt like years. She was waiting at the bottom of the ramp in the same old shirt. That was a shock. The same shirt! What did I expect? Different clothes? A different person? She was thin and brown. Her hair was shorter. She looked tough, travel-hardened. Our faces broke into old-time's-sake grins, we opened our arms. I closed my eyes in her hair, my nose full of memories. We found a hotel in Hollywood with green artificial grass in the hallways and spent the night talking, trying to find out what was left of what we had before, where we stood now, what was possible for the future.

Twenty-four hours later we were still talking. Only starting to scratch the surface. It was my second night in America. My mind, my body clock, our conversation – all this was still over on the east coast of Australia. About ten p.m. we went walking down Santa Monica Boulevard. Fiona said something. I said something back. Fiona said the next thing. We turned off Santa Monica into Ogden. A car slid to the kerb beside us. Doors flew open and two bodies were around the back of the car and yelling at us.

'Give us the money. Give us the money.'

I turned to see who they were talking to. Then my bladder opened. Then I gave them the money.

One of them had a knife, the other had his hand down his tracksuit pants pretending it was a gun. I realised this soon enough. But on your second night in America with two guys yelling at you down a dark side street, pretend don't matter. Pretend is something you work out later on.

Next day at the LAPD, Beverly Hills, a deputy took our details. Straightforward enough. Chicano kids. Cracked to the eyeballs, from the look of it. No casualties. Just money, jewellery, soiled trousers. Shock. Anger. Violation. The usual. Another LA story.

'You folks go on and enjoy your holiday,' the deputy said. 'We cain't promise we'll find the scum who did this to you. But if we do ... '

His eyes were cold, icy blue. Beads of sweat stood on his upper lip. He spared us the end of his sentence.

Fiona and I agreed any future sightseeing should be by car.

average eight-lane l.a. through street

1912	aged twenty-three, Chandler returns to US from England
1913	713 South Bonnie Brae St, Los Angeles
1916	311 Loma Dve

1919		127 South Vendome St
1920		224 South Catalina St, Redondo Beach (Cissy lived in nearby Hermosa Beach)
1923		723 Stewart St, Santa Monica (Cissy: 3206 San Marino, Santa Monica)
1924-27		2863 Leeward
		700 Grammercy Pl
		2315 West 12th St
1928		1024 South Highland Ave
1932		4616 Greenwood Pl (after dismissal from Dabney Oil)
1939	Feb	Route One, Box 421, Riverside
	Aug	Big Bear Lake
	Dec	1265 Park Row, La Jolla
1940	Jan	818 West Duarte Road, Monrovia
	June	1155 Arcadia Ave, Arcadia
	Oct	449 San Vincente Blvd, Santa Monica
1941		857 Iliff St, Pacific Palisades
1942	March	12216 Shetland Lane, Los Angeles
	July	Idlewild, Cathedral City
1943		c/- Paramount Pictures
1944	Jan	1040 Havenhurst Drive, Hollywood
	July	c/- Paramount Pictures
	Oct	6520 Drexal Ave, Los Angeles
1946	Oct	6005 Camino de la Costa, La Jolla,
1955	March	Following Cissy's death and his attempt at suicide, Chandler sells the house in La Jolla and goes to London

These were all the addresses I could find for Chandler in California up to 1955. Day Three we decided to do some business. We bumped out of the Ugly Duckling lot on Santa Monica in a gunmetal-green Buick with loose steering and a hundred stories in the cracked vinyl of the seats, and we went looking for Raymond Chandler.

Specifically, 700 Grammercy, at Melrose. Not far away, an address of the drinking years in 1927.

Melrose is your average eight-lane LA through street. We

bounced over it in our Ray Bans and baseball caps, my left arm getting some LA sun out the window as I swung the wheel from side to side to avoid the potholes. It felt like driving in the movies. All cars in LA seemed to bounce around like this, with loose steering and trampoline suspension, light as air, quite unreal, as if they really are in the movies.

At Grammercy Place I swung in and parked. We walked back to the corner. 690, 692, 694, 696. It was a small cream block of four apartments. That's where the numbers ended. We looked at each other, knowing what that meant, and turned to face the traffic. Four lanes each direction of tanned arms and mirror shades and gaping mouths and bouncing, swinging automobiles, all on the wrong side of the road.

We headed back along Melrose. Weeds grew out of the cracks in the pavement. After about five minutes we reached a cross street with traffic lights and a pedestrian crossing. Fiona pressed the button. Another five minutes and the traffic stopped. We set off across the bitumen, reached the middle, set off again, reached the other side, turned and went back the way we had come. Five minutes later we reached Grammercy Place. On the corner was a small cream block of four apartments identical to 696. Number 710.

Standing on the kerb looking out across the traffic through the thick grey air we could just make out our little green Buick parked in Grammercy. In Chandler's day Melrose was probably only four lanes wide. 700 Grammercy had died the Los Angeles death.

We walked back the way we had come. Back in the Ugly Duckling, I consulted my list and started the car. We headed west towards the sea.

good god, we have moved again

'The above address will be good for six months, I hope,' Chandler wrote to Blanche Knopf on 9 October, 1940, from the apartment at San Vincente Boulevarde, Santa Monica.

It wasn't.

'Good God, we have moved again,' he reported to Erle

Stanley Gardner from 857 Illif Street, Pacific Palisades, on 1 February 1941. 'It's better over here, quiet and a house in a nice garden. But they are just beginning to build a house across the way. I shan't mind it as much as the good neighbors bouncing on the bed springs over at the apartment house.'

Chandler didn't care for Santa Monica. In *Farewell, My Lovely* it became Bay City: 'Sure it's a nice town. It's probably no crookeder than Los Angeles. But you can only buy a piece of a big city. You can buy a town this size all complete, with the original box and tissue paper.'

The beaches at Santa Monica were a joke, a bad joke. Most of them were privately owned, the sand was grey, and the Californian ocean trudged into shore sluggish and fat and full of plastic bags.

We left the coast and wound up into the hills. The roads were steep, twisting back on themselves like a coiled snake, lined with high fences and expensive bungalows. Pacific Palisades is an affluent suburb now. When Chandler was there, during the war, it was comfortably middle class.

By the time we found Illif Street it was dark. Number 857 was older and less fashionable than other houses in the street. It was small and built of wood. I pulled in to the kerb and turned off the engine. We didn't move. We didn't speak. The engine pinged. We turned our heads to number 857. Grey TV light flickered in the window. The lawn was long, the edges scraggy, a wind-hardy weed climbed the wall from the garden.

A sheet of newspaper was wrapped around the post holding up the letter box. It was yellowed, stiff with age and weather, it'd been there for some time. I could have got out of the car and checked the date. It might have been 1941. I could have walked up the path and knocked on the door. A man in round tortoiseshell glasses might have answered, a long-stemmed pipe in one hand.

'Yes?'

Behind him an elderly woman with strawberry blonde hair would crane around the corner of the couch.

'Yes?' the man would say again.

'I'm sorry to disturb you. But ...'

'Yes?' His hand wouldn't have left the door. The woman would mouth something. 'Ray, what does he want?'

I would shuffle uncomfortably. What did I want?

I didn't even get out of the car.

We sat for a few minutes then I started the engine and wound back down the hill, got on to Santa Monica Boulevarde and drove east in silence. I looked across and Fiona's face glowed green in the lights of LA, which is a lot of lights. She looked at me and reached across and put her hand on my leg. A sudden wave of literary necrophilia seem to have put us both off colour.

The next day we took a bus north. Fiona had met a woman in Guatemala. Some potter who lived in Oregon. She'd promised we'd visit.

a small town on a big lake

The potter lived in the woods right down near the California border. The biggest town nearby was Medford.

In the 1944 Film *Double Indemnity*, which Chandler co-scripted from the James M. Cain novel, he has a minor character introduce himself to Fred MacMurray, who plays Walter Naff, the insurance salesman. 'Howard Jackson,' the character says, 'from Medford, Oregon.' He peers closely at MacMurray, recognising him but unsure where from. 'Say, you from Oregon? Ever been to Medford?'

MacMurray glances uncomfortably at Edward G. Robinson, the company investigator who can smell a rat but doesn't suspect yet that it is in the office next door. MacMurray knows Jackson has seen him on the train impersonating Barbara Stanwyck's husband, who they have killed for the double-indemnity insurance. Jackson persists, leaning forward to examine MacMurray closely. 'Ever go trout fishing up at Klamath Falls?' he asks.

Klamath Falls is in the Cascade Mountains, eighty miles east of Medford. Fiona and I drove up one day. It's a small town on a big lake. We didn't go trout fishing. But we did see a train.

let's go!

It was probably the very same train we had been on a few weeks earlier.

When we left LA we didn't go direct to Medford. We caught the Green Tortoise hippie bus to San Francisco, and from there a train to Portland. Our plan was to take out a Rent-A-Wreck, do us a little touring. Maybe see us a few (more) pine trees.

In Portland, on the advice of *Lets Go California and The Northwest*, we put up at the Jack London Hotel on South Alder Street. Dead writers seemed to be the theme of this trip, after all. But it was more James Ellroy or Charles Bukowski than Jack London or Chandler, and perhaps more like the inside of a drunk tank than anything else. We stood out in the lobby, with our bright backpacks and Gortexes, like kindergarten kids in a line-up of murderers. Men with dramatic scars and freshly bruised faces made quick use of the front door. Others slumped in front of the TV with cigarettes burning down to their fingers. The manager argued with someone about back rent. 'I don't give a goddamn fuck about your goddamn lousy clothes. I don't care a fuck where your mail gets sent. Just get the hell outa here before I call the fucking cops.'

We asked the clerk how the Jack London got its name, and without looking up from the register he shrugged. 'Someone liked the guy. I dunno.'

In the corridors at night men leant against the walls looking down at their shoes. Our room had three different bolts down the inside of the door and none of them worked. The room itself was an archaeology of smoking. Decades of it hung in the air. It was layered into every surface in burns and stains and discolourations. The ashtray was a blackened half of a Coca Cola can on the bedside cabinet. When we went out in the street the smell went with us, in our clothes, through our hair. There was no paper in the toilets, and stuffed down behind the cistern I saw a pair of men's underpants, size XXL and soiled. Under the cotton sheets of our bed were plastic ones that crunkled loudly every time we moved.

I told the guy from Rent-A-Wreck where we were staying and he shrieked like a gay hairdresser, 'Oh my God, lets go skid row!'

the net closing

Bodleian Library
5 May 1989

Dear Mr Close

Thank you for your letter of 26 April. We can certainly photocopy the Chandler material and send it to you by post, but not until we have received Ed Victor's written permission. The cost is 10 pence a sheet, plus whatever postage and packing is involved. A US dollar money order would be acceptable, but there is a minimum bank conversion charge of £5, however small the sum involved.

I think that there would probably be no difficulty about allowing you access to the Chandler/Gartrell material on the strength of your publisher's letter, but is there no one in Oregon who could act as a suitable recommender for you, as specified in the application form for a reader's ticket to the Library which I am enclosing? I am afraid that we could not allow you wider access without such a recommendation.

Anyway, I hope this answers most of your queries. As soon as we hear from Ed Victor, we can put your xerox order in hand.

Yours sincerely
Judith Priestman (Dr)

Usual bond paper and immaculate typing, and ref JAP/JAS. But why am I formalised to Mr? And why has (Dr) Judith not signed the letter? Do I detect a distancing after our recent informalities?

Ed Victor Ltd
Literary Agency
London
10 May 1989

Dear Mr Close

Thank you for your letter of 26 April requesting permission to use material in the Bodleian Library connected with Deirdre Gartrell.

I have discussed the matter with Mr Ed Victor and Mr Graham C. Greene, who have no objections to you photocopying the material you require for your book.

Best wishes.

Yours sincerely
Sophie Hicks

On stage at last! Airmail paper, letterheaded, custard yellow. Electronically typed, no visible errors, signed in blue biro. They look good. A professional outfit. Is that Graham C. on trombone? And Ms Sophie Hicks on back-up vocals?

Columbia University
18 May 1989

Dear Mr Close

I expect to be here for most of the summer, so just give me a ring when you arrive. The telephone number is – .

Best wishes
Frank MacShane

Usual paper, typed this time, ref FM:cl. My heart races. Is the net closing?

that stuff

In New York City we stayed in Flatbush, Brooklyn, two streets from where Allen Konigsberg grew up before he became Woody Allen. In those days Flatbush was solidly Jewish. But by the time we got there the corner store was stocked with plantains and pawpaw and crowded with big Haitian women in floral sarongs and flip-flops, with luscious brown-skinned babies who stared at us from where they were slung across their mothers' backs.

Our host was a friend of a friend, a painter named Katarina. She worked in colour fields and had a blind cat. She kept her cigarettes in the fridge to cut down on her smoking. Like most Americans I talked to, she wasn't sure she had heard of Raymond Chandler.

'What did he write?' she asked. I told her and she brushed it aside with an impatient shake of her head. 'I don't read that stuff.'

he's good

At least I knew the Professor read 'that stuff'. On the phone he had a soft New England voice and fell immediately to business, as if he'd been doing nothing but sitting by the phone waiting for my call, and as soon as I was out of the way he could get on with the next thing.

'Now,' he said, 'can you come next Friday? I'll organise with the library. Do you know how to get here?'

I was looking at a map. 'On the subway?' I said.

'Yes, well, that's right. Take the 'One' line up Central Park West. But make sure you get the 'Local', and make sure you get off at 116th Street. If you don't, you'll end up in Harlem and we'll never see you again.'

'Great, thanks,' I started to say.

'Good. I'll see you then. Look forward to it.'

'Yes, thank you – ' But the Professor was gone, on to the next thing.

It was a hot day. I had new shoes and was trying to look neat. Determined not to miss 116th Street, I got off at 109th and walked. There was a demo over something. A massacre in China – Tiananmen Square, or somewhere. The street was clogged with Chinese students carrying placards. Bored cops stood along the pavement drinking Cokes. I hugged my daypack close and tried to ignore my sore feet.

At Columbia the students were on holidays and the campus was quiet. Dodge Hall was an old square building across the quadrangle from the library. I climbed flights of stairs and made my way down corridors, my shoes squelching on the lino. I saw a small wooden sign above a door: WRITING DIVISION. Inside a thin young man sat with his feet up on a desk. When I came in he lowered his feet to the floor. I sat opposite him. He wore small wire-rimmed glasses and hadn't shaved very well. He wanted to be a poet. His name was Andrew. He was studying with Professor MacShane.

'He's good,' he said, nodding seriously.

'I'm seeing him about Raymond Chandler,' I said.

Andrew looked blank, nodded, and then with the smallest gesture of a shrug, said, 'Who?'

right, let's ah ...

The Professor, when he arrived, was tall and stooped. His coat was patched at the elbows and he wore a cardigan underneath. He didn't wear a tie. A large pair of sunglasses jutted out of his top coat pocket. He had a long face and thin hair. I put him in his sixties. He carried a battered leather briefcase in one hand and two plastic shopping bags in the other. He considered putting them down to greet me but muttered instead and headed into an internal office, and reappeared a moment later with his hands empty. Then he shook my hand. He did nothing to indicate he'd ever set eyes on Andrew before in his life.

The Professor patted his coat, looked around vaguely, then located the sunglasses in his top pocket.

He looked up at me. 'Right. Let's, ah ...' He stood aside for me to go out the door first.

We squelched down the corridor. 'Sorry I'm late,' he said. 'My bus got caught in Central Park.'

I nodded knowingly, and felt like a fraud. Central Park! Just the name was exotic and dangerous.

We went through a glass door and down the lino stairs I'd come up. The Professor held the door for me. We emerged into the sunlight at the bottom. As he waited for me to pass through the door ahead of him, the Professor hooked the sunglasses from his top pocket. They were chrome-framed and very large – like something you'd see on a mental patient. We set off across the quadrangle.

I reminded the Professor why I was there. I mentioned the way Deirdre had first heard of Chandler, in the *Sun Herald*.

'Yes,' he said, 'yes, oh really!' He watched his feet as he walked. 'I forget things of course. I'm working on another book now.'

He looked up and blinked, as if suddenly he'd noticed it was broad daylight. He had his hands behind his back and leant forward, like a professor from the movies – like Tintin's Professor Calculus.

I asked him what the new book was about.

'It's about the rich in America.' He kept walking, his nose in the air. 'How they stuffed things up, basically. I'm stopping at Teddy Roosevelt.' He turned then and looked at me, giving the impression he expected me to know what he was talking about.

As we crossed the quadrangle I asked by what route he came to write the Chandler biography. He had gone out to Berkeley to teach, he said, in 1960. He was advised to read Chandler as an introduction to California. Later, studying at Oxford, he met Helga's son, Graham C. Greene.

'Graham C. Greene is Helga's son?'

'Yes. To Sir Hugh Greene. He was head of the BBC. Among other things. For a time. And Hugh was the brother of Graham Greene, the novelist.'

'Ah,' I said.

In due course, he told me, he had travelled through Nepal with Graham C.

'Nepal? You weren't wearing beads, were you?'

He laughed. 'A hippie? Good heavens, no. I was on a Fulbright.'

Several years later, Helga and Grahame C. Greene invited him to do Chandler's biography.

'And eventually, after about ten years, I got around to it.'

We reached the library. The Professor waited at the door and ushered me through.

'Long time ago now, of course.'

he kept his hat on

The security guard watched us approach across the foyer.

He held the security bar open for us to pass. 'Afternoon, Professor.'

The Professor fumbled in his pockets. 'I, ah ... ' He felt his breast pocket and patted his trousers. 'I can't seem to find my ... '

'Don't matter, Professor. I know who you are.'

The Professor waited for me to pass. He still had his sunglasses on.

'Yes, ah, quite. Thank you.' He had his wallet open in one hand and was fingering through its compartments.

I stood beside him. The Professor flipped the wallet closed and replaced it in his inside breast pocket without looking at the guard.

'Thank you. I realise you're not supposed to ... Well, next time, then.'

We crossed to the lift and watched the numbers descend. The doors opened to reveal a young woman standing alone in the car.

The Professor stood aside to let me enter first. He leant

forward and pressed the button marked BASEMENT. The three of us stood in silence with our faces turned up to the indicator board above the door. I could smell the woman's perfume. I looked down at her black stockings and small black shoes.

In a letter to Helga, Chandler recalled the story of the Hollywood writer who racked his brains how to show, with maximum economy, that a middle-aged man and his wife were no longer in love. 'Finally he licked it. The man and his wife got into a lift and he kept his hat on. At the next stop a lady got into the lift and he immediately removed his hat. That is proper film writing.'

I watched the Professor from the corner of my eye. What were his wife and family like? His kids were no doubt grown up now. What did he eat for breakfast? Black coffee? A bagel? All Bran with fruit and skim milk?

When we reached the basement the professor held the doors and let me leave the lift first. The woman didn't move. The doors slid closed behind us and the lift returned up the building.

We walked down a corridor to double glass doors marked RARE BOOKS AND MANUSCRIPTS. The Professor stood aside to let me enter first. A librarian waited behind a long counter. He had a huge black moustache, almost no hair, and a gold ring in his ear.

'Um, MacShane,' the Professor said to him.

The librarian nodded then jerked his head at me. 'He stays. We go up.'

the slouch of idle curiosity

I was left in a light and airy display room. I sat at a table. I stood up. I paced. Glass-fronted cabinets lined the walls. Inside, held open with perspex markers, were manuscripts and first editions of Tennessee Williams.

(Chandler on the film version of *A Streetcar Named Desire*: 'Zero in Art. A-plus in adaption to the circumstance that where there is no art, it is possible for an ingenious fellow to simulate it without losing money.' Always easy to please.)

I craned down to see inside the cabinets. My daypack, hung over one shoulder, swung forward against my side. I ran my eyes along the lines of print and moved on to the next book. My feet followed. I took in nothing. They were old books and I was waiting. My heart pumped against my ribs. My search until this point had been haphazard, almost incidental. I'd located Deirdre, virtually by accident, and now perhaps I would have the letters. But if so, what then? It'd be serious. A gust of panic blew into my heart. After all this meandering around I might have to actually write the book.

Gradually my nerves settled. I held my hand out in front of me. It barely shook. Maybe the letters weren't here. If so it'd have to be England, and (Dr) Judith in Oxford. Try and guess what she had for breakfast. But she had already told me that the 'Bodley' didn't hold the letters. What would I do then? Hadn't this entire project been just idle curiosity pulling me on, as by a ring through the nose, from one thing to the next? You start with an interest in trivia and end up on the other side of the world with nothing concrete beneath you except a vague idea and a few notes scratched on some bits of paper.

I remembered this: 'One of my peculiarities and difficulties as a writer is that I won't discard anything. I can't overlook the fact that I had a reason, a feeling for starting to write it, and I'll be damned if I won't lick it.'

That seemed to add a bit of backbone to the slouch of idle curiosity.

There was a sound behind me. I turned. A voice. A smiling face. A yellow envelope held aloft. A ridiculous black moustache curled like a sleeping animal above a grim, set lip. A flash of earring.

The Professor beamed.

'I'd all but given up. We were sitting on the floor going through box after box, and then there they were! In the last box!'

'You were sitting on the floor?'

'Um, yes, we were.' He noticed some dust on the sleeve

of his coat and twisted his arm to brush it off. The envelope turned towards me. It was addressed to him and had Australian stamps. It was a half-quarto envelope, the size of a school exercise book.

The writing on the front was Dee's.

she told him her measurements!

I stood at the Professor's shoulder as he slipped the contents from the envelope.

'Is that it? The whole correspondence?'

He turned the package around in his hand.

'Well, I guess so. That's all there was. I have no idea why I didn't send them back when I finished the *Letters*. I must have just, I don't know, forgotten.'

The Professor opened out the sheaf of letters. The first letter was handwritten, in black biro, on pages ripped from a quarto supermarket pad. It was from Dee. My eyes rushed down the lines as the Professor started to turn the pages.

Bathurst
31 May 1980

Dear Frank!

Here are the letters! I decided to send them, rather than photocopies, because they give a strong feeling of Ray's moods at that time. They're real, so they make him come alive. Death doesn't seem to mean much, when letters can speak so clearly and personally.

Last night I read them all again. It made me feel cherished, maybe more than I . . .

The page was turned, and the next and the next. The Professor had less patience than me. Next were three letters from Helga to Dee in 1960, typed on an old manual with smudged letters and hand-corrected errors, requesting Ray's letters for *Raymond Chandler Speaking*. The paper was letter-headed, HELGA GREENE LITERARY AGENCY.

The next two were letters from Dee to Helga, replying to her request, written in a younger, yet familiar hand.

Then there was this:

London
15 February 1956

Dear Miss Gartrell

Thank you very much for your letter, and for your measurements, which twenty years ago would have made me rather excitable ...

'That's the first letter! Ray's first letter to Dee. She told him her measurements and this was his reply. She was angry and wrote back. That's how they started.'

The Professor held the pages open and turned slightly towards me.

'She told him her measurements?'

I nodded, scared to take my eyes off the page in front of me.

The Professor grunted. 'Well, no doubt he would have liked that. That's why he responded, I'm sure.'

The letter was brief, two paragraphs typed on small notepaper, signed 'Raymond Chandler' in a large looped hand. Slightly shaky, dashed off with florid pleasure, no doubt with a glint in the eye and the lips twisted.

I stared at it. Chandler's actual letter! I could barely believe it. Typed and signed by him over thirty years ago. Folded into an envelope. Addressed, stamped, licked, dropped down the gullet of a red English pillarbox in Carlton Hill on a cold blustery day in February 1956 – a few hundred yards from where, years later, the Beatles would record *Abbey Road*.

The second letter was another short note, the next was four typed nutmeg-coloured pages with the letterhead, HOTEL DEL CHARRO, 238 TORREY PINES ROAD, LA JOLLA, CALIFORNIA. This was where Chandler stayed when he returned to La Jolla in May 1956. Where they kept giving him the room beside the pool.

The letter was dated 25 June, 1956, and addressed to 'My Charming Deirdre'. At the end of the letter Chandler had typed, 'With much love (Send your photograph to me, if you have a decent one, please). And don't call me Mr Chandler. My name to my friends is Ray.' Under this, in the loose sprawled hand, was signed 'Ray'.

The Professor proceeded. The letters were all typewritten, most of them on blue paper with the italicised letterhead, *Raymond Chandler, 6925 Neptune Place, La Jolla, California.* Corrections to the typing were scrawled, often illegibly, between the lines and in the margins. Some letters needed more corrections than others. These, no doubt, were his drunk letters. The early letters were signed 'Raymond Chandler', the later letters were signed 'Ray'. Some were addressed to 'Darling Deirdre', others 'Deirdre Darling' or 'Dearest Deirdre'. There appeared to be about twenty letters in all.

I was having trouble with the reality of what was in front of me. The actual letters. Why did this so surprise me? What had I expected? Photocopies? Carbon copies? Until now all I had in mind was the search, with no thought to the goal: actually finding the letters. I hadn't thought what to expect.

I didn't touch them, but kept my hands respectfully behind my back, like a member of the royal family on a colonial tour, allowing my guide, the Professor, to lead me through them. Then suddenly it occurred to me.

'Hang on. These are Ray's letters, but where are Dee's?'

the path ends

'Whose?'

'Deirdre's.'

The Professor shuffled his feet. 'Well, um, I have no idea. But, ah ... '

He flicked back through the pages in his hands. My eyes lighted on words and phrases before they were whisked out of sight. Then a word caught my eye. One word. 'Destroyed'.

I reached forward to stop a page turning. It was a letter from Helga to Deirdre in 1960, typed on thick bond paper:

Ray destroyed all your letters to him just before he died. He was planning to go and live in England for ever, and while I was in La Jolla he went through everything and he decided that his wife's diaries, his letters to her, your letters and many others just had to go.

'Well,' the Professor said, 'that explains why there's no letters from, um, Deirdre.'

I said nothing. I couldn't speak. I felt burning behind my eyes. This moment ended what had started two years earlier, a continent and an ocean away, when I turned the page in the Professor's *Selected Letters* and the word 'Armidale' set itself in my path. Now that path had reached its end.

'Oh,' I said to the Professor. That's all I could say. 'Oh.'

anything can happen in the mail

We stood in silence.

'Well, I suppose you'd like copies of these?'

'Sorry?'

'Copies. I suppose you'd like copies?'

'Ah, yes. I suppose I would.'

'Good. We'll find a Xerox and do them.'

'What? Now?'

'Yes, now. Why not?'

I looked around. No reason seemed to present itself. The

Professor folded the letters, slipped them back into their envelope, and handed them to me with finality. Exuding achievement, he led the way up from the basement, past the security guard and out of the building into the sunshine. He stopped, looked about him as if he was taking the air on the English moors, reached into his top pocket, unfolded his lurid sunglasses and stepped out across the the quadrangle to Dodge Hall.

The Professor was a changed man. He had the zest about him of work well done. I tried to keep up. I kept a good grip of the envelope in my hand.

'Would it be possible – '

The Professor turned towards me in mid-stride.

'Would it be possible to look through these for a while? The originals?'

'Of course. No problem.'

He leant forward and kept walking.

'Could I take them away and read them?'

He waved his hand in the air.

'Of course. You can take them away.'

'For that matter, who actually owns them?' I asked. 'Does the library own them?'

We had reached Dodge Hall. The Professor stopped on the steps and turned to face me.

'No, the library doesn't own them. I just store my papers there. I can't imagine how it came that I didn't send them back at the time.'

'So you don't own them?'

'No, I don't own them.'

'The estate? Does the Chandler estate own them?'

'No, the estate wouldn't own them. They hold the copyright, but the actual letters. They belong to, to ... '

'Deirdre?'

'Yes, that's right. Deirdre.'

'Then maybe we should make copies and send the originals back to her?'

'Well, you're going back, aren't you? Why don't you take them. If you don't mind.' He looked down at me over his sunglasses. 'Would you mind?'

'Mind? No, I don't mind. But I can't believe you'd just give them to me. Aren't they valuable?'

'Well, you'll see her, won't you? You look trustworthy. You're not going to steal them, are you? And who knows? Anything could happen in the mail.'

into the underworld

The Professor set me up in front of the photocopier in the Writing Division office. 'Pleased not to have to think about it myself. I don't trust myself around these machines.'

I laid each sheet carefully on the glass, snatching at sentences before I lowered the cover. Chandler's actual letters! Still, I couldn't believe it. Everything went wrong with the copier. The paper ran out. The ink ran out. The paper jammed. The pages got mixed up. A staple got trapped in the stapler. I couldn't find extra staples.

The Professor came in looking hopeful, a sheaf of pages in his hand. He saw the mess I was in and retreated to his room.

I made three sets of copies. One for the Columbia University Library. One for (Dr) Judith at the Bodley. One set for me. These last two sets, with the originals, I stuffed into my daypack.

I presented the Professor with the copies for the library.

He looked down at them.

'Thank you. Yes, thanks. I'm sure, um, the library will be most grateful. And, um ...'

He smiled broadly, almost, I'd say, mischievously, and extended his hand. 'I look forward to the book.'

I forced a smile. 'So do I.'

I thanked the Professor and left.

I squelched out of Dodge Hall into the sunshine. At 116th Street I descended into the underworld, waited uneasily on the crowded subway platform for the 'One' line to take me down to Columbus Circle, where I would connect with the

'D' line, which went all the way down to Sheep's Head Bay – which always reminded me of Goat's Head Soup, and not pleasantly. All the time my knuckles were white around the strap of my daypack.

At Church Avenue I emerged out of the ground and ebbed my way slowly with the tide of brown faces around the corner. Thankfully the crack guy wasn't in the foyer. I never knew what to say to him. How armed he was. I got the three locks open on the apartment door and the smell of cat litter hit me. I closed the door, leant back against it, peeled my fingers from the strap of the daypack and laughed with relief. Consuela, Katarina's blind white cat, mewed her way uncertainly towards me and found her head against my hand as I crouched down to say hello.

Katarina wasn't home. She was up-river at the Poughkeepsie Art Show, shocking the locals. I went into the kitchen, pulled out a chair, sat at the table, reached across to open the fridge, took out a cigarette, lit it, drew back deeply and slipped the letters from the yellow envelope on to the table in front of me.

I can only give you words; I can only give you love

Dee's letter to Frank MacShane, 1980. Three letters from Helga to Dee, 1960. The two which Dee had written Helga in 1960 and 1961. Sixteen letters and two telegrams from Ray to Dee, 1956-57.

'I can still recall that correspondence and its effects on me with the clarity of an A1 dream,' Dee wrote to Helga in 1960. To the Professor in 1980 she commented that on re-reading the letters she realised how 'blindly selfish' she had been then, 'uncaring of the feelings I evoked'. Dee's memory filled in the gaps between the letters, but that was missing for me. I read Ray's letters as if I was watching events from the wings of a stage, getting a new angle on a drama which I'd already seen unfold. I'd read the Professor's 'Revenge', the 'official' version of Chandler's life. I'd been through his sifted edition of Ray's own version in the *Selected Letters*. I'd heard Dee's side of their story. Now I was reading the words straight from Chandler's own mouth. And a strange emptiness surrounded the letters: Ray was talking to himself, alone on centre stage with no one to feed him his lines.

The tone was much as I had guessed from the extracts in the *Selected Letters* – only more so. And what became apparent was the dexterity of the Professor's editing. Reading the whole of Ray's correspondence, I could see how carefully the Professor had steered around the personal details inappropriate for the *Selected Letters*.

Ray commented several times about Deirdre's feelings towards him, about her 'halfway falling in love with me at long distance'. And I was left still wondering what exactly Dee had written to him.

'Are all those crosses kisses?' he wrote. 'Am I entitled to them?'

'Ray wrote to me more as father to daughter, than writer to writer,' Dee told Helga. And yet in one letter Ray writes, 'So here we are again. How do I write to you? As an older brother? It just does not suit me. You say that at the university you have never been kissed. I should remedy that rapidly.' And in another, 'I should like to write love letters, but the difference in our ages is so great that it would be absurd.'

Ray was trying to field her romantic naivety while he, the single man alone in La Jolla, even in his sixties, succumbed to it to a greater degree than the extracts I had read originally indicated. Coyly, in a subsequent letter he wrote, 'Now really darling, if I said you were half in love with me at long distance, surely you didn't think I was imagining any romantic involvment? Not at my age, surely?'

It was no wonder the young Deirdre was confused. This was the man who allowed his Australian secretary to wear his wife's ring, while complaining of the demands she was making of him. He did, however, seem to know how frail he was. He wrote to Deirdre, 'My heart is in your hands. Hold it gently, it is rather tired.'

Chandler's response to Dee's involvement with Barry was here played out in full. On 6 May 1957 he sent a telegram:

I AM ANGRY IF POSSIBLE AWAIT LETTER I HAVE MANY EXACTING THINGS TO DO HAVE APPARENTLY SPENT TOO MUCH OF MYSELF ON YOU WITHOUT KNOWING SITUATION CLEARLY LOVE RAY.

Over the next three letters he is blunt, and his exasperation appears genuine:

'I don't care how much you like this Barry, he is all wrong for you ... I only wish to God you could get into bed with him.'

'Do you really want to have breakfast every morning with a man whose every word you can anticipate? ... I have only one thing left to say: ... if you become formally engaged to this chap ... you are an idiot.'

'Almost, insulting as this may sound to you, I wish that I, even at my age, could have an affair with you ... I could, I think, make you realise that love is an infinite tenderness, an infinite respect, and that if it is ever for one instant mechanical or boring, it is a far greater sin against the beauty of life, than an unconventional, but very sincere, attempt to achieve an idealistic relationship.'

With resignation, he ends the letter: 'I can only try to give you what knowledge of life I may have acquired. I can't give you what you will know twenty years from now; I can only give you words; I can only give you love.'

In personal matters he tended to be vague. By colouring memory and maintaining distance on personal detail, he appeared to be avoiding the painful immediacy of his loneliness in La Jolla. Peaks of eloquence rise above the mist covering his own affairs. There are moving passages about Cissy, about the nature of love and loss, but the reality of their marital imperfection has gone through some romantic rewriting. He was not as faithful, nor the marriage as perfect, as he wanted to remember.

Chandler's comments about Hemingway come to mind.

Chandler may no longer have been able to 'throw the high, hard one', but he didn't just walk off the mound and weep. He threw his heart instead. These letters were representative of what was happening to him at the time: he expended on correspondence the writing energy he could no longer put into fiction. He did what he could with the abilities he had left. In the letters of this period Chandler's prose still stands.

He devoted paragraphs to the spartan life of an Eton schoolboy, to a concise description of his Australian secretary's marriage breakdown, to the subtle personality of his cat Taki. He sent Dee the photo of Natasha Spender ('an English lady I am very fond of') and wrote: 'She is a superb pianist. As a concert artist she has one great advantage; she is tall, stately, very beautiful, with luminous eyes and a magnificent carriage. One rather cynical London newspaperman told me it was worth the price of admission merely to see her walk out on the stage.' These were the details Deirdre had little desire to receive.

But all this was removed from the reality of his life at the time. Most obviously, he did not once mention his struggle with alcohol. In July 1956, after spending two weeks drying out in the Las Encinas Sanitorium at Pasadena, he wrote simply, 'I have been away and not too well.' In his next letter, 2 November, he writes, 'I am not too well and have a lot of problems, as who hasn't?'

It was in the period between these two letters that he had initiated contact with Louise Delamotte, decided to marry her, and under the stress of this rushed decision, changed his mind and returned alone to sit amongst the dusty furniture of his marriage in the crowded apartment in La Jolla.

This vagueness could have been a straightforward decision not to involve Dee in the complications of his life at the time. But it could also be seen as a deliberate whitewash, concious elusiveness, unconscious denial.

Reaching the last letters, it became apparent why Dee was hurt by Ray's glib dismissals. On 8 May 1957 he wrote, 'Your snapshots don't suggest at all that you are a neurotic type. The loneliness, the inability to form close friendships ... has probably happened to many people of about your age, intelligent, clever, analytical, over-introspective people.' Such a clinical reduction would not be what a young woman would want to hear after she had emptied her heart to a distant confessor. Elsewhere he wrote, 'Your intense introspectiveness worries me. At times it seems almost morbid.'

The letter dated 4 September 1957 indicated the end that Dee had described. The illusion finally could not bear the weight of reality. 'I have the photograph you sent me, but after careful consideration I have to confess that to me it is just not right. I can't imagine a girl with your brains really having that expression: too mild, too bucolic, almost, if you won't be angry with me, cowlike.' A compliment whipped away with an insult. With this, Dee decided she had had enough.

Ray ends, 'Much love, more later.'

It was the last letter. There was no more.

I turned the page over and sat at the kitchen table in the evening half-light. Out the window it had been mid-afternoon when I started. Now the children playing on the street had gone inside and I could smell dinners cooking. The fridge whirred, the lonely aroma of used cat litter seeped into me.

So this was what the search had been all about. Sixteen letters, two telegrams. An old man standing alone on centre stage, declaiming in the spotlight, the theatre empty but for one young woman in the stalls, watching with wide eyes, sucking her pen. He was a sad character, unsteady on his feet, but proud, keeping his place on the mound, pitching them. A small table beside him, a cigarette smoking in the ashtray, a half-empty bottle of vodka, a glass.

I leant behind me and flicked on the kitchen fluorescent light. I let my eyes adjust to the brightness and picked up my pen.

Brooklyn
June 1989

Dear Dee

I've got them. I've found the letters ...

yes!

Bodleian Library
16 June 1989

Dear Mr Close

How very kind of you to send us copies of Chandler's correspondence with Deirdre Gartrell. I've had the letters bound and catalogued (MS.Facs.c.117) and they really are a most welcome addition to our holdings. Your detective work has been impeccable. I'm only sorry that Bodley isn't on your immediate itinerary, but you must look me up if you ever do come to Oxford.

It must have been good to meet Frank MacShane. I drew on his book quite heavily when cataloguing our papers. Did you know that Houghton Mifflin have commissioned another biography? Its author is due to start work on the collection in July.

Anyway, it has been a pleasure to correspond with you. Good luck with your own work.

Yours sincerely
Judith Priestman (Dr)

This was waiting for me when I got back to Australia. Ref JAP/JAS. There were two errors, both forgotten s's that she had added in biro. Oh delirious flaws! Did I care? Never! 'Your detective work'. Yes! It had all been worth it.

Part ten
green pastures parched brown

I was mistaken

If I thought it was all over then, I was mistaken – this is the story that started when I started to write the story.

Dee and I had become friends. We exchanged letters. She kept me up to date with family news, with her and Walter's efforts to sell their house in town, with progress on the plans out at The Block. I responded with stories about my life in Sydney, about my jobs, and about life with Fiona. Occasionally, between our preoccupations, we remembered Chandler.

When I first met Dee, I was mowing lawns with a bloke in Vaucluse. To earn the money to go to America, I spent a summer working as a labourer for a builder friend. To repay the Mastercard debt when I came back, I drove a florist's delivery van around the centre of Sydney. I earned money any way I could. I licked envelopes, worked on elections, tended the bar at an old girlfriend's wedding.

By the time I came to actually write the book I was working as a steward on cruise boats on Sydney Harbour. In between, I climbed the stairs to the Bondi Department of Social Security and lined up with the rest of them. Young mums with tattoos and empty strollers, cooing to the grizzling babies in their arms. Aboriginal kids with red, black and yellow beanies, packs of Horizon 50s square at the shoulders of their T-shirts. Young arties with purple hair and paint-splattered jeans; heavy-jowled blokes in suit coats and Levis, that preoccupied look behind their glasses, that desk-dwelling pallor. Each of us with a form in our hand, eyeing off the others. The great unwashed.

horizon distant, sky high

Over the years I had been welcomed into Dee and Walter's family. Sometimes I felt they viewed me almost as a surrogate son. They were keen for me to meet their children. I visited Ellen at her house in the Blue Mountains and we became friends. One night we went together to see her brother Rolf, the jazz bass player, at a club in Sydney. Svend still lived at home when I first went up to Bathurst and I got to know him through my subsequent visits. He was an apprentice carpenter with Walter's company. He spent his weekends at the local gliding club.

Dee and Walter had been generous and hospitable towards me. They had fed me and housed me and even, when I came back from the States, given me work helping out at The Block. We worked side by side manhandling rocks and attempting to rabbit-proof the fence around the property. We laid the steel reinforcing for the slab of the new shed, and Walter let me try my hand at a few courses of bricklaying. After work, cleaned up around the dinner table, I was a good excuse for him to drink more than his one-an-evening whisky.

I liked this family and their straightforward country values. I liked working with Walter out at The Block. The air was clean, the sky was high. I enjoyed the physical labour, feeling my muscles working. Weekends out at The Block made my adrenaline weekdays in city traffic seem all the more insane.

Walter and I sat down to enamel mugs of black morning tea, and the 'black and white' sandwiches (one side white, the other black rye) that Dee made for us, and I cradled my tea and looked out over the river to the blue hills in the distance. I didn't consider at all that what I was doing might cause me trouble later on.

all right, till something goes wrong

Initially, I think, Dee and Walter were excited by my interest in Dee's past with Ray. Bemused, at any rate, and curious to find out more about me, where exactly I was coming from. They answered my questions with patience and questioned me about my own life, accepting my answers with head-shaking amusement, but without apparent judgement.

Very early on, in my second letter to Dee, I had asked whether this episode of her life might not be something she wanted to write about herself. 'Are you concerned I am stealing your story?' I had asked. She reassured me that this was not a part of her life she had thought of writing about. Three decades as a mother, and life now as a grandmother, had matured her own writing aspirations. What she wanted to write were children's stories about her childhood, stories for her grandchildren, and for their children.

For the entire period of researching this book, locating Deirdre, and searching for the letters, I had put off the serious nuts-and-bolts consideration of how I would eventually write it, trusting that a route through the darkness would appear when the time came. Through the months and years of casually following each lead as it came, I don't think I once considered that what I was doing was work.

But after the search was over, after I'd found the letters and returned from America, after the trip was finally paid off and the debris from the explosion in my personal life had started to settle, I eventually sat down to consider in what form I wanted this book to emerge. That is what got me into trouble.

I began to realise that the friendship I had built up with Dee and Walter, far from being a conduit for the flow of the story, was actually censoring me. I had unwisely confused business and friendship. When it came to the writing, this book was business, but what I shared with Dee and Walter was friendship. It was like selling a car to a friend. Everything is all right until something goes wrong.

That 'something' went wrong with Dee and Walter when I realised that the book I wanted to write was not the book

I had originally imagined. When I first came across Ray's letters to Dee, my fascination was that they had formed such a close relationship without ever meeting. My idea then, although it only became clear later on, was to write a novel based upon this relationship, moving it forward into my own time, colouring it with my own experience.

But since then events had altered in my own life, new information, if you like, had come to light. That book was no longer possible. I still wanted to write about Chandler and Deirdre. ('I couldn't overlook the fact that I had a reason, a feeling for starting to write it and I'd be damned if I wasn't going to lick it.') But it would have to be another book. That book would have to be the actual story of Ray and Dee. And underneath that, of Julia, Fiona and me.

the love letters of the century

This was the story I started with.

Two people are writing to each other. They have never met. They aren't unhappy in their own lives. They've got relationships, jobs, after a fashion, friends and family. They've got real lives. But in their lives is the need to sit at a desk and write. I had a definite couple in mind. Two individuals, hundreds of miles between them, their lives at either end of a thin tarmac thread. They know nothing of each other, and then they start to write.

One of them reads a story in a magazine. It stops him. He reads it again. He puts it down and sits at his desk and stares out his window. From his window by the sea he can see this story, set in a shingled house in a country town by a river a long way away. He can smell the jasmine growing over the fence, he can close his eyes and feel the summer dusk in the air. He can see the eyes of the woman in the story. He can see the cigarette in her hand. He can feel her blankness, he can feel the waiting. The pressure in the air. Humid. Midsummer. The build up before release.

He writes a letter to the writer of the story. He sends it to the magazine with Please Forward printed neatly on the front of the envelope. He writes the letter in biro on a piece of unlined A4 typing paper. He compliments the writer of the story. He walks up to the Bondi Road post office, posts the letter and forgets about it.

He gets a reply.

The two writers talk to each other from their rooms at either end of the long thin road. They sit at their desks and write in their letters things they aren't sure they have ever thought until then. They discover things in their letters they didn't know before. They talk about their lives, their families, their friends, what they read, what movies they watch, what they do when they get up in the morning, what time the mail arrives and how they use the time until it does.

Through their letters the two realise that they want more than they've got. Something her husband, his girlfriend, their friends and jobs aren't providing. He sits at his desk overlooking the red roofs to the blue sea of Bondi and tries to imagine her life in the house by a wide river six hundred and forty-two bitumen kilometres away. Her husband's house. He imagines her sitting at her desk in the corner of the verandah that is hers, and imagines her tortoiseshell cat curling herself around her ankles, and her reaching down with her left hand to tickle its neck while she rests her elbows on the desk and puts the end of her pen in her mouth (a Lamy fountain pen, a gift from her husband, blue) and gazes out the louvred window at the bougainvillea and jasmine growing over the paling fence dividing her house, her husband's house, from the one next door.

They send no photos. They have never seen each other, except in their minds, in their dreams. I've found this quote, she writes one day: 'My favourite form of communication is in the beyond: in dreams. To dream of someone. The second choice is correspondence. Letters are a form of communicating in the beyond, less perfect than dreams, but subject to the same laws.'

How about this, he writes back: 'God I wish I'd kept those letters. They were the love letters of the century, any century.'

One day her husband comes to her on the verandah and crawls under her desk and rubs himself against her legs like a cat and turns his face up at her and says, 'Look at me. You never look at me.'

She writes and tells this to him in Bondi. She writes at the very time her husband is under the desk, and she writes what he says to her, and asks, 'What am I going to do?'

In Bondi he lies in the bed he shares with his girlfriend, holding a book he isn't reading. His girlfriend pushes up behind him and wraps her limbs around him like an octopus and he feels the skin of her cheek against his neck and he feels his heart against his ribs and he knows he must do something. One thing, anything.

But he doesn't know what the one thing is, he can't locate the one thing anywhere to know how to do it. There is, however, one thing he knows how to do. He knows the comfort of a letter. On the wall above his desk he has words written on cards. On one is written: 'He lay alone in the undertaker's parlour, reaping the neglect his indecision had earned him.'

The letters continue. For months, for a year, the two write to each other. They wonder if they will ever meet, if they should risk ever meeting. 'What if you took one look at me and regretted everything?' she asks. 'I'm not pretty. I'm just a country girl with big ears. You'd probably walk out of the room and I'd never hear from you again.'

She writes, 'My husband says he wishes he was my desk. Then at least he'd know all the things he knows I'm not telling him. He says if he's going to be a piece of the furniture he might as well be the only piece of furniture I care about.'

Her husband crawls under her desk. His girlfriend lies cold and confused in their bed. On the louvred verandah, on the closed-in balcony overlooking the street, the dreaming continues, until one day the two leave their rooms and meet.

This is what the story became. The start, if you like, of the real story.

real story

I'd met Julia. And Fiona and I had to work out what to do.

cross that border, buddy

I flew to Los Angeles on a return ticket to Sydney. Fiona had a round-the-world ticket which took her to Los Angeles, New York, London, and back to Sydney. I saw her off on the airport bus at the World Trade Center in New York and didn't expect to see her again until Sydney, two months later. We had done a lot of talking, but in those various kitchens and rental cars and hotel rooms many thousands of miles from home nothing had been really resolved. We were too far removed from our usual world. Everything seemed alien in those places, not just the issue of what our lives would amount to when we got home. We decided to put any big decisions on hold.

To get back to Los Angeles from New York I did a DriveAway, delivering a Honda Civic for an ear, nose and throat man moving from Queens, Brooklyn to Monterey, California. A DriveAway is a concept which is almost impossible to contemplate in Australia – you give your car to a total stranger who drives it a long distance, one way, which you don't want to drive yourself. You fly and the car is there when you arrive. It indicates the different relationship we have with our cars. I cannot imagine an Australian giving his car to a total stranger in anything but the most life-threatening emergency.

My companion was a 6'2" 23-year-old Eng Lit graduate who seemed to be literate, exclusively, in the Grateful Dead. My primary concern, when we went to collect the Honda Civic in Queens, was that it not have a cassette deck. Thankfully it did not. We crossed America, two six-footers in a tiny Japanese car, listening to local C & W stations and trying to locate a mutual understanding of English Literature, as learnt on different continents, both of them a world away from England. Chandler's letters lay asleep in my pack on the back seat. A yellow envelope waiting to happen.

On the West Coast I had arranged to stay with Fiona's sister-in-law's brother in Irvine, south of LA, and I called him from a kerbside payphone behind Cesar's Palace in Las Vegas to confirm our arrangements. 'It's you,' he said. 'There's someone here who wants to talk to you.' Fiona had changed her ticket to fly home via Los Angeles. When I uncurled myself from the lap of the Civic in Irvine she was there, walking down the path to greet me.

Over the next few days, in that condo on the edge of the orange groves, we had discussions. Eucalypts hung over the balcony railing, taunting us with their promise of home. We knew we couldn't go on like this. We both wanted things to change. If we were going to go back to Sydney as a couple, we wanted something firmed between us. On that balcony, thousands of miles from home, we made arrangements. We decided a few things.

The next day at the Ugly Duckling lot in Irvine we took out another gunmetal green Buick (with loose steering) which, we were told under threat of every car rental law in the US, we could take anywhere in the world but Mexico. 'Cross that border, buddy,' the bloke said, 'And ...' He shook his head and raised his hands in the air.

But that Saturday afternoon we took the 1-5 south and did cross the border into Mexico. We left the Ugly Duckling parked in a Tijuana backlot and three hours later, joined the queue to cross the border back again. Not thinking about the US rental car laws. Not thinking once about the remains of Raymond Chandler, only a few miles away in the Mount Hope Cemetery, San Diego. Not thinking.

It takes along time to cross the border back into the US at Tijuana on a hot Saturday afternoon in July. Hawkers wind through the queue of stationary cars, selling everything from chewing gum to carved marble statuetes of Mary Magdalene. I dozed off and woke, God knows how long later, but it felt much later, and Fiona was looking at me and the look was different to any other look before, and she said, 'I'm trying to imagine you at sixty-five. I think you'll be all right.'

We got through the border, headed north up the 1-5 and took the San Diego turnoff, winding along the beachfront, not quite as Marlowe had after driving Terry Lennox to his Tijuana escape in *The Long Goodbye* – 'through a town, down a hill, along a stretch of beach, through a town, down a hill, along a stretch of beach' – but the reluctant, overdeveloped equivalent forty years on.

We even stopped in La Jolla but I doubt I thought about Raymond Chandler even once that afternoon. Perhaps we drove right past Chandler and Cissy's house at 6005 Camino de la Costa and never realised. Perhaps we even stopped outside the apartment at 6925 Neptune when we parked the Ugly Duckling and went for a walk on the beach. Perhaps we trod the sand that Chandler had trod. Perhaps. Maybe. Didn't matter anyway. That afternoon Chandler didn't enter my mind.

We found a black dog-chewed frisbee in the sand and I tried to teach Fiona how to throw. That frisbee. It was more important to me that afternoon than Raymond Chandler ever was. How can I explain this thing? It got out of hand. We argued over it. It came between us. It was crucial to me that Fiona know how to throw that stupid piece of black plastic. I remember the gravity of this in my mind. What mattered that afternoon in La Jolla wasn't Raymond Chandler or his letters to Dee or his grave on the hill looking over us. What mattered to me was that Fiona should know how to throw the frisbee, because we were married now, we were together for life.

the mail

Or so I thought.

The first thing I did when I got back was fall on my knees and kiss the clammy winter sand of Bondi Beach. The second thing was ring Dee. The third, with the yellow envelope in my daypack, was go down to Central and buy a ticket on the XPT to Bathurst.

It was a clear and sunny winter day. Ben Chifley's

locomotive had gone from under its special roof outside the station. On loan to somewhere for something. Back in service on the Puffing Billy nostalgia circuit, maybe – the only trains these days with a hope of earning their keep. The sun was high and I set off to walk from the station, my daypack slung over my shoulder.

Dee answered the door. I held the yellow envelope in my hand, smiling broadly.

'The mail,' I said. 'Special delivery.'

the past

She greeted me warmly but put the envelope aside without even looking inside. It wasn't the reaction I'd expected. It certainly wasn't enthusiastic. We didn't sit down and go through the letters together laughing and sighing, nothing like that. I spent the afternoon with Walter out at The Block and when we got back I asked if she had read them. Yes, she said, she had. She was standing at the sink in the small downstairs kitchen peeling potatoes for dinner.

'And?' I said.

She shrugged, and kept her eyes down.

the present

Dee and I have never discussed the letters. Perhaps by that stage things were already starting to clam up between us. The letters were sad, was all she said. They were my business now, my future. For Dee they were the past. A part of her childhood, of her growing up.

I left in the morning and went back to Sydney and got on with married life. I got the job driving the van delivering flowers. Dee and I kept writing.

the future

Fiona and I found a place down in Bondi Beach, with a cat called Yoyo. Yoyo came with the flat. He was a grey longhair with green eyes and a sensual disposition. He liked a good back massage. And he liked women better that men. He always liked Fiona better than me. We changed his name to Kevin and moved in.

Philip was boarded out with his uncle. I had visiting rights, of course. Some days when I had finished work I'd stop in at my brother's little house behind Charing Cross, and Philip and I would walk across to the rocks overlooking Queens Park and watch the sun set over Randwick Racecourse and talk about things.

Fiona and I weren't happy. It wasn't right. We ate like strangers across the dinner table. The room was loud with silence. We were supposed to be at the start of something new but the past was thick in the air like noxious gas. It deadened our limbs. We couldn't move.

Fiona's conditions were that I stop writing to Julia: I didn't see her, I didn't talk about her, she's over. She's gone. She's the past. I agreed. We had both wanted to come back to Australia with the future ahead, not the past to go back to.

But I wrote Julia one more letter. I told her Fiona and I were married. I told her I wouldn't be able to see her, to write to her, to think about her.

Julia had always said she didn't mind if I stayed with Fiona. It'd be easier if I did. Then she wouldn't have to decide for herself whether to abandon the security of married life and go off into the unknown with me. Instead, what she hoped for was some sort of clandestine relationship, extending comfortably into our parallel futures. When she heard my news these hopes were dashed.

I found this out by postcard, from her. She had left her husband and moved to Sydney. She found a job in a library. She was staying in Bronte, which wasn't very far from Bondi. Not far enough at all.

Once again everything changed.

stalking phantoms, reaping neglect

I moved out from Fiona, scooped up Philip, and found a flat in an old crumbling mansion in Coogee. I had the old billiards room out the back. It wasn't bad. Philip had a friend, a nervous black kitten who had been adopted by tenants of the flats. He stalked phantoms in the long grass at the back of the building while the kookaburra who lived in the tree outside my window tilted its head to watch. Someone had named the kitten Desmond Tutu. Desmond and Philip used to wrestle in the grass – a big ginger tom with his skittish black shadow.

I kept Dee informed of developments. She had been excited about our Mexican marriage. She had sent a wedding card and offered us a weekend in The Shack by the river for a honeymoon. She expressed sadness at our abrupt separation. She had never met Fiona.

It wasn't long before Julia left Sydney and moved to her parents' farm where, she said, she planned to write a novel. We went back to writing letters, letters every week, every day, aching with our situation. I kept driving the van. Sometimes she would ring while I was driving, trapped in a gridlock on George Street or speeding out across the Glebe Island Bridge with a sour-smelling flower arrangement in the back destined for an advertising agency at Balmain, the massive afternoon clouds boiling in the sky over Blackwattle Bay.

'What's it like up there?' I'd ask, and her voice would come out from under the dashboard, thin and distant. 'The storm has just started,' she'd say. 'I can see it moving over the river. I'd better hang up. I miss you. I want you. What are we going to do?' And then the line would go dense with static, and she'd be gone. We had no idea what we were going to do. I'd keep driving, rounding the lights at White Bay into Victoria Road and leaning over the steering wheel at the turn-off into Mullins Street with a thick muggy desolation in my stomach.

I had to keep driving. I had to pay for the divorce now, as well. I apologised to Fiona so many times that we both got sick of the sound of my voice. I lay alone at night, reaping the neglect my indecision had earned me. To otherwise engage my mind I tried to work out how on earth I was going to write this book.

I wrote to Dee. I told her that a novel didn't seem to be the way any more. I said that perhaps I should come up and we could discuss it. She wrote back saying she thought that was a good idea.

hard times

It was summer. Bathurst was hot and dry and still with that choking inland heat you forget about on the coast. The green paddocks were parched brown, thin stalky grass stood hard and dry in the ground. It hadn't rained since November. Out at The Block the grass crunched underfoot and the boughs of the eucalypts drooped low and still as if the trees themselves were gradually succumbing to thirst. Small rainless clouds drifted high in the hot blue sky.

Dee and Walter still hadn't sold the house in town, but they were ready to make the move when a buyer did come along. They had packed their belongings in carefully labelled boxes and taken them out to The Block and stored them neatly on demountable shelves in the big shed, which had been a square grid of steel reinforcing laid on industrial orange plastic on the ground the last time I'd seen it.

They spent more time out at The Block now. Walter had retired, and they stayed over in the little shack by the river whenever they could. In town they lived in the downstairs guest flat and kept the upper floor empty and clean. Svend had moved out and was living in a flat in town. One night he came to his parents' place for dinner and sat at the table with his arms around his plate. 'Do you guys know how much it's cost me to move out of this joint? Two thousand dollars.' He shook his head. 'They never told me it'd cost this much to grow up.'

The other kids had had their share of change as well. Ellen had moved to Sydney to try to find a job which wasn't there.

Rolf's girlfriend had asked him to move out, and he'd found a flat in Bondi with a woman called Fiona, which I didn't believe when Dee first told me. The oldest brother, who I hadn't met, had broken up with his wife, with Dee and Walter's only two grandchildren caught in the fray. Dee's mother, aged eighty-six, had fallen and broken her leg, and although she was out of the wheelchair and walking with a stick and crutches, they were both forced to face the fact that when you're eighty-six you don't get better forever.

Everything stable for Dee and Walter seemed to be falling away around them. They believed in hard work and family values and had tried to invest in their children as much of that wisdom as they felt they'd learnt. But over a period of months, none of this seemed to be adding up to anything at all.

When Dee met me at the station she gave me a hug and said, 'Hard times all round, eh?'

thank god for green beans

The country around might have been dying of thirst, but the Place of the Trees was on town water and Dee's vegetable garden was leafy and green. In the cool of dusk we went out to pick greens for dinner. We talked softly as we worked our way down the trellised rows, snapping fat purple beans from their stalks.

'I love this garden,' Dee said. 'Being able to come out here by myself and potter around with nothing else to think about has been the only thing keeping me sane over the last few months.'

She puffed out a laugh.

'I think Walter and I must have been getting too pleased with ourselves. We had our thirtieth anniversary last December, you know. More than half my life.' She sighed. 'I suppose we were getting complacent, and God decided to shuffle a few things around to remind us of our place. It's been hard for both of us. We've had to reassess so much of what we believe. The world has changed and the values we gave the kids don't seem to apply anymore. Ellen applies for job after job and finds sixty other applicants in front of her and has to go on the dole. We can't sell the house because of the recession we had to have. Rolf's girlfriend decides she wants more space so he's got to move out. Erik's wife isn't sure she wants to be married any more, so she takes the kids and leaves. As far as we're concerned none of this should have happened. And it all seems to have come at once. Thank God for green beans and cherry tomatoes, I say. And thank God Walter and I have got each other.'

She looked out across the yard to the golden horizon behind the trees in the west. 'More than half my life. And it's gone so fast.'

two people

When I started out to write fiction I had the great disadvantage of having absolutely no talent for it. I couldn't get characters in and out of rooms. They lost their hats and so did I. If more than two people were on a scene I couldn't keep one of them alive. This failing is still with me, of course, to some extent. Give me two people snotting each other across a desk and I am happy. A crowded canvas just bewilders me.

The following morning we took our places at the round table upstairs. The windows were open. The long hanging leaves of the gum tree glowed in the morning sun. Small green wrens flittered along the wooden railing of the balcony, twittering over the rim of the bird bath and sending out a fine spray of droplets as they washed and shook themselves dry.

It was hot already. Walter had gone off to The Block under the broad brim of his straw hat, his styrofoam water cooler clattering with iceblocks. Inside the house it was pleasant. The tabletop was cool against the undersides of my forearms.

Dee laid her hands in front of her on the table.

'So. Tell me what you've got in mind.'

'Okay. The more I think about it, the actual story of you and Ray is too interesting to muck around with. That's what I want to write.'

She looked at me, saying nothing. Her hair, quite grey now, was clasped up on top of her head. She was wearing a soft-green cotton blouse. Beneath the table she had on jeans and light white sandals.

She said, 'So what does that mean exactly?'

'It means the true story: Ray's life at the time, and your life, and how it was, out of these different worlds, the two of you wrote to each other – and why, for your own reasons, you kept writing.'

She nodded, keeping me in her gaze.

'That's the past. Then there's the present ...'

She waited.

'Which is the story of how I came across the extracts in the *Selected Letters*, and how I started looking for this Deirdre who I knew nothing about, except that she was at university in Armidale in 1957. How I rang the university, then sent letters off around the world, until eventually I found her – you – by looking up the Sydney telephone book. And, I'll talk about getting the train up and meeting you and Walter, and how you couldn't find the letters anywhere, and how eventually I went to America and found them in New York, and, I suppose, to round that off, what my motivation was for being interested in the first place.'

I emptied my hands into the air.

'That's about all. That's enough.'

She didn't move.

'And my idea is to print the letters in full at the end of the book.'

'All the letters?'

I nodded. 'They're the reason for the whole thing, after all.'

'And you definitely want to include Walter and me?'

'Yes.'

'But you'll change our names?'

'If you want me to.'

'Absolutely we want you to. You don't seem to realise

what you're asking. When your letter came we sat down and talked about this. We don't like this idea. We don't want you to do it.'

'Okay.' I could feel myself blushing. I said softly. 'What part don't you like?'

'Well, we certainly don't want you to put our names in. And we aren't all that keen on actual details from our lives being in there either. When you first came here you said you were researching for a novel. That was fair enough. We saw no harm in that. We never thought that our lives now would end up in a book.'

She kept speaking before I could answer.

'Look. There's something I've got to get off my chest. Something you said in a letter which really made me angry. I didn't know if I was overreacting, or if I really did have reason to be upset. But, well, it might as well be dealt with now.'

She kept her eyes fixed on mine.

'You suggested in a letter that I "had the hots for Walter". I hated that. I did not "have the hots" for Walter. That's a horrible modern expression, something dogs get for each other. What I felt for Walter and what I still feel . . .'

She took a breath.

'I was a virgin when I met Walter. I felt desire but I had no idea what it really meant physically. I yearned for him, but in a deeply romantic way. I knew he was special. It wasn't just sex. It was much more than that. I felt him in my heart. That is not what I call "having the hots". How you could even use an ugly term like that I don't know.'

I lowered my head into my hands. Oh God. It was a throwaway phrase I had used when I was trying to work out the chronology of Dee's life at the time. I raised my head. Dee was looking at me with such gravity I couldn't hold back a gurgle of laughter.

'Dee, I'm sorry. I had no idea you'd take it that way. I was being flippant. I apologise. I'm sorry. I had no intention of demeaning your relationship with Walter. I'm sorry. Really.'

She kept the hardness in her eyes, then looked up to the ceiling.

'The thing is ...' She sighed hard, breathed in deeply, and lowered her eyes to meet mine. 'Walter and I welcomed you into our house, we gave you our hospitality, we opened our lives to you. We took you out to The Block, our private place, our retreat. We fed you and gave you a bed. We trusted you. We told you our stories because you were interested. You never told us you would be using what we told you privately in your book, and if you had, if you'd had a tape recorder in our faces as we spoke, we would have spoken differently. We did all this because we liked you. We still like you.'

She pinned me again with the hard gaze.

'Please don't let us regret it. You want to print the letters in full. That's something we've never discussed. I don't know if I like that idea either. They were private letters written personally to me. It doesn't matter how long ago they were, they're still my life. They still have meaning for me. I don't mind you taking extracts. But I don't think I want you to print them in full. You never said you wanted to do that. And Walter. Why do you have to have Walter in it at all? It hasn't really got anything to do with him, has it?'

'Dee, Walter is a big part of it. He was there before you ever wrote to Ray. If you'd been involved with Walter, you agree you probably would never have written.'

She stared at me without answering then looked away. The house was silent until she turned back. 'I just don't see why you have to do this. Don't you think it'd be better for you to write your own story? I still think this is the issue. You're hiding behind Ray. And now you want to hide behind me. And Walter. You're not confident enough to go out with a book under your own name. You need the name of Raymond Chandler on the cover. That's what I think is the real issue here. You don't trust yourself. So you're using Ray, and you're using me. And you're using Walter.'

For a minute or so we said nothing. The temperature in the room had dropped about ten degrees. Even the little wrens had jumped ship. There was no sound. No twittering, no wind, not the passing of a car on a faraway street.

'Dee, it just seems pointless to make something up when

the real story is as good as it is. What's interesting is that you, a girl from Orange, NSW, Australia, should have had this correspondence with Raymond Chandler, probably the best known crime writer – '

'See, you're just in awe of him.'

I took a breath, closed my eyes and opened them. 'It's not that. It's not that I'm in awe of him. It's a great story, that's what it is. That you should have formed the relationship you did. Purely by letters. Without ever meeting. And you didn't even like his books. You didn't even read them!'

She turned back to me, her eyes glassy.

'Dee, the fact that your relationship with Ray actually took place is what's interesting. I've stumbled, quite innocently, across this fascinating story. What am I supposed to do? Throw it away, ignore it, because I didn't think it up?'

Dee looked down at her hands. Very quietly she said, 'I don't know.'

'It's a great story, Dee. Really. Walter. Barry. Everything. It all fits in.'

She looked away again out the window. I watched the side of her face.

'You want to use Barry as well?'

'He is pretty central. Ray's reaction and all.'

'But you'll change his name too?'

I paused. She turned to look at me, and I kept her gaze for a moment. I said quietly, 'Yes. If you like.'

'I would like. And Margaret?'

'Margaret? I hadn't thought of her.'

'Ray mentioned her in one of the letters – jumping up and down on the bed when he rang and I told her about him for the first time.'

I smiled.

'You're right. I'd forgotten about that. Do you want me to change her name too?'

Dee nodded once, with great tiredness, and closed her eyes. 'Yes, I do want you to change her name. I want you to change all the names.'

hands

'Dee, we don't have to fight. This doesn't have to be a battle.'

Dee shrugged.

'No, we don't have to fight. I don't want to be enemies. But I want you to see our point of view. I don't want you to think you can run all over us just because you're holding the pen.'

She kept her hard stare, then the corners of her mouth cracked into a smile.

'A blue biro, Bic medium point. On unlined A4 paper.'

'Dee, I'm not out to tell lies.'

'You might not mean to.'

The room was silent. Outside a bough of the tree moved against another, a harsh scraping sound. When she looked up tears had filled her eyes.

'It's just, this is our life. For you it's just a story and you'll walk away from it. We can't do that. And at the moment ... at the moment I just couldn't bear for anything else to go wrong. I just couldn't bear it.'

I reached across the table.

'Dee?'

Her eyes were rimmed with tears. She looked down at my hand, lifted her own and laid it tentatively in mine.

The house creaked around us. Our breathing was loud, the only sound in the room. We looked at each other and didn't speak. Then a wren landed on the verandah railing. We both looked over.

I gripped her hand.

'Dee? Really, we don't have to be enemies.'

She held hard on to my eyes for a moment, then nodded once. I looked down. I felt her hand squeeze mine.

they eat their young

This is where we left it.

In my preoccupation with my own upheaval in those months, I am sure I didn't realise how much strain Dee was under and, looking back, I realise I was naive in my hands-open attitude to Dee and Walter's privacy. I tried to put myself in their position, but in the end I think it was impossible. There was a fence between business and friendship, and we were on either side of it. And I am sure as a writer I saw things differently. Our job is to open doors and look under beds. Fiona left a note on my desk one day, something Dennis Potter said. 'Never trust a writer. They eat their young.'

Dee and I agreed I would show her the manuscript when I had finished. My publishers made it quite clear that without her written release the book would not go ahead. For them her approval was crucial to the future of the book. They wanted to be certain there was no possibility of legal action.

My greatest concern was that Dee might object to this last section. Despite having changed the names of her family and friends, I worried that she might still find my discussion of the real circumstances of her life too close to home. My guess was that she would approve the body of the book, perhaps with amendments, but that this part would have to be substantially altered because the details of her contemporary life would leave her feeling that her privacy was compromised after all.

I was completely wrong.

several years later

I finished the manuscript in 1993, several years later than I thought I would, and posted it to Dee in Bathurst. Some weeks later a card arrived. She had finished reading and suggested we meet to talk – in Katoomba, halfway between Bathurst and Sydney.

'Looking forward to meeting you again,' she wrote. 'Love from Dee.'

That was positive, I thought, but I was disturbed by her suggestion that if we could find no other place to meet, we might have to do a café crawl 'with our manuscripts and pencils and pads'. What did she have in mind? I realised, for the first time, that I might have over-estimated the likelihood of her approval.

I rang her. She was quite certain that she wanted to meet on neutral ground so I talked to the administrator of Varuna, the former home of the writer Eleanor Dark, now a residential writers' centre in Katoomba. Having been a guest in their early days, I had a small connection to the place. No problem, I was told. The living-room wasn't being used. We could meet there.

When I arrived at Varuna Dee was already there, out talking to a small bent woman in a terry-towelling hat. I approached them across the gravel drive. 'Here he is,' I heard Dee say.

It was four years since we had seen each other. Dee was taller and stouter than I remembered. Her hair was greyer. I opened my arms to her and we smiled and she let me hug her. But it was dry and perfunctory. Not at all like our first meeting.

We went inside and Dee laid her copy of the manuscript on the table in front of us. A neat stack of paper awaiting its fate. I lined the edges nervously. Dee had a businesslike air I didn't remember from before and she took a breath and got straight to the point. She would not approve this version I had given her. It was a compromise between fact and fiction in which she was too easily identifiable. She wanted a complete rewrite of all the sections relating to her. If she was going to be in the book at all she wanted it to be the truth. Her real name, and the details of her life correct. Without embellishment, distortion or invention.

Two inches of manuscript, many years of work, lay on the table between us. As Dee talked I glanced at the cover page, the proposed title, and noticed that she had suggested an amendment even to that. My heart sank. While the birds sang in the trees outside on that brisk Katoomba morning, I wanted to get up from the table and walk right away from the whole thing.

wrong, wrong, wrong, *wrong*!

I have never had a piece of fiction 'corrected' before, and I cannot recommend it as an uplifting experience. If felt like putting a poem through a lie detector test. It took two days. We started at the title and negotiated each page, line by line, to the end. If there was any mist on the moors at the start of this process, I can tell you, the sun was well and truly beating down by the end.

Dee had been very thorough. In the sections relating to her, she had written copious pencil notes questioning the version of her life which had taken root in my imagination. In many instances she was angry that I could have been so 'wrong' about her. There were exclamation marks and underlinings and upper case emphases, and sometimes all three at once.

Pointing out certain character peccadillos of which I was completely unaware, she drew my attention to the number of disfigured minor players I had set in the background to her story. My original version of Barry's father, for instance, had no arm, the result of a shunting accident. The university's postman had a harelip and, due to a 'childhood accident', no fingers – which at some point, I suppose, I thought was an interesting dilemma for a postman to face.

Dee protested strongly. 'The university didn't even have a postman! And you had to invent one who called me 'Eedwee' and only had stumps for fingers!'

'YUK!' she had written in the margin.

My imagination had led me astray. I had, for instance, made Dee's relationship with Barry a major event in her life – an emotional deflowering, if not an actual one. In my version, if not actually scarred by the emotional intensity I had bestowed upon the relationship, she had at least been bruised. But no, this had not been the case.

Dee's involvement with Barry, in fact, lasted only about three weeks. He was one of her many attempts to find romance, and whatever his attributes as a suitor, he was noteworthy primarily because of the fuss Ray created around him. Dee had already seen the last of Barry by the time Ray reacted so strongly to his presence.

Dee insisted that she was substantially more robust than I had imagined her. When Barry produced his packet of condoms, my Dee had burst into tears of shocked confusion. In fact, Barry's confidence that contraception would ease his way into Dee's heart only served to reinforce her suspicion that he was not the man for her. She reacted calmly and asked to be driven home, and never saw him again.

I had my Dee spending a lot of time staring out of her college window with her pen in her mouth, excruciatingly sensitive, a social inadequate who lived almost exclusively in her intense and self-sustaining fantasy life.

Not at all, Dee said. She might have been ill at ease with her surroundings and her contemporaries, but she had a lot of friends, or at least several faithful ones, and they were, she insisted, the most interesting people at the uni. It was the squealing girls and larrikin boys who she had no time for.

The young Dee was certainly naive, her middle-aged version told me, but she had a strong sense of what she wanted, of what was right and what was wrong. When Ray described her photo as 'cowlike' she did not wither in hurt and confusion, but instead knew his behaviour had crossed a line beyond which she did not feel comfortable, and she began the process of withdrawing.

And Dee's friend Margaret was not the vapid airhead I had made her, jealous and gossipy of Dee's 'famous American writer'. No, Margaret was nothing like that. She was an intense and spiritual woman who lit candles and laid out tarot cards. And Margaret did not even know about Dee's friendship with Ray. No one did. It was Dee's secret, until the day he rang up and Margaret happened to be in the room – only then did Dee decide to tell her.

I was wrong in much of my invention about Dee's family – her father was not the gruff hairy-armed outdoorsman I had made him – and some of my invented details of Dee's relationship with Ray were also way off. As I progressed in the story, for instance, I had distilled my own version of how Dee had found out about Ray's death. I had decided that Dee would stumble upon Ray's death notice in the *Sydney Morning Herald* on the very day

Walter visited to declare his interest in her. This was too dramatically neat to risk finding out what the truth actually was. I didn't want to know the truth. The truth would just confuse me.

But the truth is what Dee insisted upon. Her interest in Ray towards the end of 1957 had simply waned, and as she had no relationship with the public Chandler, she didn't bother trying to keep up with him. She carried on with her life, with her new penfriend Helmut, and soon enough with Walter, and, in actuality, she didn't realise Ray had died until a year after the event, when she received Helga's letter.

In the midst of all these changes there were passages Dee had marked with approval. The essence of her relationship with Ray was right enough – the 'why?' of it. We had, after all, discussed this at length. The desire to uncover the 'why?' of their story was what motivated me to search for Dee in the first place. It was the 'how?' which Dee decided didn't look enough like her.

I think at the start of our meeting I was in a state of shock. Dee was asking me to lift the engine out of the book, strip it down, rebuild it, drop it back in – and then tune it again, ensuring, as best I could, that the book was indeed 'firing on all twelve'.

The prospect of this was, to quote Chandler about the business of redrafting a film script, 'about as fascinating as scraping teeth'. But page by page, as Dee fitted together the jigsaw of actual events which added up to her real life, my intended version became irrelevant. This might not have been the route I would have chosen, but it became exciting to have Dee's real story to tell, at last. What started as a frosty meeting became gradually more relaxed. I grew less hostile to the changes Dee was asking me to make, and as the hours wore on she seemed to treat me less as an enemy. It was in this spirit of compromise that we parted, some degree of friendship, I think, at least partially restored.

another room

Things ended with Julia. She stayed on the farm and I moved up and joined her. During this time my divorce from Fiona came through, but by then Julia had already changed her mind about us and she called it off soon after. I made my way back down to Sydney and lay alone in another room of the undertaker's parlour.

Of course I wondered many times what would have happened if Julia and I had never met. She might have stayed with Gavin and I might still be with Fiona. But on one level I knew that what happened had to happen. In the same spirit that Dee wrote to Ray, Julia and I were both looking for an escape from lives that, for reasons we didn't understand, were not satisfying us. And I guess we got it.

One dayI ran into Fiona down at the beach. She had heard, of course. What could we say to each other? She could have been unkind, she had many reasons to be, but she wasn't and we looked at each other with that great sadness of personal history behind us, of what might have been and what wasn't to be. We talked for a while and then kept walking, both hugging the shoreline, her going one way, me going the other.

the last say

And the dribbler Philip is gone now. He ran out under a car at my brother's place when I was up on the farm with Julia. I got a phone call and my brother buried him under the grevillea in the backyard. Philip, mate. I'd like him here now to leave his pool of ambivilence on this pile of paper. Stake his territory, lay his claim, leave his mark. He always did like the last say.

And my affection for Chandler? It hasn't diminished. I still open the *Selected Letters* to look something up and find myself half an hour later turning a page I've read ten times already, shaking my head with a smile on my face.

Yes, there are always the letters.

Part eleven
the letters

For reasons of privacy, four names have been altered, as they have been in the book throughout. Otherwise the letters are complete, and as written.

all of r.c.

Judith Priestman to Alan Close

> Bodleian Library
> Dept of Western Manuscripts
> 28 May 1993

Dear Mr Close

If you really sent your letter on 17 March you must be wondering why you haven't heard from me. The fact is, I only received it on 26 May. I hope you are still at the same address.

You may certainly have the Library's permission to publish my letters to you, though presumably you won't want to quote them in their entirety?

Anyway, I look forward to the appearance of *The Australian Love Letters of Raymond Chandler*. The Bodleian would very much like to have a copy of this work, which will be of great interest to Chandler scholars, I'm sure. Perhaps you can send me publication details nearer the time.

With best wishes, from a wet and cold England.

Yours sincerely
Judith Priestman (Dr)

The familiar letterhead, immaculate typing, again the ref JAP/JAS. Home after a long exile! (Dr) J's concern about my address was warranted. Every letter I had sent her over the years was from a different address. But why, after all this time, was I again formalised to Mr? Bloody hell, and if she could be Dr, why couldn't I?

> Bodleian Library
> Dept of Western Manuscripts
> 22 June 1993

Dear Dr Close

If you don't mind, I think I prefer Alan and Judith, now that we have had a five-year epistolary acquaintance. In my stuffy, English way I judge that this is about the right length of time to justify abandoning formal prefixes, although I am not sure that I should be writing to you at all in view of the state of play in the second Test Match. (And the first; and the series before that, and before that ...)

I wasn't, in fact, touting for a free copy of the *All of RC* for the Bodleian, but it will be most gratefully received needless to say.

I regret that I have never watched *Sylvania Waters*. Not an everyday story of Oxford library folk, I gather from the reviews. Well, fastening my bun more tightly and buttoning up my cardigan, I must pedal off on my bicycle. Now where are my wellingtons?

All the best
Judith

Now we're getting places. Cricket and cardigans. Should I tell her I went to school with Allan Border? Small kid, thick moustache.

Deirdre Gartrell to Frank MacShane

Bathurst
31 May 1980

Dear Frank!

Here are the letters! I decided to send them, rather than photocopies, because they give a strong feeling of Ray's moods at that time. They're real, so they make him come alive. Death doesn't seem to mean much, when letters can speak so clearly and personally.

Last night I read them all again. It made me feel cherished, more than I realised at the time. I was an exasperation too! That was my most egocentric and introspective stage, and I was blindly selfish, looking for a safe repository for my soul-searchings, uncaring of feelings I evoked, except maybe a little flattered.

I'd make a more appreciative correspondent these days! But now I'm forty-one, almost forty-two, not eighteen. Life must have had some effect on the bland clay I was then.

I'll always wonder how we would have reacted to each other in the flesh – probably complete disaster!

Would you like a summary of what I did do with myself after Ray and I ceased writing to each other? (Just you try to escape it!)

I finished my Arts degree, majoring in English and History. During this time I established a long and loving correspondence with a psychology student in Eastern Germany; it was cathartic to express my feelings in letters, and to daydream about their recipient. But gradually I made 'real' friends in the college, and began to date 'real' men. When I disclosed this to my

German penfriend, he reacted angrily, just like Ray, and rushed off and married another student!

In Sydney I studied for a Diploma of Education, and finally succeeded in attracting a fascinating German-Danish carpenter who'd ignored me for four years. (He very wisely decided to wait until I'd matured a little!) After one year's teaching, I married him.

Heart and soul have been happily poured into the marriage by us both, so here we are, twenty years later, still together, and richer by four children. Just now Walter, mein Mann, is in Germany, introducing Rolf, our sixteen year old to his German and Swedish relatives, and to Europe. Walter will be back in 27 days, but Rolf will stay until September.

Our eldest son is there too. Erik, eighteen is studying hotel-motel catering, in southern Germany this year, and in Lausanne, Switzerland, in 1985, if he can wait till then!

At home we are three; me, Ellen (twelve) and Svend (nine). We're lonely, but think the projects are worthwhile.

I love them all so much! There's no doubt in my mind that I'm the old fashioned woman who loves one man for better or worse till death us do part. It's corny these days, but that's how I am! Country bred, you see!

I've dabbled in music, writing, dancing, (folk dancing), educational matters, psychology, ecology. But the core of my life is my family. It takes a lot of creative energy to keep a love affair alive and well for twenty-two years, and to raise children from squirming mites to independent, adaptable, enduring loving adults. Puff! Puff!

I'd still like to write, but I'm still scared of it. ('If I try, I might find out I can't!') Plus I have a strong streak of laziness. But maybe the next few years will see the combination of opportunity and courage which I need.

What of you? How is it you have come to write a biography of Ray? (Today in a bookshop here I saw five of Ray's novels lined up, looking so modern. I wonder if his readers today guess how long ago those thrillers were written? There was an article in the *Australian* newspaper here recently, too, on how he used alcohol to free him to write that three-week screenplay.)

Well – here we are then! (Do you like English comedy?) Bow your head while I confer my blessing on you in your writing efforts. BONK! There! Feel blessed!

Best wishes!
from Deirdre

Helga Greene to Deirdre Gartrell

>Helga Greene Literary Agency
>61 Eaton Mews West,
>London SW1
>29 March 1960

Dear Miss Gartrell,

I feel sure you know that Raymond Chandler died almost exactly a year ago. Anyway I hope your newspapers reported this so that it is not a shock to you now. I was Ray's literary agent for some years and if he corresponded with you right up to the time of his death then I feel pretty sure you have heard of me. I am the Executrix of his last Will and am writing to you now to ask whether you have kept letters of Ray's which you would be willing to lend for publication. I had better explain that Houghton Mifflin in the US and Hamish Hamilton here are going to publish excerpts from his letters and that these are being edited by Miss Dorothy Gardiner in New York. She is also writing a short biography for the book. When I say excerpts I realise that Ray was often quite libellous and this is to be a serious book and not a gossipy one at all. The letters we are mainly interested in are those where he writes about his own writing or that of others; or where he gives advice to young writers; or where he says something particularly witty or revealing about himself. Until now our method has been for me to go through all his letters libel and all, and I have done the preliminary choosing for Dorothy Gardiner. I send her on what I think might be useful and the letters themselves right back to the recipients. In that way his friends don't feel that they lose sight of their letters from Ray for months at a time whilst this book is being got ready for the press.

I do hope you will decide that you can contribute. Naturally I will disregard the too personal bits his letters are full of! I have no doubt that if Ray did keep up the correspondence with you which he told me about then there are many passages unsuitable for publication. I can assure you I am used to that by now and nothing he said could make me blush any more ... Perhaps you would like to know who Dorothy Gardiner is too: she was for many years secretary of the Mystery Writers of America and knew Ray well too. And he and she and I were together in New York only two weeks before he died. When you write to me do please ask any questions you like about the book and Ray himself. Also let me know if you would have liked something of his to remember him by.

Yours sincerely,
(Mrs) Helga Greene

Helga Greene Literary Agency
61 Eaton Mews West,
London SW1
23 November 1960

Dear Miss Gartrell,

In March 1960 I wrote you the enclosed letter, but I have not heard from you in the meantime. I therefore wrote to the University of New England and they have given me your present address. I do hope to hear from you.

Yours sincerely,
(Mrs) Helga Greene

Deirdre Gartrell to Helga Greene

Orange
9th December 1960

Dear Miss Greene,

Your first letter did arrive, some weeks after you sent it. It must have sat in the G-cubicle at New England University several weeks, unclaimed, and then been forwarded. It's two years now since I dusted my shoes of Armidale soil. I have a B.A., and Dip Ed, and one year's teaching experience, since then, and tomorrow week, I'll be marrying Walter —, a Danish/German building contractor (even though Ray warned me that Germans don't make understanding mates!)

In the interlude, the atmosphere and thoughts of the years of letters to Ray are becoming misted over, unrelated to today. But I can still recall (when I want to) that correspondence, and its effects on me, with the clarity of an A-1 dream. Ray wrote to me more as father to daughter, than writer to writer. He used to worry about my developmental problems (nothing spectacular about them!) give me advice, sometimes by cable, or even telephone, when I appeared on the brink of some madcap scheme, and sigh with relief when I recovered from my foolishness.

He guessed immediately why I wrote to him. I wanted an anonymous outlet for my written thoughts. He expected me to be irritated when he took notice of me and responded to my introspective unburdenings, and I was. First flattered and incredulous, then irritated (nasty young girl!) at losing my iceberg confidante; then? Gradually we changed; Ray realised I had shown him only one aspect of myself, and so he felt a little cheated and disillusioned. So the two idealists drifted apart, letters fizzled out.

All his correspondence is intact, Helga. (Pardon my calling you this, but that's how I think of you – besides it's an unusual name, rather pleasant, and I like using it!) So, since your second letter has convinced me you're serious about this editing, you are welcome to the whole series.

Ray sent me an autographed photo of himself (Penguin edition, with captured cat), and his books I purchased out of 'satiable-curiosity' (do you read Kipling, O Best Beloved?), so there is really no need for a reminder of him. His letters do that most satisfactorily.

So, Miss Greene, Literary Agent! Expect a middle-sized parcel one of these days.

Did Ray have all my letters to him destroyed? I wish I could now meet Ray, as friends. I'd appreciate him much more now. You seem to miss him, so he must have become close to you. He needed someone, once his wife died, since he didn't appear to have the roots of a regular job, or a home of the family kind. I gained the impression he respected you and was fond of you. He liked many women, he said. But I never knew how much to believe. He's a bit like me; his words sometimes ran away with him.

10.45 p.m. Being a barbarian Australian, unsophisticated variety, I'm tired (up since 5.30 a.m). So what do I do? Make a round of the clubs? Eat pep-pills? Drink coffee? Go shooting kangaroos? No, my dear friend, I go to bed.

Sorry to be so silly, Helga. Perhaps it's getting married that makes one so frivolous, semi-detached, perhaps? Do you enjoy Christmas? Hope this one is a peaceful, joyful occasion for you.

Best wishes for the future, in which I hope to receive a word or two from you.

Yours sincerely,
Deirdre

Helga Greene to Deirdre Gartrell

Helga Green Literary Agency
61 Eaton Mews West,
London SW1
29th December 1960

Dear Deirdre,

I can't tell you how pleased I was to get your letter. Of course I am serious about the editing project, and in fact it is now most urgent that I get your letters from Ray as the book itself is almost ready to go to Hamish Hamilton and Houghton Mifflin. Any suitable extracts from your series will have to be inserted in the appropriate places. So I do hope that you managed to send them off before you got married. I can imagine that what with the wedding and Christmas you might have put it on one side to wait for a later date – but *please* send your parcel off as soon as possible if you haven't already done so.

Ray destroyed all your letters to him just before he

died. He was planning to go and live in England for ever, and while I was in La Jolla he went through everything and he decided that his wife's diaries, his letters to her, your letters to him and many others just had to go.

While I am sorry that Ray did not write to you as writer to writer, because those bits would be the most useful ones for the book, I quite expected that he took a rather avuncular line. I am very much hoping though that he may have told you, even if it is only in an occasional sentence, something autobiographical about himself which might fill out any gap we have. I laughed when you wrote he used to worry about your development problems and that there was nothing spectacular about them really, because this is so very typical of Ray. Not that he had any other girl of your age to write to, but he certainly gave advice by cable and telephone to those of his friends whose welfare particularly concerned him, and of course you will know only too well that he sometimes got the wrong end of the stick and got worried about all the wrong things.

I am glad you have an autographed photograph and his books, and of course you will have the letters back quite quickly.

You are quite right in thinking that after Ray's wife died he needed people and particularly someone who could have looked after him and made him less lonely. It's a shame he never had any real home or family ties after her death. And again you are right in saying that if he had had a regular job things would have been easier for him. From a business point of view he was really splendid to deal with, drink notwithstanding, and even before I became his literary agent we were great friends. It wasn't always easy to stay neutral amongst the many women around him because he had an almost devilish way of wanting to put one up against the other ... I do wish you were over here and we could talk about him rather than write about him. Perhaps you and your husband do plan a visit to

Europe some time soon. That would be fun. Anyway I'd like to meet you, and if I were in your place and had had a correspondence without ever actually meeting the man, I would be absolutely fascinated to check up if most of my impressions were right or not.

It's nice of you to like my name, which I haven't really cared for all that much. But it is actually Norwegian, because my mother came from there. You might tell your husband that one of the reasons Ray admired me as an agent was because I could check up on the German and Scandinavian translations of his books for him. His own German was quite good but a little rusty and he had (quite rightly) suspicions about the adequacy of the German translations before my time. I expect you know that he had been to Heidelberg just before the First World War, but he may not have told you that if it hadn't been for knowing that there was going to be a war quite soon he had almost decided to settle there.

Do write again if you have time and there is any question you want to ask. My very best wishes for 1961 and to both of you for your married life.

Yours,
Helga

Deirdre Gartrell to Helga Greene

Orange
10th January 1961

Dear Helga,

I'm afraid you were correct in thinking that our wedding, honeymoon, and setting up house would oust the posting of these letters. Truly, I'm very sorry, and hope that, despite my tardiness, you will be able to make use of anything relevant.

On re-reading the letters, I think that there is more of use to you than I had remembered. Also, more to make me blush for myself there!

Just the same, I'm not asserting that the Deirdre of 1960 is any great improvement on Deirdre of 1956-57. I'm a lot happier, a bit more stable, and I haven't made a dull marriage! But Ray might, if he were alive, prefer me as I was. You never know.

Thanks for your best wishes to us both. You seem to be a very understanding woman.

With apologies, but optimism that I'm not too late.

Yours sincerely,
Deirdre

Helga Greene to Deirdre Gartrell

Helga Greene Literary Agency,
61 Eaton Mews West,
London, S.W.1.
1 February 1961

Dear Deirdre,

I think it was very good indeed of you to send me Ray's package of letters and you will be glad to know they arrived safely. Your letters did not come too late, although the publishers have the book and I would have to think where a sentence or two could be fitted in when it comes to proof stage.

I would think that you and Ray would have got on very well if you had actually met. He had an amazing charm, and was wonderfully easy to get on with except when he was eating too little and drinking too much. The drink wouldn't have done him so much harm if he'd kept to eating regularly, but of course his home life with its regular routine went all to pieces when his wife died. It unsettled him completely, quite apart from the feeling of loss he had which he never really got over. It was fascinating reading his letters and seeing, rather as I had expected, that he had obviously got worried and upset about all sorts of unnecessary things from time to time. I am afraid that did happen, and you must have found it rather infuriating sometimes.

Thank you again very much indeed for sending the letters which will go back to you shortly by registered post.

Yours,
Helga

Raymond Chandler to Deirdre Gartrell

49 Carlton Hill,
London, N.W. 8
15th February 1956

Miss D. Gartrell
Orange
N.S.W. Australia

Dear Miss Gartrell,

Thank you very much for your letter, and for your measurements, which 20 years ago would have made me rather excitable. But you know perfectly well that in writing to me you are just expressing yourself.

However, it was a nice letter, it was a kind letter, it was a friendly letter, and if you wish to write to me again I shall be only too responsive.

Yours sincerely,
Raymond Chandler

49 Carlton Hill,
London, N.W.8.
9 May 1956

Dear Deirdre,

I have neglected you I know but somehow I never find the time to write the kind of letter you would like to receive.

Now I am leaving for New York on Friday next and it will be some weeks before I reach California. When I get settled down I'll write you a decent letter.

Yours ever,
Raymond Chandler

Hotel Del Charro
2380 Torrey Pines Road
La Jolla, California
25 June 1956

My Charming Deirdre:

You must not scold me if I don't write as often or as long as you would like me to. I have a massive correspondence, most of which I cannot dictate to a secretary, since no one likes to get dictated letters from personal friends.

Your two letters dated May 15th, and May 16th, arrived this morning. They had been to Carlton Hill, to my London agent[1] (and very close personal friend) a daughter of the fabulously wealthy Guinness family, then to Old Chatham, New York, then to the Grosvenor Hotel in New York City, then here. Although they were airmail it took all this time for them to catch up with me.

Incidentally a couple of my best friends in London

are Australians, but neither has any trace at all of the Australian accent (which is bloody awful) and one of the two, a very pretty girl painter, has the most affected English accent I ever heard, although I don't really think it is deliberately affected. She is too nice a person.
I suppose you realise, baby, that I am old enough to be your grandfather, if I had married very young. I am all alone in the world now and live alone. My nearest relatives are first cousins, of whom there must be dozens in Ireland and England and various parts of Africa, since my British mother (Anglo-Irish, not Catholic) was one of a family of ten, all fertile. I have a sister-in-law here who is much older than I am and some kind of second cousin who is a crashing bore. That's all. I have leased an apartment at 6925 Neptune Place, La Jolla, and you should write to me there until I get a Post Office box. They are all taken now. It's only a two bedroom place, but rather chic and across the street from one of the best beaches we have. La Jolla has a superb climate, but with few exceptions nothing from the neck up. Most of the people I know here are well-to-do and some of them filthy rich. Of course I know all the people in the shops also, most of the police and post office employees. I am a well, but not always favourably, known character and one of the very few La Jollans listed in *Who's Who*. But as far as any minds to commune with, blah! I really depend a great deal on letters from England, for which I am already homesick, but to which I dare not return very soon, for fear of being tagged for British Income Tax, which ain't funny.

Now don't be silly about your not having read my books. That sort of touchiness I never had, and even if I had had it once, it would have been kicked out of me long ago. A writer with a reputation doesn't get only praise; he also gets malice, envy, and some abuse, sarcasm, malignant reviews from jealous little men, and in time he becomes quite indifferent to all of it, and realises that most of it is really a back-handed compliment.

You sound as if you had a pretty full schedule. I hope

Australian education is better than ours. Here people who go to the public schools seem to learn nothing, but somehow acquire enough credits to get into a state university, but not an exacting one like Stanford, Harvard, Yale or Princeton. Those who go to good private schools don't seem to learn much more. All our state-run institutions are co-educational and there is too damn much sex in them. On the other hand we don't breed sodomites like the English boarding schools. I'm not against sex – in fact I'm very much in favour of it, but it takes up too much time and attention in high schools. There is too much necking. A promiscuous girl in school or college is not respected, but it is a hell of a strain on young healthy girls and boys to neck almost up the point of coition and then stop short. However, perhaps I should not be so frank with you. I'd like to say this to you, though, from a man who knows a great deal about women, that no girl is ever as safe as she thinks she is.

I didn't use the subway in New York. The cars are dirty and sordid and you have to walk such immense distances to get to the trains and to get to the street from them, that the whole thing is a bore. I rode the Fifth Avenue bus a couple of times, but for the rest I used taxis, which are very cheap in New York. The London tubes are far better, cleaner, with cushioned seats, and are very fast. But I'm sorry that they have substituted enormously long escalators for the lifts they used to have. I don't mind short escalators in a shop like Harrods (easily the best department store in the world) but the long ones at the tube stations got me down. I didn't go up the Empire State Building this time nor even watch the skaters at Rockefeller Centre. These are things you do once and you have done them. I didn't go to a theatre or a film. If a show is any good in New York, you can't get tickets except at exorbitant prices, from scalpers. It's not like that in London, which has over 40 active theatres and all you pay the agencies is a fixed fee. I saw several plays in London and a number of films. If Italian films come your way, don't miss *La Strada* (The Highway). It is quite wonderful. I had a boring trip from London to NY. Due to mid-Atlantic storms we went by Iceland and Gander and took 20 hours; then, as we arrived three hours late off-schedule, the Customs were unusually brutal. The American Customs can be bloody awful. Not always. A couple of suitcases I sent direct from London to La Jolla by air freight were passed without being opened.

The women here are awful after London ladies. They are all brown and sundried, with harsh skins and flat voices, and when they dress up for a dance or a cocktail party, they look like hell. I have $20 000 worth of furniture in storage and out of that I have to pick what I can use in a four room flat. God knows what I'll do with the rest. Sell it for a quarter of its value, no doubt.

With much love (send your photograph to me if you have a decent one, please.)

And don't call me Mr Chandler. My name to my friends is Ray.

Ray

Raymond Chandler
6925 Neptune Place,
La Jolla, California
24th July

Darling Deirdre:

I am deliberately addressing you thus as an overemphatic gesture. We may never meet and most probably won't, but if we do, you will not have to think of me as a menace. I am certainly not a man who makes love to 18 year old girls. So much for that.

I am sorry not to answer your adorable letters more promptly, but I have been away and not too well.[1] I am sure you understand that I have a terribly exacting correspondence and that it is only by something approaching to rudeness, at least by my standards, that I have left any time to work. In fact, the only reason why I write to you at all is that I sense in you some very unusual quality. I suppose writers are doomed to that sort of thing – the love of what is in a person, however remote from them, however estranged by years or distance, some living vital poetic thing in a world which morons or near morons have become standard equipment. We may die of the H.bomb or of TV. It doesn't seem to make much difference anymore. At least to me, but it must to you. I say, it *must*. Otherwise what in the hell is the use?

I don't know just how to write to you. Yesterday happened to be my 68th birthday. I found the idea quite revolting.

But people send me telegrams and cables as though it were an important occasion, instead of one I should prefer to forget. What the hell do they think a man is? Do they think he enjoys counting the years to his death?

So here we are again? How do I write to you? As an elder brother? It just does not suit me. You say that at the University you have never been kissed. I should remedy that rapidly. I have a talent for women, and the basis of it is this: You never treat them except as something to be adored and respected and you never lay a hand on them until you know that they are ready and willing to get into bed with you. (This is the shock system.) I think a man of my sort never thinks of protecting himself, but lies awake all night trying to protect others. But of course he never gets any credit for it. People don't understand pure motives. They assume a certain dirtiness in any familiarity, and this is something of which I am incapable, but as long as it is assumed, one must somehow try to dispose of it. But try is the operative word. One can always find evidence for one's sins, but almost never for one's virtues.

The furniture was all here, and my sister in law will sell it for me after I am gone. I am living with some of it, but it is quite painful. One buys things like this for a woman one loves, and when she is gone the reason for their existence suddenly disappears. And yet such mounds and mounds of hand-embroidered linen, such piles of all sorts of things such as pink sheets and pillow cases, sterling silver, all of which I worked for since I inherited nothing, and now all of this becomes worthless to me. Yet I have friends in England who live, by our standards, almost in squalor, to whom I should be so happy to send some of these things, but it's impossible. You have to pay Customs Duty and Sales Tax and by the time you get it there you could have bought it cheaper.

After all, darling, what can one know, really know, about anyone else!

Yours with much love,
Ray

Raymond Chandler
6925 Neptune Place
La Jolla, California
2nd November, 1956

Dear Deirdre:

You are a sweet child, but if you knew how many letters. I have to write, you would not scold me for being so long in writing to you.[1] I am not too well and I have a lot of problems, as who hasn't? I seem to have given you the impression that they were financial, and I did have a spell of worrying because I couldn't seem to get much interested in writing, but I got over that.

So all you have to do is climb up a hill and sit

under a tree and scribble, scribble, scribble, Mr. Gibbon. (The allusion is not lost, one hopes.) You have no real worries: you will pass your exams standing on your head, you evidently come of a prosperous and loving family, and your only emotional entanglements are over some silly girl who hurt your poor little feelings so that you cried all the way through a symphony. Be of good heart – all my girl friends are easy weepers. I'm rather the Continental type myself – rather than the stiff-upper-lip and dead-pan Etonian. What those boys go through shouldn't happen to a rhinoceros. I drove one of my girl friends down to Eton last January on a Sunday to visit her younger son, a somewhat supercilious but very brainy type, and take him to lunch. He was in his last year at Eton and was attired in what is with you also, I suppose, called morning dress, except that he wore a dab of white stuff in place of a tie. It seems only the head of a house is permitted to wear an entire white tie. The door of his little room had to be wide open, his narrow bed folded up against the wall, and there. was no heat, although we had just come through a horrible cold spell so severe that I wore a Norwegian ski cap to keep my ears from falling off. It may be nice to have gone to Eton ... I went to a school called Dulwich College, not one of the big five, but likely in the next ten – but I'm damned sure it is not too nice to go there. I can't see any reason for all this Spartan nonsense. The food is bad at Eton, too. I guess the theory is that if you can survive Eton, you can stand anything. And it seems to be a fact that after the first year of agony most of them stand it easily enough.

Your 'philosophy' seems reasonable enough, but a little remote from me, naturally. I don't think you are smug at all. It is just that I no longer have any ambition to reform the world or even myself. The latter task I regard as hopeless and the former beyond my ambition.

This isn't much of a letter; I hope to do better next time. But at least it will tell you, with my love, that you are not forgotten nor have I grown tired of writing to you.

Do you study any foreign languages?

Con amore,
Ray

>
> Raymond Chandler
> 6925 Neptune Place
> La Jolla, California
> Feb 12, 1957

Dear Deirdre:

You don't write to me anymore, so therefore I must presume either that I have in some way offended you (not with intention, of course) or that you have found a new and closer interest. In the latter I should of course give you my love and understanding, in the former I must offer you abject apologies, and hope that you may forgive me. I don't know exactly what I am apologising for, but to a lady one more or less assumes oneself to be in the wrong.

I am leaving for England on April 1st, probably for a long time. I don't know where I shall be, but you may, if you wish, always reach me through my agent, the Helga Greene Literary Agency, 61, Eaton Mews West, London. S.W.I.

Yours always,
Ray

Raymond Chandler
6925 Neptune Place
La Jolla, California
2nd March, 1957

Dearest Deirdre:

Damn it, I am answering your letter the very day I received it. I've been worried about you a good deal, although we have never met and our ages are far apart. But the sort of emotional, introspective, highly intelligent but inwardly rather lonely girl such as yourself is always apt to fall in love, or think she has, with the wrong sort of man. Naturally, I hope you will find the right one, but I didn't feel at all sure. Perhaps Australian boys are not like ours. Ours seem to think that if they can't get a girl in bed the first time they meet her, they are not quite male. Very silly. I have always had a much greater respect and even veneration for women than they ever seem to have for themselves.

I had, as I suppose I must have told you, a long and very ideal marriage – except for the last few years when I had to watch my wife die by half inches of fibrosis of the lungs. When I was a young man I had many love affairs, but never with a girl for whom I did not have some real affection, and I don't think I ever hurt one. There was never any angry parting.

I know almost too much about women; several whom I know say so. Love is a difficult thing; atavistically, I suppose a woman has some vestige of thought that she must get or hold a man with her body or the promise of it. We ought to have outgrown that. It is very easy to seduce a girl; she is human and has desires that may be aroused at the wrong time, the wrong place and by the wrong man. Sometimes it could scar her for life. Of course a lot of them don't care, but I always think of the others.

I'm so glad that you passed all your exams. And as

for writing to me, you couldn't do it too often, except that I should feel very guilty at not writing to you so often. I have a mass of correspondence: I never really catch up with it. So much of it is at least semi-personal that I feel I must answer it myself. By the way you'll be interested to know that I have an Australian secretary, a delightful girl with a beautiful accent. I think I could dictate almost anything to her, except for a few close friends (ladies, of course). I seem to have some sort of talent for women, and please don't assume the worst.

Why do I want to go to England and endure that beastly climate. Well, for one thing I have friends there who are stimulating. For another I can live on a third of what it costs here, for another I love the country, and for a fourth but not final reason, I want to see whether I can write plays and England is the best place to get a chance. They have so many active theatres and the Continent is full of theatres that are almost desperate for plays. Of course I don't know that I can, but my English agent thinks I should be able to, as she regards me as about the best dialogue writer in the world. I should add, perhaps, that her opinion, even if quite mistaken, is not venal, since she is the daughter of an immensely rich man – so rich indeed that he has been forced to establish residence in Ireland (where he was born – he is one of the Guinness clan, the banking side, not the brewing side.).

It's an experiment of course and I have no idea of giving up my American citizenship, nor am I anti-American except that I have grown very tired of the gangsterism in this country. Organised crime seems to be getting worse and worse, its connection with business and politics seems to grow more and more intimate. Our Government seems quite powerless to do much about it. Also, if I stay out of the U.S.A. for 15 months I need not pay any tax on income earned abroad, and for quite a long time now, except for occasional TV deals, I have received much more from

Europe and the Continent than here. I hope this satisfies you. There are also a few ladies I am fond of, but that would not make me uproot myself. How long will they be fond of me? One never knows, does one?

No, I am not worried about money anymore in the obvious sense. What I am worried about is that the British income taxes are so exorbitant, and that there are people I have to take care of, with no tax benefit. I don't terribly care to have to wear patches on the seat of my trousers.

My Australian secretary adores Australia. She wants to go back and she says such lovely things about it that I am tempted. But I know that it is not the place where I could earn any real money. I am sometimes accused of thinking too much about money, and usually by someone on whom I have spent large sums because no one else had it to spend and perhaps her life depended on it. But so few people know that many a man, like myself, doesn't want money for himself, but that it is a sort of power that one can use benificently [sic], and that one has to be pretty tough to get it. I always knew that in Hollywood I should have to lay my head on the block in any negotiation, that these people could throw me out on my ear with the greatest ease, and that all I had to trade with was a certain way of making them believe that I had something to give them. I wrote very caustic articles about Hollywood and no one of importance ever objected. In fact, I got my most lucrative assignments afterwards. I really had a lot of fun fighting the moguls, and in the end I don't think they minded at all. There are so very few who ever stands up to them.

I'm afraid this must sound like bragging, but anyone who knows me would bear me out. I was probably the only writer in Hollywood in 20 years who had been suspended for refusing an assignment. I may have been the only writer to do a number of outrageous things, all of which I thought had to be done, and I am almost certain I was the only writer in

Hollywood, in my time, at least, who wrote an original script in 21 days, always only a day behind the camera (because a certain actor was going to be called up for military service) and the whole film was shot, cut, and finished in just over three weeks. And it was not a cheap film.[1]

Well, enough of that, and really I don't know why I wrote it, except perhaps to tell you that your boyfriend (don't take that seriously) was no pushover for anyone. Since I got malaria I am not so tough, but there was a time. Courage is a strange thing; one can never be sure of it. As a platoon commander very many years ago I never seemed to be afraid, and yet I have been afraid of the most insignificant risks. If you had to go over the top somehow all you seemed to think of was trying to keep the men spaced, in order to reduce casualties. It was always very difficult, especially if you had replacements or men who had been wounded. It's only human to want to bunch for companionship in face of heavy fire. Nowadays war is very different. In some ways it's much worse, but the casualties don't compare with those in trench warfare. My battalion (Canadian) had a normal strength of 1200 men, and it had over 14,000 casualties.

Well, to conclude on a lighter note, I may perhaps tell you a couple of funny things, one actual, and the other a story, but not the kind you can't tell a lady (I know far too many of those, but they must be witty.)

Some nights ago the telephone rang and the ensuing dialogue, as well as I can remember it, followed.

'Mr Adams, you will have to stop annoying Carol.'

'I'm sorry, but my name is not Adams and I have not been annoying Carol and don't even know who she is.'

The voice was young but very firm. 'Oh yes you do, Mr Adams. I recognize your voice and I know your telephone number.' She then told me the number and it was quite correct.

'My dear lady, I assure you that my name is not Adams. If you would look in the directory under the name of Raymond Chandler, you would see where I live, and that there must be some mistake.' (Incidentally, I hated to tell her my name, because I am too well known and it costs a good deal to defend even an entirely unjustified action.)

'I don't have to look it up, Mr Adams, because I know who you are, and I am telling you that if you don't stop annoying Carol, I'll call the police.'

'My dear unknown lady, if you would give your name and address, I should be most happy to call the police myself and save you the trouble.' So she hung up. The next day I ordered my telephone number changed and put on what we call the unlisted or unpublished list. That is to say, it is not put in the directory and Information won't give it out. Of course, it's a damn nuisance because you have to notify everyone who you might wish to be able to telephone you, and that's quite a lot. And some people are certain to think you are highhat and don't realize that twenty or thirty telephone calls a day from people who are trying to sell something can be very exhausting.

But I do feel a bit curious about Carol and Mr Adams. After all I've had the telephone number since last June, and it seems to me that Mr Adams must have been annoying Carol rather more recently than that. So the only guess I can come up with is that Carol somehow got hold of my number and told it to her mother or elder sister (the voice could have been either). Also, if she knew Mr Adams well enough for him to annoy her, don't you feel that she would have known his Christian name? But it does seem to me that in the circumstances, and considering the annoyance and even humiliaton I was put to, that I should be in all fairness allowed to annoy Carol just a teeny bit – that is, if she seemed worth annoying.

The other is a story about a man with a small men's clothing store in New York who had only one salesman and for reasons of economy, and no doubt his own laziness, also allowed the salesman to be his buyer. In a moment of aberration the salesman bought a perfectly awful green and purple checked suit. This hung up on the rack and no customer would buy it for so long a time that the proprietor got angry. One day he said to the salesman:

'I am going to lunch, may be gone an hour and a half. If that damn suit ain't off the rack when I get back, you ain't got no job.'

When he came he looked where the suit had hung and smiled.

'Boy, you sure had it in the clutch.' Then he looked at the salesman and saw that he was barely able to stand up, that his suit was so torn that he looked somewhat as if he had been dragged by a truck (lorry to you). 'Whassa matta, boy? You have trouble with the customer?'

The salesman said weakly: 'No trouble at all with him boss. Very polite kind of guy. Liked the feel of the material, bought the suit right away – but his seeing-eye dog damn near killed me.'

End of the performance and much, much love, sorry for all the mistakes. It is 2.30 a.m. and I haven't had more than 3 hours sleep a night for five days. I should have waited until I had rested.

Ray

P.S. Wouldn't it be awful if I came to Australia and looked you up, and everything you may have imagined about me turned out to be completely disappointing. I always say that if you like a man's books, take care never to meet him.

R.

Raymond Chandler
6925 Neptune Place
La Jolla, California
March 20th, 1957

Darling Deirdre:

My, we are getting ahead, aren't we? Thank you for your delicious letter. Are all those crosses kisses? Am I entitled to them? Do you kiss Old Wise Owls? Thank you also for the snapshots. All I can say is that you look very nice indeed, but not a raging beauty – who is in a snapshot? I look like Grandma Moses. I can't find my professional photographs. Some were good and some bad. They must be in storage. I have some of my furniture here in this apartment, or flat, and a lot more in storage, because we had a large house, and now I have only a two bedroom apartment, but a very nice one, with a private patio (which I don't use) and storeroom full of the most impossible agglomeration of books, manuscripts, screenplays, tools, electrical equipment (I used to like changing switches and receptacles and so forth), a collection of foreign language translations of my stories which the University of California wants, and so on. Also lamps and glasses and all sorts of things which accumulate during a long married life, but which have ceased to have much meaning for me.

Love is a strange thing. I smoked a pipe from morning to night when my wife was alive and I loved it. I can't smoke cigarettes at the typewriter. I'm not much of a smoker anyhow. I used to drink a great deal of tea, and my wife loved that, just as she loved to see me smoking a pipe. I have a large collection of them, all English. Since she died I don't smoke a pipe or drink tea; I suppose it may be wrong, but everything intimately connected with her likes has died in me when she died. I don't mean I am unhappy – not at all. I was for a long time, but not now. The irrevocable can finally be endured. It would in a way be far worse if she had divorced me (this is just an example, we adored each other) and had married some other man and I had to think of her living with and loving that man, and saying to him the same tender things she said to me.

My Australian secretary is going through hell. She is a Catholic and married an American officer (Italian by birth) who had a good, a very good war record, but became a paranoiac. He is a doctor and, she says, a good one, if he is in some institution where he is under control. A paranoiac – I know a good deal about them – can always behave quite normally when he wants to. They have their up and down spells, like manic depressives. She has two very charming and polite children. The boy was obviously badly hurt psychologically, but has picked up a lot since the father walked out taking all the money and leaving all kinds of unpaid bills and no money at all. By some strange coincidence I had advertised for a secretary, since my secretary of many years had become a teacher. I had many replies, but hers was in a long telegram, which she could not afford, and something in it attracted me. I asked her to come and talk and I took her on the spot, and I walked into another problem. I have spent most of my time trying to hold her together, trying to make her realize that she had to divorce him to protect her children, that she was entitled to support herself and for them. She comes of an old and quite well-to-do Australian family and she sold at least $50 000 worth of property she owned there to give it all to or spend it all on her husband at various times when he was ill or had behaved so badly that he couldn't practise. What women will do for love!

There was no 'veiled' hint about my coming to Australia. I should like to very much. But the practical and sensible thing at the moment is what I told you. The snag is whether the British tax authorities are going to consider money transferred from here as taxable income in England, even if it comes from capital sources. If I can't get a positive assurance on that point, I may go as a visitor, but certainly not as a resident. I estimate as well as I can that on an income of, say, £7500 a year, I might with a good accountant to help me, be able to keep £4000. That is bearable, because after all the money goes much farther in Europe, and here prices are rising all the time. Our national talent for making things fast and efficiently in great quantity was wonderful during the war, in spite of the grafting that went with it. But now it has got a bit out of hand. There are so many things made that no one really needs, and there are ferocious advertising campaigns to convince you that what you bought six months ago is obsolete, that the motor car you bought last year must immediately be replaced by a new and shining model. And the suckers fall for it. Working men get a lot of money here, but they are up to their ears in debt on installment (time payment) contracts. If we had a depression, it would be worse than the last one. Billions and billions are spent on military and naval stuff, because in a sense we *are* at war, but if that ever stopped (I don't think it will in my lifetime), if the Soviets ever became decent people, I think we should collapse like a pricked balloon. This country is enormously rich – much too rich, probably, except in intelligent foreign policy, but the more you have, the more you have to lose.

You pay me a great compliment in feeling sure and happy when you put your thoughts and feelings in my hands, but you are quite right. I do have a strange sort of instinct for understanding people, especially women. And I can always be trusted, although by bourgeois standards I am no moralist. I am more than twice your age and it may be out of place for me to be saying these things to you, but it is nevertheless a simple fact that I could never hurt, cheapen or demean a woman, and often, when I was young and unmarried I had to think for the girl too, to prevent her sometimes from doing something which I knew would shame her later. I always seemed to know. I don't have any idea why. I don't go too far with this, because after all I am writing to a well-bred young lady, and I don't want to offend her. I could go much, much farther, but would it be right?

Surely you realize, that when you write so frankly to me, it is because I am far away and because we may never meet. I rather hope we shall, unless it destroys an illusion. You need the illusion. And it might be that if we did meet, and even if I didn't too much disappoint you, you would never again be able to open your heart to me. As for your being born too late or I too early, I shouldn't have had the marriage I had, if it had been otherwise. Do you understand what it is to love a woman so deeply and be so deeply loved that no day in thirty years was not in its way a courtship? I always held her chair for her at the dinner table – until she couldn't come to it any more. I always opened the car door for her and helped her in. I never let her bring me anything. I always brought things to her. I never went out of a door or into a door before her. I never went into her bedroom without knocking. I suppose these are small things – like constantly sending her flowers, and always having seven presents for her birthday, and always having champagne on our anniversaries. They are small in a way, but women have to be treated with great tenderness and consideration – because they are women.

As to your emotional difficulties in making friends, I know that is trying, but it is better than being cynical. And as for your sort of halfway falling in love with me at long distance, that may be a good thing too. It might help you not to throw yourself into the arms of some nice but insensitive man who would never really understand you. What you say about the Australian husband is very much like my perception of the English husband. But very few people are acute about these matters. If you find a man that is, you will be frightfully lucky. But don't settle for being a housekeeper. You have far too good a mind. I don't know how Australians regard career wives, but when a woman has the sort of mind that has to be used, she should use it in something and for something that widens her life, instead of narrowing it. If there are children, and if there is enough money, there can always be someone to look after them for part of the time. Anyhow, it is much better for parents not to have their children underfoot all the time. Then their children regard the company of their parents as a privilege and a pleasure, instead of whining all day. The loss of the nanny has spoiled the manners of English children very much.

The American husband is too subservient to his wife, and the wife is too possessive – exceptions, of course. He can't take another woman to dinner; if he is late at the office, she suspects he is carrying on with his secretary. (A lot of them do, and I don't blame them in the least, if they have possessive wives). When he comes home he is only the vice-president in his own home. If he tells the brats to do something, they may very well answer: 'Mom says I don't have to.'

The English, and perhaps also the Australian husband, goes too far in the other direction. He is too insensitive to what a woman is, what makes her happy, what she needs to make her happy. One of my English lady friends said to me: "My husband allows me a good deal of freedom to have other men friends." I said "What do you mean by 'allows'? Do you have to have permission to have friends?" She seemed surprised that I asked the question.

I know one chap, and in many ways he is a nice man, very polite and considerate to his friends, who came home after a month's trip somewhere on the Continent, picked up a pile of letters and marched into his study, sat down at his desk and proceeded to read them, while his wife sat on a couch in silence. After quite a long time she got up to go. He noticed her enough to say, "Please don't go." So she sat for another half hour. You may wonder how I should know this. Never mind that. I do know. I scolded her for not going the first time.

Another thing they will do (and I apologize if this is something I should not write) is wake up in the middle of the night and grab their sleeping wives and decide they want to make love. None of the delicate approaches, none of the caresses, just a grab. This sort of thing is hateful to a woman. She feels as though she were being treated as a convenience.

You can love me anyway you care to. I should be honoured. At a distance it may be good for you to set up an ideal, even though overidealised, which would make you unlikely to fool with inferior types. As for height, I am just under six feet. I weigh when I am in condition 170 pounds, or 12 stone 2. I am in perfect physical condition, but often very tired, because I don't get enough sleep. A doctor who made a rather drastic physical check-up on me not very long ago (it took him two hours) was quite annoyed about it. He said: "In a man of your age or considerably younger a doctor can nearly always find some suggestion of a weakness of an organ or a malfunction which will suggest to him what the patient is likely ultimately to die of. In your case I can't find a damned thing. You have the prostate of a schoolboy, a perfect liver, a perfect set of kidneys, better than normal blood tests, all reflexes exactly right. I don't think – apart from accident or some virulent infection – that there is anything of which you can die except exhaustion." He *really* seemed a bit annoyed about it.

Well, you said I didn't write primarily about myself. This time I'm rather afraid I did. I can't send you a decent photograph of myself at the moment, so I'll annoy you by sending you one of an English lady I am very fond of.[1] She is a professional pianist and has toured in Australia with Goossens. She didn't like Australia at all, and I suppose you know what happened to Goossens, but not at that time. She is a superb pianist, is married to a poet, has two children, and has been very ill, but is now fairly all right. She had an American tour recently – not an important one – and she spent several weeks with me in Arizona and Palm Springs while I tried to get her over a nervous breakdown and a concussion and necksnap in a Boston accident. I think I succeeded – up to a point – but then she had to go back and once in London everything seemed to close down on her again. She has written a couple of rather depressed letters to me. I think she has begun to hate England, its foul climate, its too many lascka-daisical people. She adored Arizona. Nevertheless, she is getting somewhere. Her TV appearances seem to have gone well – I've never seen her play in public – and she has a concert at the the Albert Hall in July. You don't get that without being someone. The trouble is – I don't know if you are musical at all – that a pianist even a very good one, must spend six to eight hours a day for three weeks preparing a programme she already knows and has played. Well, if you have two demanding children, a household to manage, and numerous social engagements, you simply can't do it all. Something has to give. And with her, it has given more than once, and will again, unless she radically changes her way of living, refuses to be interrupted when she is working, or to go out to dinner parties when she is tired, or to arrange them herself. As a concert artist she has one great advantage; she is tall, stately, very beautiful, with luminous eyes and a magnificent carriage. One rather cynical London newspaperman told me that it was worth the price of admission merely to see her walk out on the stage. I've never seen it, myself.

Of course I agree with you that money is not everything, but the lack of it can be pretty awful. Also, to get it you usually have to fight, and I love a fight. In ordinary life I am a very polite good-natured sort of man, but when you deal with powerful people, and you are after all only a writer, there is only one way to deal with them. I think I must have said all this before.

My darling little secretary thinks she knows your family by repute (bakery business?) and she suspects but is not at all sure that she once knew your mother a little, if your mother's name is Dorothy. I told her I thought time might rule that out. She is a Catholic, very well-bred, very well educated, and she is having a horrible time over this divorce. She went to Melbourne University, France and England, but much prefers Sydney. I don't like very hot weather and I assume that where you live it must be very hot in summer.

It is Sunday, March 24th, now, and I started this several days ago. I have been writing letters etc. all day from eight o'clock until now, 5 p.m. and I'm beastly tired. So I am going to knock off with a couple of stanzas from a poem by a man named Terence Tiller (you never heard of him, most probably) but these two stanzas express so perfectly something which is very close to me – and yet very far.[2] They would look better double spaced, so please turn the page over.

Sometimes in cages of work, in night
that is not of the heart,
as once in another year, another dark,
she is there across the room, reading; gilt
by a common lamp, tired by a common end,
that part us though they join; so she would go
and be tomorrow's contradiction.

Our love appeared to us in little
gestures, in words; and yet
our lonely rooms knew granite, knew the battle,
knew the air, of love that was not spilt over
apparent lips, but lay profound
in a drift of images, immediate, though
denied the link and lamplight of an action.

P.S. I always said I should make a lousy Abelard. I may have to be one just the same.

R.

Raymond Chandler
6925 Neptune Place
La Jolla, California
April 8th, 1957

Dearest Deirdre:

I'm terribly sorry about your friend's miseries, but I don't think you are right to assume that you did her no good by talking to her half way through the night and being sympathetic and so on. She seems to be an oversensitive neurotic, but it may be only a phase. I don't know how sensitive young ladies of 18 or 19 feel, never having been one and never before this having had one confide in me as you do. I had no such desperate feelings at that age, although all was not soft music and pale pink roses. If it is *not* a phase with Margaret, if she is one of these people whose destiny, like that of Virginia Woolf, is to suffer terribly over trifles, then I'm afraid she won't get over it, and no one can really do much for her. But Virginia Woolf, however brilliant she may have been as a writer (I never met her, but I visited Leonard Woolf at his house in Sussex) was clearly a manic depressive. She was a number of times in a nursing home for mental cases, and she told her intimate friends that the awful part was the suffering of getting back to normal. This was what she was finally unable to bear, and when in 1941 she knew another attack was coming on, she left a note for her husband and threw herself into a river with a strong current and her body was never found – not that this last has anything to do with it. Please believe that you have nothing to blame yourself for, that you did all that anyone could do, and that it would do absolutely no good for you to feel guilt where there is nothing but kindness, or to destroy yourself by the emotional outpourings (basically self-pity, you know, as I found out in myself) of someone who lacks the emotional stability to accept life as it is.

Once I asked a Dominican why, if God were all-knowing and all-powerful, he allowed so much suffering and cruelty, so many abominations to the innocent, so much of the jungle in His world. The Father said: 'He wanted to create man free to mould his own destiny.' I said: 'Well, man has had at least ten thousand years to work at it, and he doesn't seem to me to have made much progress, if Belsen and Dachau and Buchenwald are still possible, if the Russians can destroy a nation as a political move, if ordinary decent people can be tortured until they lose their minds or "brain-washed" until they become semi-idiots. And apart from man, what about animals? I suppose God made them too. The very existence of animal life in the wild depends on the killing of the weak by the strong. Is that the sort of world God wanted?'

The Dominican said: 'I don't know. But I must believe.' He wasn't very pleased with me, nor I with him. Of course one must believe in something, of course one can't understand everything, but when they hand me 'credo quia impossible' it sounds to me like a very convenient gadget and nothing more.

You are very penetrating in so many ways. Those who grow up in a conventional society really do find themselves fixed in it before they have made any choice. Then they can only rebel, and rebellion usually goes too far. A girl who rebels against the humdrum semi-Victorian rules and postures of her society may easily become a promiscuous Greenwich Village wench. But somehow I think I'd almost rather have her even that than imbedded in the cast-iron mould of a dull, conventional marriage. From what I have heard our society is freer than yours, but if so, it is also more hypocritical, more shallow, more selfish and basically less moral. Too much fuss is made about sex here, both for and against. I've always been against co-education for that reason, but now I am not so sure. Is it better for young men and women to go to the same university and take their chances on learning how to behave to one another, with certain risks, or is it better for a lot of girls to go through what you call 'growing pains' in an environment where they, in a sense, prey on one another emotionally? Might it not be better for an emotional girl to be concentrated on a girlish love affair with a young man – even at the risk of its going too far, than for her to concentrate her whole being on trying, and failing, to become close to some other girl in whom, eventually, she finds nothing at all; no response, no real friendship. There are risks either way. In English Public Schools there are risks of sodomy and, I suppose, in girls schools there are risks of Lesbianism. In some cases, but relatively few, these things become permanent, but if they do, the tendency was already there.

I myself take sex in my stride, subject to a code of behaviour which I think I tried to suggest to you. I don't think it is either unimportant or that it is the whole of life. But to deal with it well is certainly an art.

My secretary's name is Betty Bluefields.[1] She would like to write to you, if you permit, and tell you about her family connections and so forth. Also, she has been about ten years or more away from Australia and (this is confidential), wants to go back, and she is curious as to whether it has changed and if so in what ways. Between the two of you I shall probably be driven to go there and see for myself. Australia as a background for fiction is almost untouched, and we have many – Betty has convince me – very false ideas about it. The few films made in Australia which I have seen – except possibly *Bush Christmas* – haven't helped at all. The little fiction I have read gave me no true feeling of Australian life. Katherine Mansfield wrote rather good stuff about Tasmania,[2] but none of it stayed with me. She was another of these lost, over-sensitive people.

Now really, darling, if I said you were half in love with me at long distance, surely you didn't think I was imagining any romantic involvement? Not at my age, surely. I accept the difference in meaning between loving and being in love. Of course, I always have.

Being in love involves a sexual content which, though it is completely masked, as it often is with idealistic people, is inevitably present. A young man for the first time puts his girl on a pedestal. He hardly dares touch her. If she lets him hold her hand, it is ecstacy. A kiss is almost too much. At night he will stand outside her house for hours, across the street, happy to know that she is in there, although he can't see her. When he meets her, his throat tightens and he can hardly get a word out. He wouldn't dream of trying to paw her; it would be sacrilege. Or so it was with me. But a man so seldom marries his first love. He is not yet in control of his life, nor she of hers. Parents interfere, he hasn't enough money to support her, or they are separated by some necessity, such as war, or the family going to another place, and the whole thing fades. He never quite forgets her, but as he grows older and more cynical, he sometimes wonders whether this extravagant infatuation was not simply an awakening to love itself, rather than love for a particular girl. Of course, he never finds that out. She has married someone else long since.

So you call me tall. I thought Australian men were very tall. In California anyone under six feet one or two is practically a midget. My wife was just about your height. I like tall women. Also, I'm sorry I sent you the photograph of my English friend – one of them – bad joke. So I am sending you one I dug out of myself. It has been used on the back of Penguin books (I don't know whether you get them in Australia) but very much cut down. This was taken about ten years ago, and my hair is much greyer now, alas. You will notice that I had to hold the cat's tail to keep it from wagging. This cat was a pure-bred Persian, black, and lived to be almost 20 years old. Black Persians are not a fixed species, they are really sports. Sometimes you get one in a litter of five. This one, whose name was Taki, had a red Persian for a father. She was a wonderful cat, completely intelligent, and a bit snobbish. If she came into a room she would march straight up to a cat-lover and never which is now part of Eire. A couple of my cousins married farmers, a couple more were doctors, one a solicitor, one an officer in the Connaught Rangers, one is a film actor. He played the Dauphin in *Henry Vth.*, the film made by Olivier (about the only actor I have known who seemed completely natural in manner on stage, but not so his wife, Vivien Leigh – she played to an audience all the time). And so on. I think I am the only one of the lot who had an American father and was born in America. Curiously enough, my father also came of a Pennsylvania Quaker family.

I think that should be enough for now, don't you? Be of good heart, and don't take the problems of growing up too damned seriously, if you can help it. It's a difficult time for any sensitive person, but many of its agonies will fade like a mist when the sun comes up. On you they will leave no scars; on some, the weak ones, they will. My heart is in your hands. Hold it gently, it is rather tired.

With much love,
Ray

Raymond Chandler
6925 Neptune Place
La Jolla, California
April 23rd, 1957

Deirdre Darling:

This has to be a little short, because I am up to my neck in various struggles preparatory to my going to England.[1] If and when I go, you may always reach me through my agent: Helga Greene Literary Agency, 61 Eaton Mews West, London, S.W.1, England. But don't write to me there until I cable you that I am on my way. I don't know how long I can stay, because information I have received from the British Information Services in

New York indicates that any money transferred by me to England would be regarded as taxable, and on an income of, say £10,000, I should have to pay a tax of over £6000. Since during my efforts to write a play I might have to transfer funds from here, I can't accept that situation. It wouldn't leave me enough to live on decently. I guess I'm spoiled, but I can't face a situation where you bring dollars into a country and are then almost pauperised for bringing them.

Betty had your letter and was very pleased. She says she is a bad letter-writer, and she may not answer at once. But don't blame her too much – she is in a lot of grief and trouble. I help her all I can, but I can't cure her grief and humiliation in so degrading a situation. She has nothing to blame herself for, and I have met enough of her friends, professional mostly, to know how highly they regard her devotion to her beastly husband.

You need have no fear that any confidences you do me the honour to confide will ever be seen by any other eyes. I keep your letters locked up. If I ever feel that they could be endangered, I should destroy them, much as I should hate to do that. And if I should – however unlikely – drop dead tomorrow, my lawyer will destroy all my private correspondence unread, as also my own and my wife's diaries. It is in my will, and he is an honourable man.

You Australians seem rather more prudish than we are. Or more proper, might be the better word. I didn't realize that your university was co-educational. I am very glad that Margaret got something out of your delicate and enormous kindness to her. I rather think she will find herself. No amount of kindness will make a weakling strong, but she doesn't now sound like a weakling. You can kiss yourself on the back of the neck for having done a kind and generous thing.

You ask about my latest romance. I haven't one. No, you didn't exactly ask, you only made an allusion. Since my wife died in 1954, I suppose, after the shock had passed off somewhat, that I did try to find someone to love. But it didn't work very well, since the women who attracted me and were attracted by me were all in some sort of trouble or difficulty or unhappiness, and the one who was my real flame[2] and who did so much to bring me out of my depression and despair is beyond my reach. It has taken me quite a long time to understand that her life is fixed in a pattern which she will not change, and of course I have no right to ask her to change it, except that she is destroying herself by trying to live three lives at once, the life of an exacting professional pianist, the life of a mother of two adored children and a manager of a home, and a social life, rather exacting at times. The last she could give up to a large extent, but I don't think she really wants to. So she will probably go from breakdown to breakdown. A man can give only so much for a lost cause, especially when it is deliberately lost, and unnecessarily lost. I have given a great deal; I have owed a great deal. But if what I give achieves nothing permanent, disillusion sets in.

Your sweet little flirtations make me feel very fond of you. Your skill in preventing them from going too far makes me respect both your intelligence and your character, even more than I respected both already. But please do not *ever* think of yourself as immune. No one is ever immune to the sudden flare of infatuation. But for a young girl you have shown what to me seems enormous resources of character. Of course, I can't know whether or not you were ever really tempted to a dangerous point. Australian girls may be rather more fortified than ours or English girls. Kisses may be many things. But if you ever feel yourself beginning to tremble, run like hell. Love is an unpredictable emotion, and the physical manifestations of it even more so. I wish I could tell you how to grow up, but of course I can't. What I should dread in your kind of society is that you should find yourself married to some quite nice and decent man, and should find yourself bound to him by children, and yet know in your heart that you had been frozen into a pattern which was not at all what you really wanted of life, and could, in fact, have had of life, perhaps. I suppose the accent is on the 'perhaps'. Most people make do with what is available and seemingly appropriate to their condition. Ferocious romantics of my sort never make do with anything. They demand the impossible and on very rare occasions they achieve it, much to their surprise. I was one of those, one of the perhaps two per cent who are blessed with a marriage which is forever a courtship. I can't, as I think back, find any reason why I should have been so favoured. Above all, since as a young man I was anything but virginal.

The photograph I promised you is much too big for a letter, and has to be sent separately. It will be sent – in fact it is already packaged to post, but I have to find out about the Australian postal regulations. It won't cause you any ecstacy, but it is the best I have.

You will never lose dignity with me, since it is obviously a part of you. To answer one question, I never proposed marriage formally to anyone. My wife and I just seemed to melt into each other's hearts without the need of words.

With much love,
Ray

telegram from Raymond Chandler to
Deirdre Gartrell

6 May 1957

LA JOLLA CALIF

MISS DEIRDRE CARTRELL
HUT C
NEW ENGLAND UNIVERSITY
ARMIDALE

YOURS APRIL 30 RECEIVED I AM ANGRY IF POSSIBLE AWAIT LETTER I HAVE MANY EXACTING THINGS TO DO HAVE APPARENTLY SPENT TOO MUCH OF MYSELF ON YOU WITHOUT KNOWING SITUATION CLEARLY LOVE
RAY

Raymond Chandler
6925 Neptune Place
La Jolla, California
May 5th, 1957

My Dearest Deirdre,

I suppose you have had the cable I sent you last night and I suppose it puzzled you. So this letter has to be very frank, and if it is too frank, I can only hope you will forgive me. My motives towards you have always been completely altruistic. I have probably, in fact certainly, spent more time and consideration on you than I ever spent on anyone who wrote to me out of the blue, whom I had never met and very likely never shall meet, than on anyone else with whom I was not personally involved in some way. I have even left things undone which I ought to have done, in order to answer your letters. I suppose I felt drawn to you by the obvious intelligence and sensitivity of your mind, and of course I assumed that at your age, being a strong and healthy girl, you would have certain normal impulses and desires.

But until your last two letters you never spoke of them. I can hardly blame you for that. I am not your father confessor and you had no way of estimating my discretion. I had assumed that your university was for women only, and that as you were a boarder, you would not, except on certain days, meet any boys or young men. I had assumed from one letter, the one about Margaret, that there was a sort of ingrown, esoteric atmosphere about the place which might be unhealthy and at the very least could, to you, be trying. Then, all of a sudden, I hear about your love affairs, a term I use only in the politest manner. Call them mild flirtations, if you like. I certainly never assumed anything sexual, except that between a man and a woman that always exists, however carefully hidden. Well, if you were going to confide in me as much as you did on many other subjects, I do feel that I should have been told the whole story or none of it. Letter after letter gave me the picture of a well-bred sensitive intelligent girl living a completely virginal life, certainly in action and as far as possible in thought. I am no damn fool, usually, but this time I think I have been one, so that I was probably much more angry at myself than at you to find in your last letter that you had a real love affair going on with a man who attracted you very much, who is probably a very nice person, but what am I to say except what I think? If it is wrong or useless, that is a privilege you have given me. I didn't ask for it.

No man can really judge the deepest hopes and desires of a girl so far away and living in a society which is probably much more Puritanical than ours. But just to clear my own soul I am going to say exactly what I think, and in saying it I know I may be all wrong, but unless I say it, this correspondence between us has been entirely wasted, and really rather unjust to me. I am a working writer with many problems and a large correspondence, some of which I can dictate, some too private for that. I have given you a lot of myself. What I have to say is the best I know how to say. I think I have earned the right to say it.

My marriage happened to be one of those rare enchanted things. But I have seen dozens of marriages, based on a swift infatuation, which turned to abject misery in the end. Sometimes I think that the marriages arranged by parents might well be the best – if one had the right sort of parents, as I gather you have.

So here it goes, straight as I know how to make it. (And I am much too experienced in life to expect what I say to have any influence on you). I don't care how much you like this Barry, he is all wrong for you. In two years he will bore you to death. I only wish to God you could get in bed with him, but by your standards I expect that is impossible. So you will visit his parents and there will be an engagement of two and a half years, and so on. And during that two and a half years you will be under an intense nervous strain, if he attracts you sexually, and this will do you a great deal of harm. At the end of that time you will feel duty-bound to marry him, even if you have doubts. I gather from Betty that you Australians are a generation behind the English and two generations behind us in dealing with these situations. I admit we go too far; divorce here is commonplace, but at least we recognize that happy marriages, of which there are and must be few, are not based on whether the husband has a safe job and a nice disposition and comes of the right people. They are based on the mingling of two minds and two bodies in such a way that some sort of continuing ecstasy is created. It is rare, but you too are rare. Nothing less is good enough for you.

Girls of your age, and men or boys of the same age, have certain almost unbearable physical cravings. We have never really solved the problem of how to deal with them. In my country they do the obvious thing, more often than not. But in doing it, they certainly lose some of the idealism which belongs to love. I suppose there is a price for everything. Love affairs, in my sense, may make people cynical about love. Not always. I have had many, before and after my marriage, and I am not cynical about love. I am not cynical about any facet of it. But love has no qualifications. If there is a single doubt, a single thought that diverges from pure passion (clichés), then it is not love, it is only an infatuation or an attempt to reconcile the possible and the impossible, an attempt to accept the second-best. There *are* no second-bests. There is only the misery of trying to make them into something they could never be.

You want someone to love, someone to hold in your arms, someone to kiss, someone to caress you. You find a nice man who can do all these things in a nice way. And you think you have found what you want. And you give up everything your soul desires in order to be a nice, respectable, engaged young lady, engaged to a nice respectable young man who, whether he intends to or not, will put you in a cage. How can you know at your age? If you were just an average rather insensitive sort of girl who just wanted a husband, a home for 'gracious living', the respect of your circle, I couldn't have a word to say. Somehow – although I may be wrong – I don't think you are that sort of person. He *does* sound nice; I admit that. But not for you. Now I am going to be a little crude, and you may loathe me for it, except that you must know that I have no axe to grind (I borrow this phrase from Barry), that all I am trying to do is tell the truth as I see it.

If you are a passionate and sensual type, you will find that he will be no good in bed. You described the fairly typical Australian husband to me in a letter. That sort is not for you. If you marry him and have children (I don't know how you feel about children, of course), you are anchored for life. If you don't have children (and I don't suppose Australians are so innocent that you don't know how to avoid them, or have never heard of diaphragms), then in two years you may want to get out. But the pressure of your social group will make that very difficult, and of course I know nothing of the Australian divorce laws. Perhaps, in Australia, a divorce is a disgrace. It used to be in England but no longer. Here it goes too far; both of my sisters-in-law's sons have been married six times. We are a corrupted society of course, but the whole world is corrupted in our generation. I had only one marriage, but I was lucky. Divorce is a beastly affair in any circumstances, but it is far better than a life which is only a submission to a code of behaviour of no real validity.

   I expect you are going to hate me for all this. Hatred is often the price one pays for being completely honest. One learns to accept it. You will, of course, do what you will do. The most I could possibly accomplish would be to make you realise to some slight extent that at your age one wants love, and that one will make perhaps too many compromises to find it. Almost, insulting as this may sound to you, I could wish that I, even at my age, could have an affair with you. It might harm your self-respect, but what is that self-respect? Is it real or is it only conformation to conventionality? But I could, I think, make you realise that love is an infinite tenderness, an infinite respect, and that if it is ever for one instant mechanical or boring, it is a far greater sin against the beauty of life, than an inconventional, but very sincere, attempt to achieve an idealistic relationship.

   I have no real justification for what I have written here. I am what might be called a religious agnostic. One of my best friends is an Episcopalian vicar. I don't go to his church, and he never talks to me about that. He knows, as I know, that I was not born on this earth for myself alone. Perhaps that gives me some sort of excuse for saying what I have said, perhaps not. You will have to judge. I can only try to give you what knowledge of life I may have acquired. I can't give you what you will know twenty years from now; I can only give you words; I can only give you love. None of it may help at all, and all of it may easily be wrong. But I am sincere. What more could be asked of a man?

Yours with as much love as you grant me,

Ray

>Raymond Chandler
6925 Neptune Place,
La Jolla, California
May 8th, 1957

Deirdre Darling:

Your last letter, written evidently before you got my cable and the following letter, and dated May 1st., seems to make everything clear to me, especially the part where the three girls were having such a good time and hardly knew you were there, or noticed when you slipped out. Your snapshots don't suggest at all that you are a neurotic type. The loneliness, the inability to form close friendships, must come from something else. But this is the key. Loneliness. It has probably happened to many people of about your age, intelligent, clever, analytical, over-introspective people. So you find a nice kind young man with whom you can be on terms of intimacy which you could not achieve with any of the girls. Please believe that I understand that he *is* a nice young man, that you really feel yourself in love with him, that he relieves that loneliness and makes you feel at ease with someone who can give you real affection.

    I suppose I have to admit that this is a situation in which it is impossible for me to say the right thing and almost inevitable that I should say the wrong one. But without any real hope of doing good, I am nevertheless compelled by your confidence in me to say what I believe to be true, and beyond all question true.

May I comment on the fact that in none of your letters to me have you ever told me about anything external to your own thoughts? You have never described your room, your university, the buildings, the place, the atmosphere, the climate, what sort of place Armidale is. You may think this unimportant, but to me it indicates a state of mind; a state of mind which must be unhappy. I am interested in Australia, in everything about it, what it looks like, what its houses are like, how many rooms they have and what sort, what flowers grow there, what animals and birds are there, what the seasons are, what the ordinary life of people of your sort consists of. You tell me a great deal about your thoughts, but nothing about the life around you. Do you suppose I became one of the most successful mystery story writers of any age by thinking about me – about my personal torments and triumphs, about an unending analysis of my personal emotions? I did not. And you should know that very well. But from you all I hear about is you. This is not said to blame you or accuse you of being egocentric at all. It is said because to me it builds a picture and explains an infatuation with a nice young man who would be inexpressibly boring to me, but in whom you find some sort of refuge, because you can't make friends among girls of your own sort. You expect too much. You expect that all these girls should live on your own level of thought and emotion. If they don't, then you feel discarded. Isn't that a bit too arrogant? I can talk all sorts of languages to all sorts of people, and they may not love me, but at least they know I am friendly. You ask what is almost impossible, a girl who is exactly like yourself, and not finding one, you throw yourself into the arms of a man who, though kind and considerate, is clearly only a proof of your failure.

Do you really want to have breakfast every morning

with a man whose every word you can anticipate? Who never has a wild imaginative thought, who never in any circumstances says anything that could possibly be other than discreet and circumspect and utterly dull? If that is what you want, of course I have no more to say. If I am intruding on your life, I apologize. God knows you have intruded on mine. I have only one thing left to say, and it may be the last thing I shall say to you, because I can't spend my life writing useless letters to you. It is this: if you become formally engaged to this chap, and if it is a formal engagement in your circle, you are an idiot. Have him for a friend, a lover, a companion as long as you like, but the instant your families make it formal, you are out of my world.

I could, of course, be quite wrong. It may be what you really want. But please, darling, give yourself time to know that it is what you want. In the meantime, would you care to have me supply you with a list of clichés, in case his run out? I shouldn't be terribly excited by the task, but I think I could accomplish it, if it would help.

What is a man like to say to a girl like you? I have no axe to grind (courtesy Barry), nothing to gain except possibly to save a nice girl from an idiotic mistake. And I have nothing to lose except failure. And whatever I say is useless. I know that, so why do I say it at all? Why do I stay up until 2 a.m. writing letters to you when I am already exhausted and really am not sure that I am saying anything near the right thing. Is there a right thing? How could I possibly know what it was? You are either going to make a fool of yourself, or you are not. Nothing that I can say or write will make the slightest difference. Because he is there in the flesh with a warm kind smile to comfort you, and I am thousands of miles away with nothing but what I have learned from life.

I give up. To say any more would be a loss to both of us. I hope that at some future time you may realize how much I have had time to give you [sic], against many other things, and how little you have had the right to make me do it. But I have done it and willingly up to the point where you make a fool of me. After that, I can't accomplish anything. I hope very much that you and your Barry will be happy. And after that formal wish I have nothing more to say. I don't mind your making a fool of me. I terribly mind your making a fool of yourself. But it is now out of my hands – it never was in them, really – and I have had it.

With much love and some hope
Ray

telegram from Raymond Chandler to Deirdre Gartrell

20 May 1957

LA JOLLA CALIF RETRANS FM ARMIDALE UNIVERSITY

MISS DEIDRE GARTRELL
ORANGE

THANK YOU FOR LETTER AND UNDERSTANDING I SHOULD ADORE YOUR MOTHER AM WRITING IMMEDIATELY MUCH LOVE ... RAY

Raymond Chandler
6925 Neptune Place
La Jolla, California
May 20th, 1957

My Dear Deirdre,

Probably you have my cable thanking you for your letter. I tried to telephone you but they said you were on vacation, or on holiday as I suppose you would call it. I was afraid that I had offended you, but I felt that I had to say my piece, even if I said it wrongly. I see now that you are much more perceptive than I realised. Nevertheless, in a situation like this, a young girl might doubt her own judgement, and what I said could not harm you, it could only at the worst have made you angry with me, a risk which I thought justified, because what I thought might possibly have re-inforced what you yourself thought.

    I can't blame you for not confiding things to me and I apologise for thinking you should have. In America we have many Universities for girls alone, and ordinarily girls of your class would go to one of them. (To lighten this a little, do you remember what Dorothy Parker said about Bryn Mawr "If the girls were laid end to end, I shouldn't be surprised."?)

    I'm sure you realise that I have not been selfish about this but that somehow in your letters you have come so close to me I feel an obligation to protect you in any way I can. Surely I could have some understanding of the problems of a nice, normal girl in a conventional society. We all go through these torments, difficulties, uncertainties. The hunger of the body can be a terrible thing, but if one wants a happy and enduring life one must wait for the right person, or else consider oneself of so little account that any answer could be the right answer. Since I was sure you were not this type of person, I felt that I had to do my best to prevent you from making a silly mistake and I'm glad your mother and you yourself have been on my side. These situations are more difficult for a girl than for a man. When she sacrifices her virginity, if she still has it, she gives far more than a man could possibly give. She risks far more, she could be shamed far more, but nevertheless she has the same emotions. I have them too, I am still alive and still human.

    If you should ever feel yourself slipping, and it could happen, hop a plane and come to see me, of course as my guest in every possible sense. There is no recourse from a bad mistake, for the sort of person you are. It would dwell with you all your life. The sins of the flesh may be to some people unimportant but the sins of the mind and the soul are irrevocable.

In case I sound too god-damn stuffy, I am herewith sending you a limerick which I must have made up in an idle and not very proper moment.

'A charming young lady of Ghent
Was rather too often enceinte,
When her father screamed, "Who?"
She replied with a coo;
"I don't know, he just came and he went."'

Ray

> Raymond Chandler
> 6925 Neptune Place
> La Jolla, California
> July 25th, 1957

Darling Deirdre:

The spectacle of Margaret bouncing up and down on the bed when I telephoned you was really excruciating. The conversation or whatever it was is a bit vague in my mind too, because I was carted off to the hospital the next day. It seems that I have a serious anaemic condition. Not fatal, but quite serious. These diagnoses never make much impression on me, since I have lived my whole life on the edge of nothing. Once you have had to lead a platoon into direct machine-gun fire, nothing is ever the same again.

The extravagance of the telephone call may be this or that, but I am one of those wild people who do what they want to do, and count the cost later. You write me such sweet letters that I hardly know how to answer them. I should like to write love letters, but the difference in our ages is so great that it would be absurd. I am greatly concerned that you should have a happy life, that you should not make an impetuous mistake and find yourself tied in the wrong knot, but after all, I can do so little except to say that second bests are never good enough. A girl of your age has certain physical urges which are, in themselves, natural and proper, but in your society it seems one can only make them proper in one way. In ours or in English society of people of our class it is accepted that these urges may be satisfied in 'affairs' that do not commit one to a life. This may be wrong or right; I don't presume to judge. I was one of the lucky ones, and found a love too great to be betrayed, too wonderful to be dull.

I don't quite know why you are so close to my heart, but you are. In some mysterious way you have put me inside of you, so that I have to lie awake at night and worry about you – you a girl I have not even seen. It must sound ridiculous to you. All I can say is that in some strange way you have become a part of me, so that I wake in the night and wonder what is Deirdre thinking or doing, is she making a fool of herself with some nice but stupid man, and if she is what can I do about it? All very silly, but there is a certain devotion in it also, entirely because of your letters. I have had thousands of letters, and I suppose I have written thousands. A collection of my letters is to be published when I can weed them out. But that is not the point. Why should I take Deirdre into my heart when hundreds of charming people made no impression on me at all deeply?

The older you get, the less you know.

Anyhow, I love you and I send you love, but I am a little diffident about sending you kisses at the moment, since I haven't shaved for two days.

With all my love,
Ray

Raymond Chandler
6925 Neptune Place
La Jolla, California
August 14th, 1957

Darling Deirdre:

This will have to be rather short as I have only one hand to write with. I am a man who moves too fast, whose mind is always ahead of his body; a cup-upsetter, a soup spiller, but not somehow a breaker. On August 1st I chased out of the front door for the paper, tripped over a tangled rug caught in the door and did a nose dive down the steps, landed with full force on my left wrist and smashed it to pieces. They X-rayed it, put a temporary splint on it, and carted me off to the hospital so that they could get nurses and keep me drugged until the excruciating pain eased off. For two days nothing worked: absolute hell. Then it did ease a little. On the sixth day they X-rayed it again and put on a permanent cast. After 11 days I managed to talk my way out of the beastly place, but my doctor (I have two – a neurologist and neurosurgeon, and a bone surgeon) insisted that I have nurses with me, so this a bloody expensive piece of foolishness on my part.

I was reading over and admiring the letter you wrote to me on June 16th, the one in which you described your experiences at Gladesville, your efforts to avoid being seduced, and then told me about Sydney and other places.[1] A very wonderful letter. I have been kicking myself at least every other day for intruding into your private affairs. It was pure insolence – justified I thought in the circumstances. Anyhow, I love you, and as soon as I have two hands I'll write you a decent letter.

With love as always,
Ray

Raymond Chandler
6925 Neptune Place
La Jolla, California
September 4th, 1957

Darling Deirdre:

I'm still one-handed, although I can use my left hand on the shift bar, and by putting part of a rubber glove over the bottom of the cast and my fingers, I can take a tub bath, but not a shower, and can wash dishes and as a bachelor living alone in a four room apartment (flat to you, I suppose, as in England) I do have to wash dishes. Betty is often here for dinner, but not always, and even if I could drive, going out to dinner would pall in a week. The standard of cooking is very low here except in the best restaurants: La Jolla is a rich town and has half a dozen good restaurants, although many places of this size have none worth going to. By the way you did write to Betty, but you did not tell her whether your mother used to know some people named Pixley. If she did, Betty knows just who your mother is.

I'm not writing this soon enough to send to Orange, I'm afraid. Our post seems very erratic; I get letters from England in three days, but mine to England often take a week. There is no excuse for this. It is less than ten hours to New York and about 13 from New York to London. The new Pan American Polar service (I flew it once on the Scandinavian line, which pioneered the polar route) will make it in 21 hours from Los Angeles to London.

Your intense introspectiveness worries me. At times it seems almost morbid. And why should your mother and father and your girl friends wonder why you write to me? I have no evil intentions. I might have if I were younger. At 19 I was too busy preparing for a difficult exam to think much about girls, or about myself. (I made up for this later on) Of course I am glad that you are still intact, but the way you mention it makes me wonder whether *you* are glad. I never understood why you went to Sydney to work in that service station, why you accepted a room with no lock on the door, or why you recently went back to Sydney.[1] By the way, the best defence against intruders is a good loud scream. A friend of mine, a lady, woke up one night not long ago and heard someone moving in her room. When the children didn't answer she let out a bloodcurdling scream and the prowler vanished. He was caught a few nights later and turned out to be an exercise boy at the Del Mar race track, where the annual meet is on. I was at Betty's house last Sunday night – no, Monday night – Monday was Labor Day, a holiday comparable to the August Bank Holiday in England and perhaps with you also – and about 4 a.m. the dog kicked up a fearful racket, so I grabbed a revolver and put lights on and searched the house, and also put outside lights on. I saw nothing, but there were some strange footmarks near the fishpond next morning. It's a bad season for that sort of thing, and Solana Beach where Betty lives is near the race track and on the north-south highway, so it is vulnerable. La Jolla has low mountains behind it and only two roads of access. Also it has a far better police force. They can block the roads in minutes. One never knows about these prowlers; some come to steal and some have rape in mind: these are dangerous. I'd shoot one without hesitation if he actually laid hands on a woman, but usually you never have to use a gun if you have one. Of course I'd hate to shoot anyone; apart from my natural feelings about it, I'd get a lot of distasteful publicity. The papers gave me a trying time in London. If you are not friendly, they can do you a lot of harm. If you are friendly, they won't, but they will distort what you say in an interview, put words into your mouth you never said at all, and generally present a picture which is not at all accurate. One just has to swallow it.

From your letters I can't really tell whether you would make a writer, but you are certainly far more subtle and adept at analysing your own feelings than I could have been at your age or much later. It takes most people quite some time to become writers, even if they have a bent that way. I must have had some bent or I shouldn't have tried it at all, but it took me a long time to overcome the intellectual snobbery fostered by a classical education (and possibly a bit endemic also). To do this and go back to the primitives was the great difficulty. In London as a young man, very young, I wrote verses, essays, sketches, book reviews, paragraphs swiped from foreign newspapers, and in fact everything except what would have made a living. If I tried to write fiction, I couldn't get people in and out of rooms or get rid of a man's hat. So be not discouraged. You have plenty of time.

Yes, I got your last letter, the one before the one from Orange (I thought your family lived in Brisbane) and I also have the photograph you sent me, but after careful deliberation I have to confess that to me it is not just right. I can't imagine a girl with your brains really having that expression: too mild, too bucolic, almost, if you won't be angry with me, cowlike. It's not you, it's the photograph. I'm sorry but somebody will have to do better.

Much love and more later,
Ray

Raymond Chandler
6925 Neptune Place
La Jolla, California
30th December, 1957[1]

Darling Deirdre:

A Happy New Year to my growing-up girl, a lot of love and every kind of hope and good wish for her. But here I flunk out again. My lawyer has told me I can't go to Australia yet. I'd like to tell you the reasons, but they concern someone else, and that someone else should have the right to explain or not explain the situation, as she chooses. I've no doubt she will be quite open and honest about it when the time comes, because she is an utterly honest person. In the mean time, to borrow a phrase from Barry, my lips are sealed.[2]

Soon I shall be going to London. I told you I was going, but I am going much sooner. I'll be there off and on for a couple of years, but my agent, with whom, absurd as it may sound at my age, I have found the certain sort of close friendship which is rare in this world, and I intend to do some non-fiction books together, and try, if her business lets her, to get out of England in the bad months and work together. One of the books (forgive me if I said this already – I rather think I did) will be about Australia. Two keen minds might, with the help of friendly Australians, learn enough about the country and its ways in three months to be able to tell the rest of the world just how little they know of Australia. The kangaroos, the koala bears, the shark patrol, the desert-like middle of the country, and the great variety of climate, people do know (people who know anything, at least) but there is a lot more to it than that. If you ever felt like helping me with this notion, you might suggest what sort of topics or chapter headings you would like to tell about yourself. In one letter when I asked you to, you did tell me a lot. Australian writers, so far, seem not to be able to interpret their country to the rest of the world, because they are so close to it that they don't realise how much of it and its life are almost unknown.[3] I'd like to tell the wonderful story of how the wharfies beat MacArthur when he tried to act like royalty. I never could stand the man myself. Neither could the American Navy. I thought his escape from Corregidor was shameful. The British commander at Singapore could probably have got away too, but no British officer would desert his troops. The idea that MacArthur was too valuable to be taken prisoner is all bosh. He did some good work – yes – or someone did it for him (you can never be sure with big shots or V.I.P.'s) but his advance from Seoul to the Yalu was one of the worst military mistakes ever made. The hell with him.

If you really do go to Germany while I am in England, I hope you will fly over to London to visit me, as my guest in every sense of course. I might even, if Helga has time to go with me, go to Germany to see you. She speaks German like a native. I was good once, but it was long ago. And I am not terribly fond of the ordinary German.[4]

Palm Springs is a wonderful place. The dry air suits me. There are fine restaurants – better than in La Jolla, there are lovely houses, and there is an atmosphere of luxury and fine living about the place. It's almost too expensive, but if I come back to California, I'll live nowhere else. In the summer the heat is terrible – up to 125 degrees and even more – but with air-conditioning a house may be comfortable, and you just don't go outdoors, if you can help it, until evening. P.S. is right up against a big mountain and the sun sets behind the mountain, so it gets dark and cool here an hour earlier than in the open desert. And when there are sandstorms which occasionally happen, P.S. gets the wind, but not the sand. Sometimes, after a heavy rain, the water pours down the mountain sides and makes a regular river in the desert, but it only lasts for a few days. I have an apartment over the garage, but the garage is only used for storage. The air is so dry that there is no need to put a car away at night. There is a very good pool (do you call it a plunge) which is warmed, but not hot, and I have a lot of fun diving off the board. I used to be rather good off the thirty-foot board, but my knees aren't strong enough now to do anything but rather simple dives.

Please write to me when and if you have the mood. I love your letters, even if I am a bit doubtful about some of the things you do or want to do. I was pretty tame at your age, almost afraid to speak to a girl. But I made up for it later.

Yours always,
Ray

footnotes to letters

25 June 1956
1. Helga Greene

24 July 1956
1. Chandler had again been in the Chula Vista clinic, attempting to dry out.

2 November 1956
1. In the three months since his last letter Chandler had become involved with a widow from San Francisco (her name has been altered in this book) who had written him a letter of sympathy after his suicide attempt in 1955. He intended to marry her, and even altered his will in her favour, but after a quarrel they parted company. In the midst of this turmoil, another bout of drinking ended with Chandler spending two weeks in a drying-out clinic, Las Encinas, in Pasadena.

2 March 1957
1. The film was *The Blue Dahlia*, the actor was Alan Ladd. In order to complete the screenplay before Ladd was drafted, Chandler made a deal with the studio. He could only do it drunk. He would work at home, but two limousines were to stand outside the house at all times. These would fetch the doctor, when necessary, for Cissy, take the maid shopping, and deliver the script to the studio. Secretaries were to be on hand at all hours for dictation and typing. As Chandler did not eat properly while drinking, he also requested round-the-clock nurses and a doctor to administer regular vitamin shots. Under these conditions, in a semi-stupor, Chandler completed the script in less than two weeks.

20 March 1957
1. The photo was of Natasha Spender.
   Only after this visit in 1957 did Chandler accept that the hopes he had of their friendship were out of kilter with the realities of her commitments. Soon after, he wrote her a letter acknowledging that his dreams could only ever be just that, and that perhaps he was 'just bedazzled by something happening to me so suddenly, when I had more or less given up the idea of anything ever happening to me except an eternity of sorrow.' [to Helga Greene 25 May 1957]
2. Terence Tiller was a poet Chandler met in London.

8 April 1957
1. Not her actual name. In his biography, 'for reasons of privacy', Frank MacShane called her 'Anne Jameson'.
2. Chandler was confused. He presumably meant New Zealand.

23 April 1957
1. Chandler did not go to England because of his unresolved dispute with the English Inland Revenue.
2. Natasha Spender.

14 August 1957
1. Deirdre had taken a holiday job in a service station.

4 September 1957
1. Chandler was perhaps referring to Deirdre's stay in a hotel in George Street.

30 December 1957
1. This letter was not among those in Professor MacShane's papers. I retrieved it some time later – photocopied from Chandler's carbon – from Judith Priestman (Dr) at the Bodleian Library. Dee is unsure if she ever received it.
2. The woman, presumably, was 'Betty Bluefields'. Chandler had, about this time, made Mrs Bluefields his heir.
3. Chandler's glib dismissal that 'Australian writers, so far, seem not to be able to interpret their country to the rest of the world' is a sad example of how at this time of his life, when in doubt, he led with the mouth. One of the most powerful impressions of Australian life, Patrick White's *The Tree of Man*, was published in the UK in 1956 – although probably it is exactly the sort of literary novel Chandler would have loathed.
4. Deirdre, at the end of 1957, was considering a trip to Germany to meet her penfriend Helmut. Because of her studies and the great cost at that time of air travel, she never went.

notes on quoted material

Quotes in the text, other than letters reproduced in their entirety, have been taken from the following two sources. Where more than one quote appears on a page, these are listed in order of appearance.

Items preceded by an asterix are taken from *The Life of Raymond Chandler*, Frank MacShane, Jonathan Cape, London, 1976. Those without an asterix are taken from *The Selected Letters of Raymond Chandler*, Frank MacShane (ed), Columbia University Press, New York, 1981.

The quotes on pages 13 and 85 are fictional. The first and third quotes from page 212 are taken from *Mean Streets*, Issue 2, 1991.

one

	4–5	RC to Hamish Hamilton 5 January 1955
*	5	pp 229–30
	13	fictional

two

	32	RC to Charles Morton 19 March 1945
	44	RC to Hamish Hamilton 10 August 1948
	44	RC to Hamish Hamilton 19 August 1948
*	48	p 162 [RC to HN Swanson 5 January 1953]
	48–9	RC to Mrs Robert J Hogan 7 March 1947
	50	RC to Hamish Hamilton 12 March 1949
*	51	p 15
	51	RC To Alfred Knopf 12 January 1946
*	51	p 268
	53	RC to Edgar Carter 5 February 1951
	53	RC to Hardwick Moseley 23 April 1949
	53	RC to Hardwick Moseley 23 April 1949
	53	RC to Cleve Adams 4 September 1948
	54	RC to Hamish Hamilton 27 April 1955

	55	RC to Hamish Hamilton 30 May 1946
	55	RC to Jessica Tyndale 12 July 1956
	56	Lauren Bacall, unsourced
*	56	p 126
*	56	p 111
	56	RC to Lenore Glen Offord 6 December 1948
*	56	p 110
*	56	p 181 [RC to JB Priestley]
*	56	p 244
*	56	p 212
	57	RC to Roger Machell 15 March 1953
	57	RC to Edgar Carter 15 November 1950
	57	RC to Blanche Knopf 14 June 1940
*	57	p 187
*	57	p 214
	58	RC to Hamish Hamilton 16 May 1957
*	60	p 192
	60	RC to Dale Waren 15 September 1949
	60	RC to George Harmon Coxe 9 April 1939
	60	RC to Dale Warren 2 October 1949
	61	RC to Juanita Messick 12 August 1953
	61	RC to Hamish Hamilton 16 May 1957
	61	RC to Juanita Messick 12 August 1953
	61	RC to Bergen Evans 18 January 1958
	62	RC to Hamish Hamilton 12 March 1949
	62	RC to Edgar Carter 3 June 1957
	62	RC to Hamish Hamilton 16 May 1945
	63	RC to Hamish Hamilton 5 January 1950
*	63	p 136 [RC to Dale Warren 8 January 1948]
	64	RC to Hamish Hamilton 16 May 1957
	64	RC to Alex Barris 16 April 1949

three

*	67	p 240 [RC to Roger Machell undated October 1955]
*	67	p 240 [RC to Roger Machell 27 October 1955]
	68	RC to Helga Greene 13 November 1955
	68	RC to Helga Greene 19 June 1956
	68	RC to Ian Fleming 9 June 1956
	70	RC to Jessica Tyndale 12 July 1956
	73	RC to Hardwick Moseley 23 March 1954
	76	RC to Paul McClug 11 December 1951
	85	fictional

four

    100   RC to La Jolla Post Office 13 August 1951
    111   RC to Bernice Baumgarten 13 February 1949
    116   RC to Helga Greene 21 June 1956
*   116   p 260

five

*   153   p 4
*   153   p 5
*   153   p 12
*   154   p 5
    154   RC to Michael Gilbert 25 July 1957
*   154   p 8
    154   RC to Deirdre Gartrell 20 March 1957
    154   RC to Helga Greene 28 April 1957
*   155   p 10
    155   RC to Deirdre Gartrell 23 April 1957
*   156   p 32
*   157   p 38
    158   RC to Helga Greene 14 June 1956
    158   RC to Hamish Hamilton 16 January 1953
    158   RC to Hamish Hamilton 15 July 1954
    159   RC to James Sandoe 28 December 1949
*   159   p 234
    160   RC to Jean de Leon 11 February 1957
    160   RC to Helga Greene 19 June 1956
    161   RC to Helga Greene 20 October 1957

six

    164   RC to Michael Gilbert 3 January 1957
    165   RC to Helga Greene 4 February 1957
    166   RC to Helga Greene 12 October 1958
    173   RC to Jessica Tyndale 3 February 1958
    173   RC to Dale Warren 25 April 1952

seven

   196   RC to Hardwick Moseley 23 March 1954
   196   RC to Charles Morton 19 March 1945
   212   Ian Fleming, 'Raymond Chandler', *London Magazine*, 12 December 1959, quoted in *Mean Streets*, issue 2, February 1991
* 212   p 258
   212   *Mean Streets*, issue 2, 1991

eight

* 231   p 43
   232   RC to Blanche Knopf 22 October 1942
   232   RC to Blanche Knopf 27 March 1946
   235   RC to Charles Morton 9 October 1950
   236   RC to Alex Barris 18 March 1949
* 254   p 267

nine

   264   RC to Deirdre Gartrell 20 March 1957
   277   RC to Helga Greene 30 April 1957
277–8   RC to Fredrick Lewis Allen 7 May 1948
   278   RC to Mrs Robert J Hogan 7 March 1947

ten

   307   RC to Paul Brooks 19 July 1949